BEN TEMPLESMITH

WORMWOOD

GENTLEMAN CORPSE

★★★★★★★★★★★★★★

MR WORMWOOD

GOES TO

WASHINGTON

Facebook facebook.com/idwpublishing
Twitter @idwpublishing
YouTube youtube.com/idwpublishing
Tumblr tumblr.idwpublishing.com
Instagram instagram.com/idwpublishing

ISBN: 978-1-68405-037-6   21 20 19 18   1 2 3 4

Originally published as WORMWOOD GENTLEMAN CORPSE: MR. WORMWOOD GOES TO WASHINGTON issues #1–3 and WORMWOOD GENTLEMAN CORPSE: CHRISTMAS SPECIAL.

Justin Eisinger
Alonzo Simon

Collection Design by

Shawn Lee

Templesmith logo by

Babe Elliot Baker

Publisher

Greg Goldstein

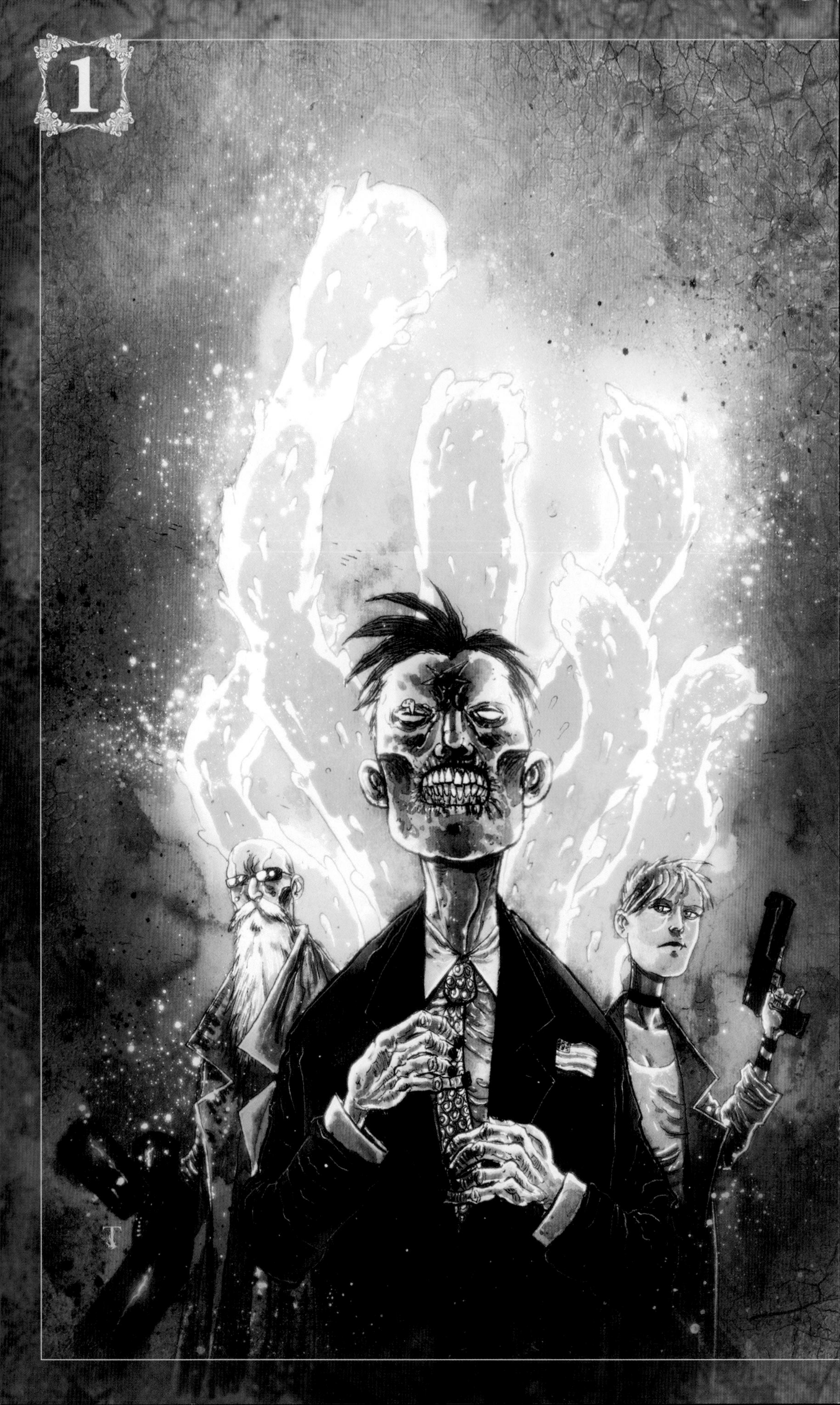
1

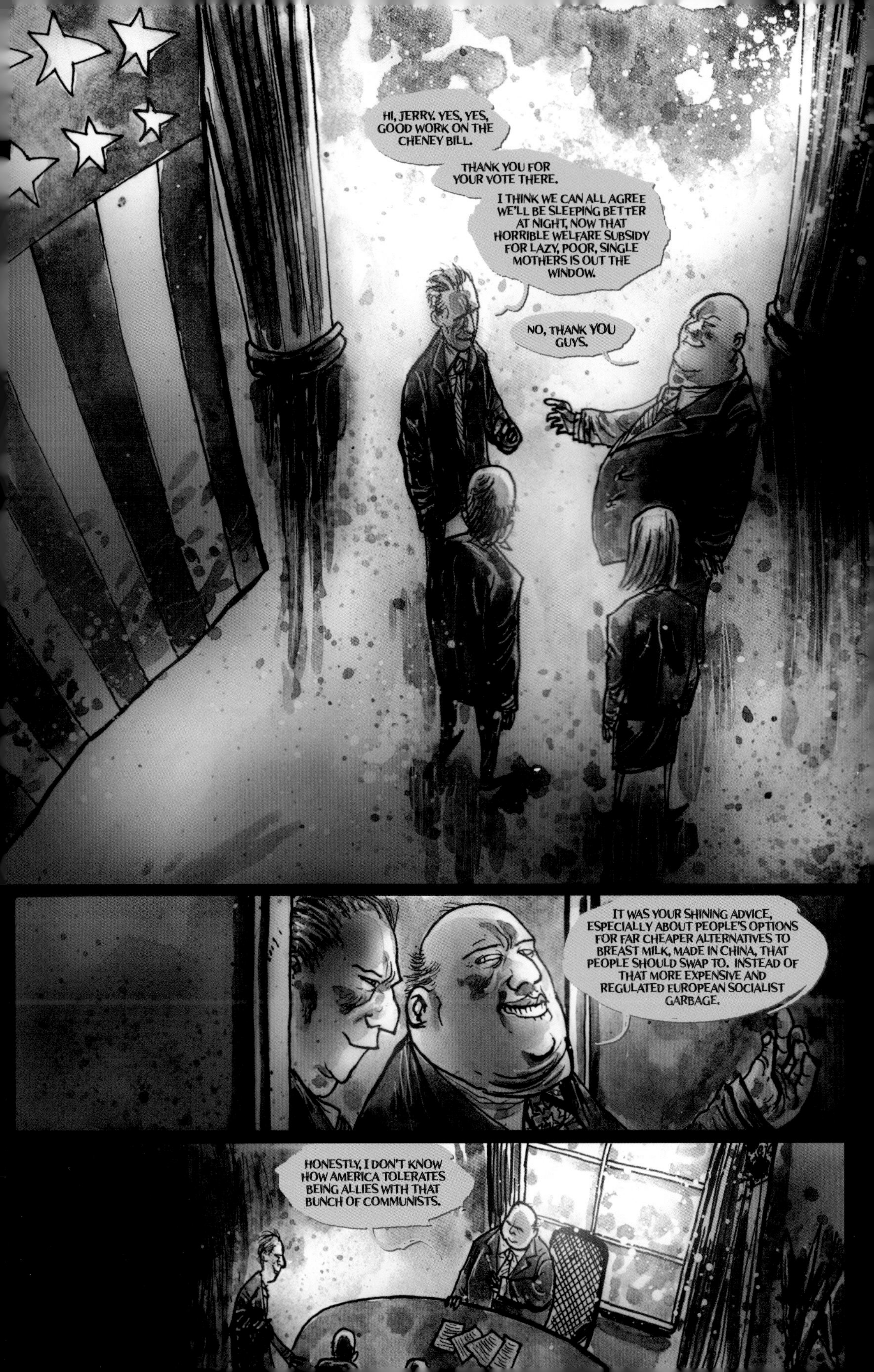
HI, JERRY. YES, YES, GOOD WORK ON THE CHENEY BILL.
THANK YOU FOR YOUR VOTE THERE.
I THINK WE CAN ALL AGREE WE'LL BE SLEEPING BETTER AT NIGHT, NOW THAT HORRIBLE WELFARE SUBSIDY FOR LAZY, POOR, SINGLE MOTHERS IS OUT THE WINDOW.
NO, THANK YOU GUYS.
IT WAS YOUR SHINING ADVICE, ESPECIALLY ABOUT PEOPLE'S OPTIONS FOR FAR CHEAPER ALTERNATIVES TO BREAST MILK, MADE IN CHINA, THAT PEOPLE SHOULD SWAP TO. INSTEAD OF THAT MORE EXPENSIVE AND REGULATED EUROPEAN SOCIALIST GARBAGE.
HONESTLY, I DON'T KNOW HOW AMERICA TOLERATES BEING ALLIES WITH THAT BUNCH OF COMMUNISTS.

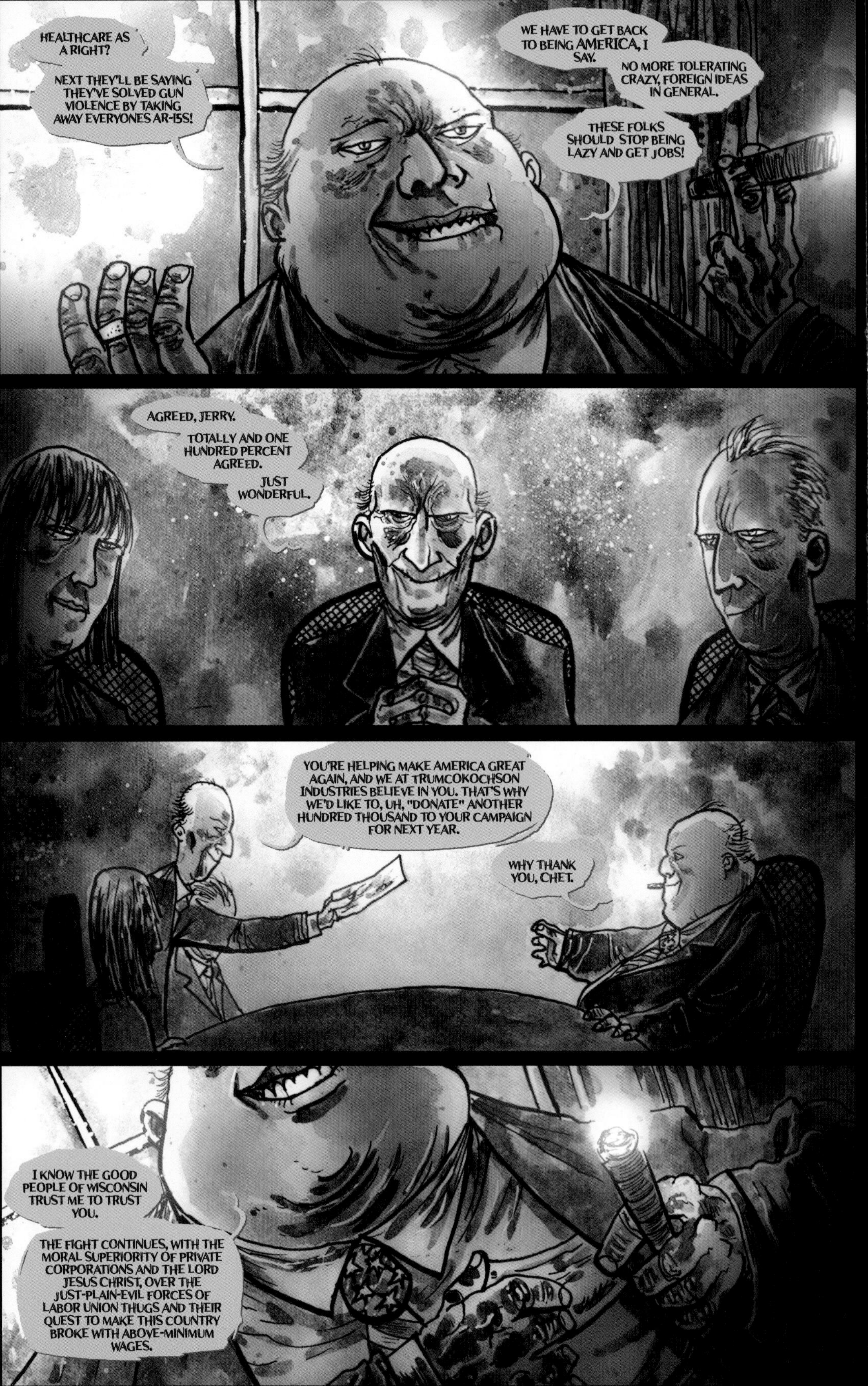
HEALTHCARE AS A RIGHT?
NEXT THEY'LL BE SAYING THEY'VE SOLVED GUN VIOLENCE BY TAKING AWAY EVERYONES AR-15S!
WE HAVE TO GET BACK TO BEING AMERICA, I SAY.
NO MORE TOLERATING CRAZY, FOREIGN IDEAS IN GENERAL.
THESE FOLKS SHOULD STOP BEING LAZY AND GET JOBS!
AGREED, JERRY.
TOTALLY AND ONE HUNDRED PERCENT AGREED.
JUST WONDERFUL.
YOU'RE HELPING MAKE AMERICA GREAT AGAIN, AND WE AT TRUMCOKOCHSON INDUSTRIES BELIEVE IN YOU. THAT'S WHY WE'D LIKE TO, UH, "DONATE" ANOTHER HUNDRED THOUSAND TO YOUR CAMPAIGN FOR NEXT YEAR.
WHY THANK YOU, CHET.
I KNOW THE GOOD PEOPLE OF WISCONSIN TRUST ME TO TRUST YOU.
THE FIGHT CONTINUES, WITH THE MORAL SUPERIORITY OF PRIVATE CORPORATIONS AND THE LORD JESUS CHRIST, OVER THE JUST-PLAIN-EVIL FORCES OF LABOR UNION THUGS AND THEIR QUEST TO MAKE THIS COUNTRY BROKE WITH ABOVE-MINIMUM WAGES.

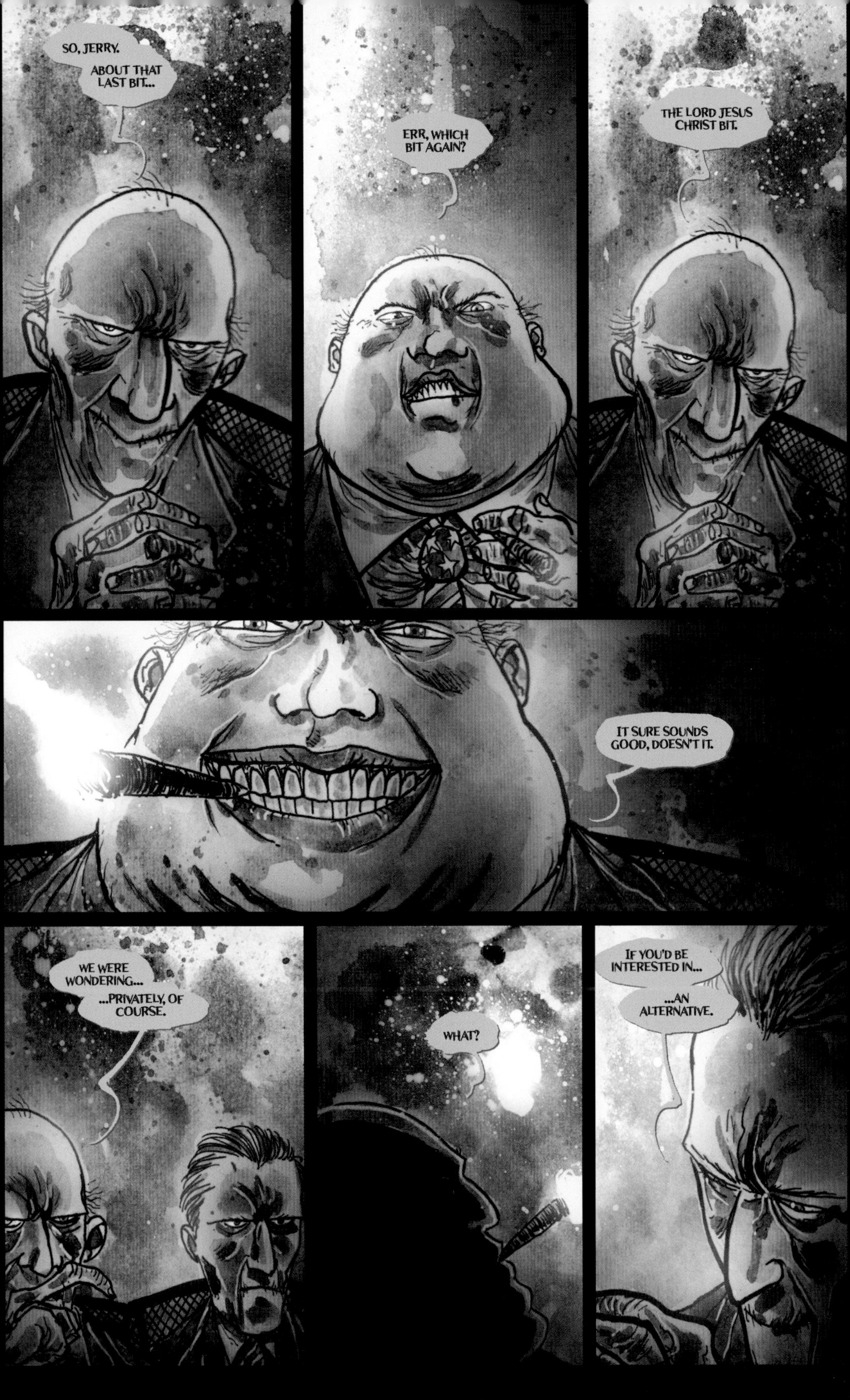
SO, JERRY.
ABOUT THAT LAST BIT...
ERR, WHICH BIT AGAIN?
THE LORD JESUS CHRIST BIT.
IT SURE SOUNDS GOOD, DOESN'T IT.
WE WERE WONDERING...
...PRIVATELY, OF COURSE.
WHAT?
IF YOU'D BE INTERESTED IN...
...AN ALTERNATIVE.

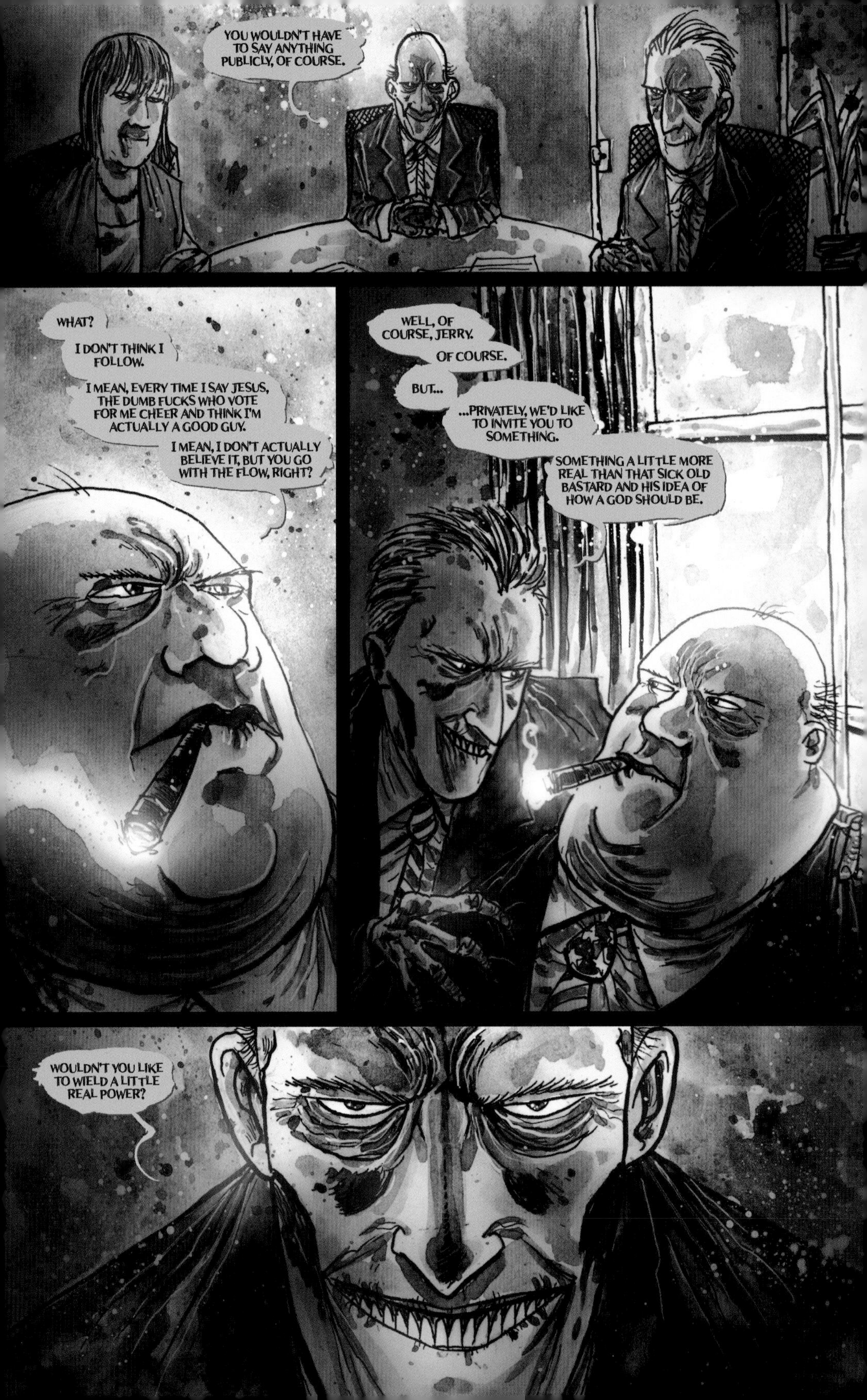
YOU WOULDN'T HAVE TO SAY ANYTHING PUBLICLY, OF COURSE.
WHAT?
I DON'T THINK I FOLLOW.
I MEAN, EVERY TIME I SAY JESUS, THE DUMB FUCKS WHO VOTE FOR ME CHEER AND THINK I'M ACTUALLY A GOOD GUY.
I MEAN, I DON'T ACTUALLY BELIEVE IT, BUT YOU GO WITH THE FLOW, RIGHT?
WELL, OF COURSE, JERRY.
OF COURSE.
BUT...
...PRIVATELY, WE'D LIKE TO INVITE YOU TO SOMETHING.
SOMETHING A LITTLE MORE REAL THAN THAT SICK OLD BASTARD AND HIS IDEA OF HOW A GOD SHOULD BE.
WOULDN'T YOU LIKE TO WIELD A LITTLE REAL POWER?

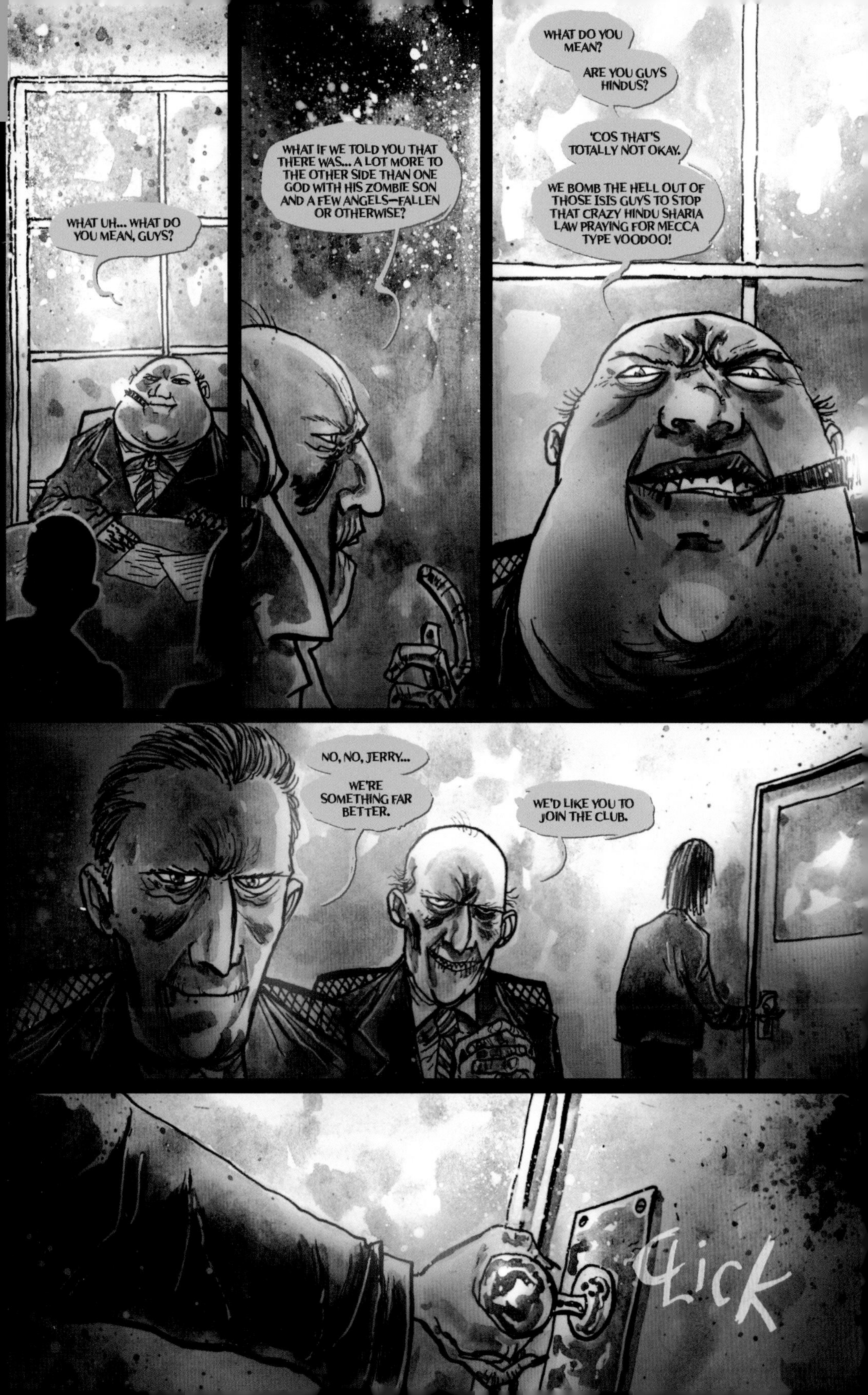
WHAT UH... WHAT DO YOU MEAN, GUYS?
WHAT IF WE TOLD YOU THAT THERE WAS... A LOT MORE TO THE OTHER SIDE THAN ONE GOD WITH HIS ZOMBIE SON AND A FEW ANGELS—FALLEN OR OTHERWISE?
WHAT DO YOU MEAN?
ARE YOU GUYS HINDUS?
'COS THAT'S TOTALLY NOT OKAY.
WE BOMB THE HELL OUT OF THOSE ISIS GUYS TO STOP THAT CRAZY HINDU SHARIA LAW PRAYING FOR MECCA TYPE VOODOO!
NO, NO, JERRY...
WE'RE SOMETHING FAR BETTER.
WE'D LIKE YOU TO JOIN THE CLUB.
CLICK

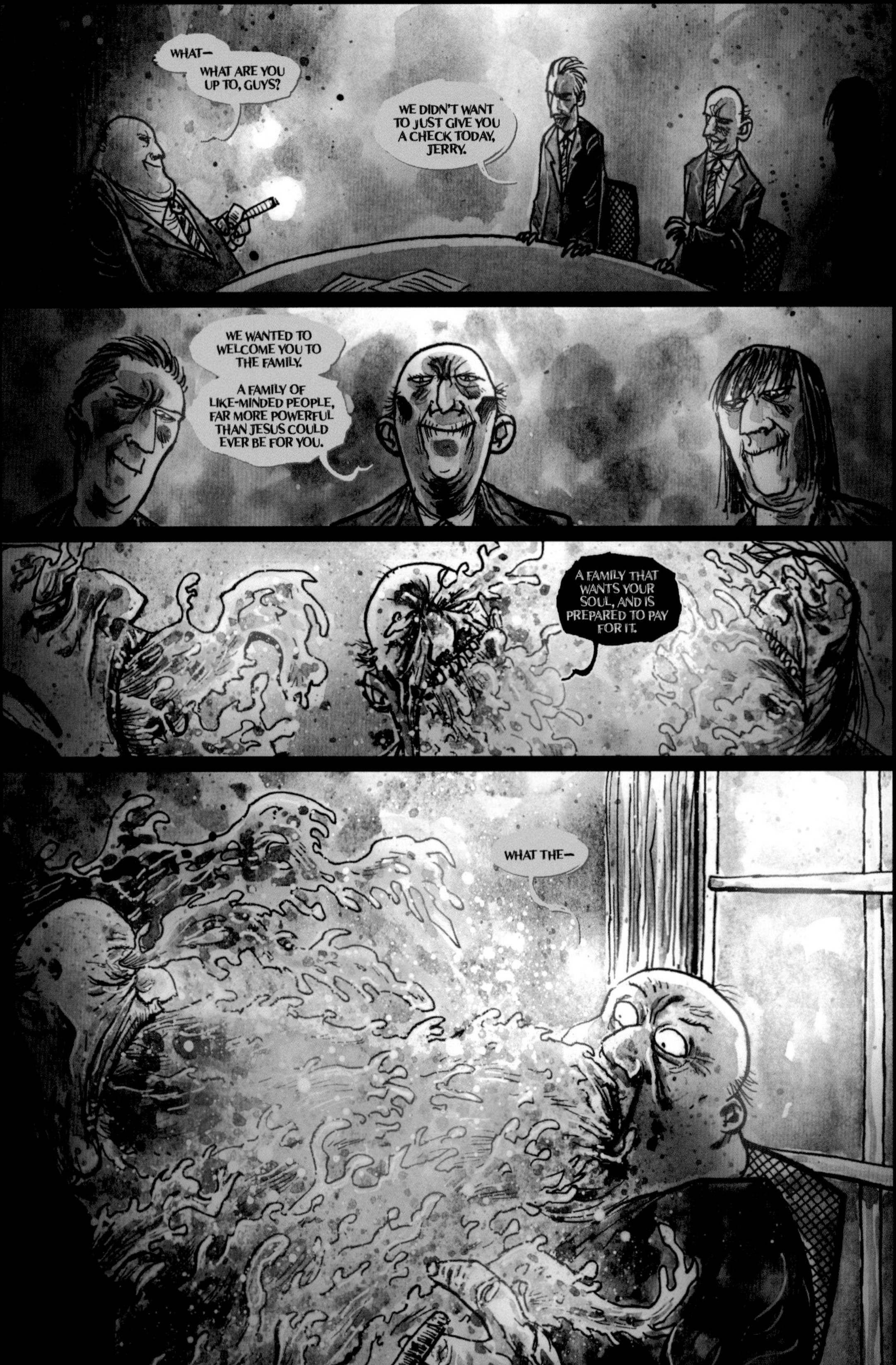
WHAT—
WHAT ARE YOU UP TO, GUYS?
WE DIDN'T WANT TO JUST GIVE YOU A CHECK TODAY, JERRY.
WE WANTED TO WELCOME YOU TO THE FAMILY.
A FAMILY OF LIKE-MINDED PEOPLE, FAR MORE POWERFUL THAN JESUS COULD EVER BE FOR YOU.
A FAMILY THAT WANTS YOUR SOUL, AND IS PREPARED TO PAY FOR IT.
WHAT THE—

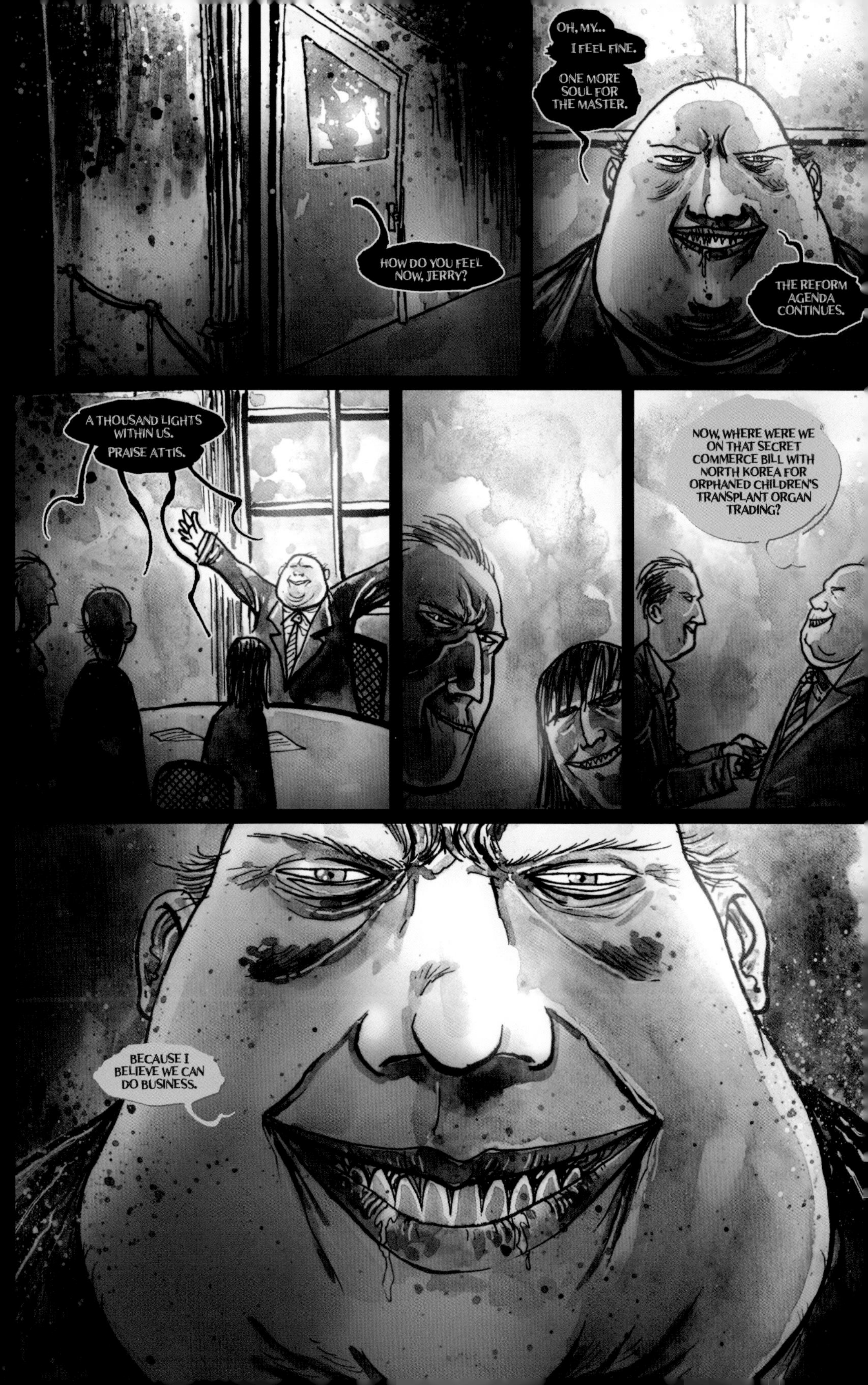
HOW DO YOU FEEL NOW, JERRY?
OH, MY...
I FEEL FINE.
ONE MORE SOUL FOR THE MASTER.
THE REFORM AGENDA CONTINUES.
A THOUSAND LIGHTS WITHIN US.
PRAISE ATTIS.
NOW, WHERE WERE WE ON THAT SECRET COMMERCE BILL WITH NORTH KOREA FOR ORPHANED CHILDREN'S TRANSPLANT ORGAN TRADING?
BECAUSE I BELIEVE WE CAN DO BUSINESS.

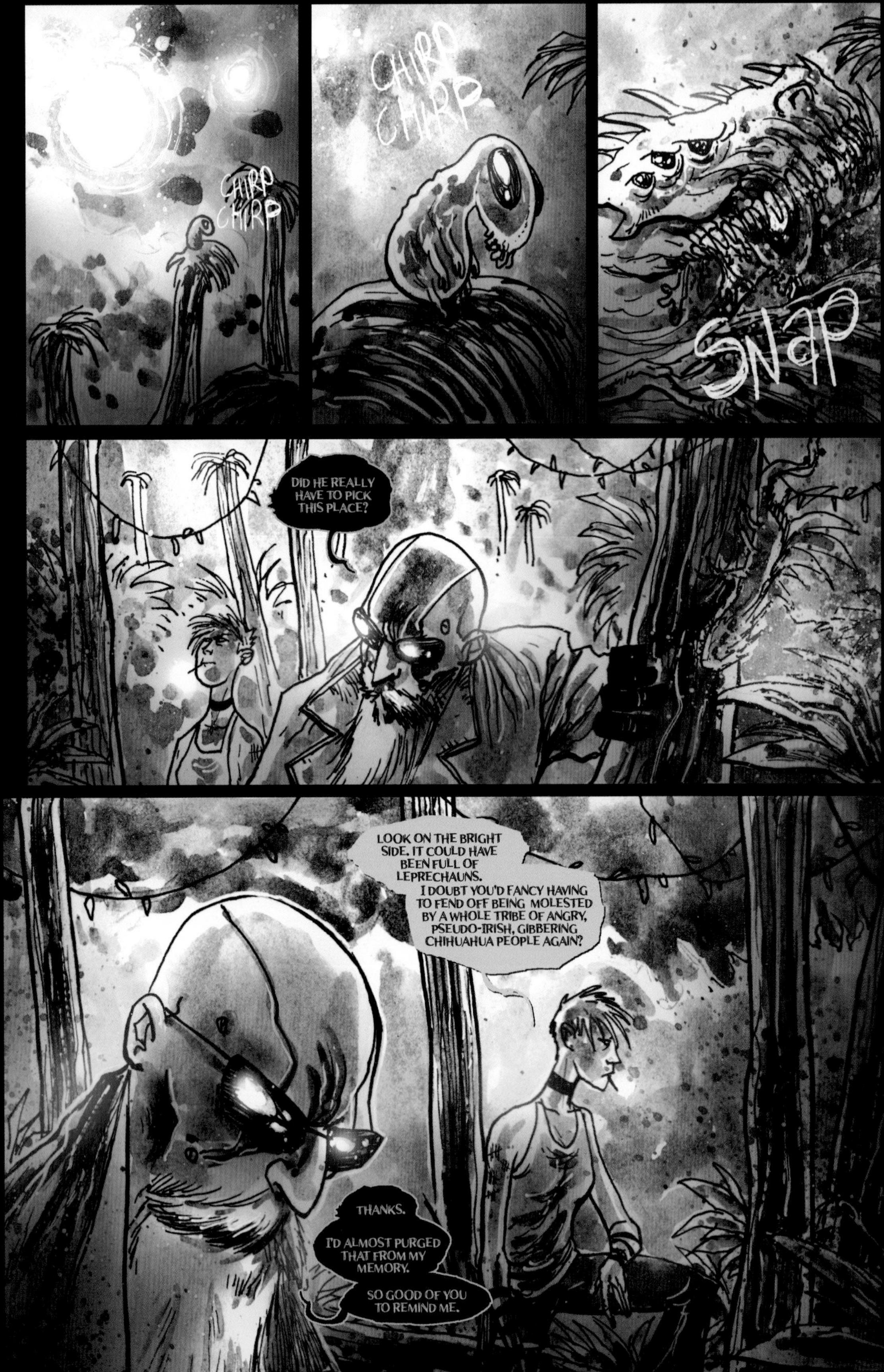
CHIRP CHIRP
CHIRP CHIRP
SNAP
DID HE REALLY HAVE TO PICK THIS PLACE?
LOOK ON THE BRIGHT SIDE. IT COULD HAVE BEEN FULL OF LEPRECHAUNS.
I DOUBT YOU'D FANCY HAVING TO FEND OFF BEING MOLESTED BY A WHOLE TRIBE OF ANGRY, PSEUDO-IRISH, GIBBERING CHIHUAHUA PEOPLE AGAIN?
THANKS.
I'D ALMOST PURGED THAT FROM MY MEMORY.
SO GOOD OF YOU TO REMIND ME.

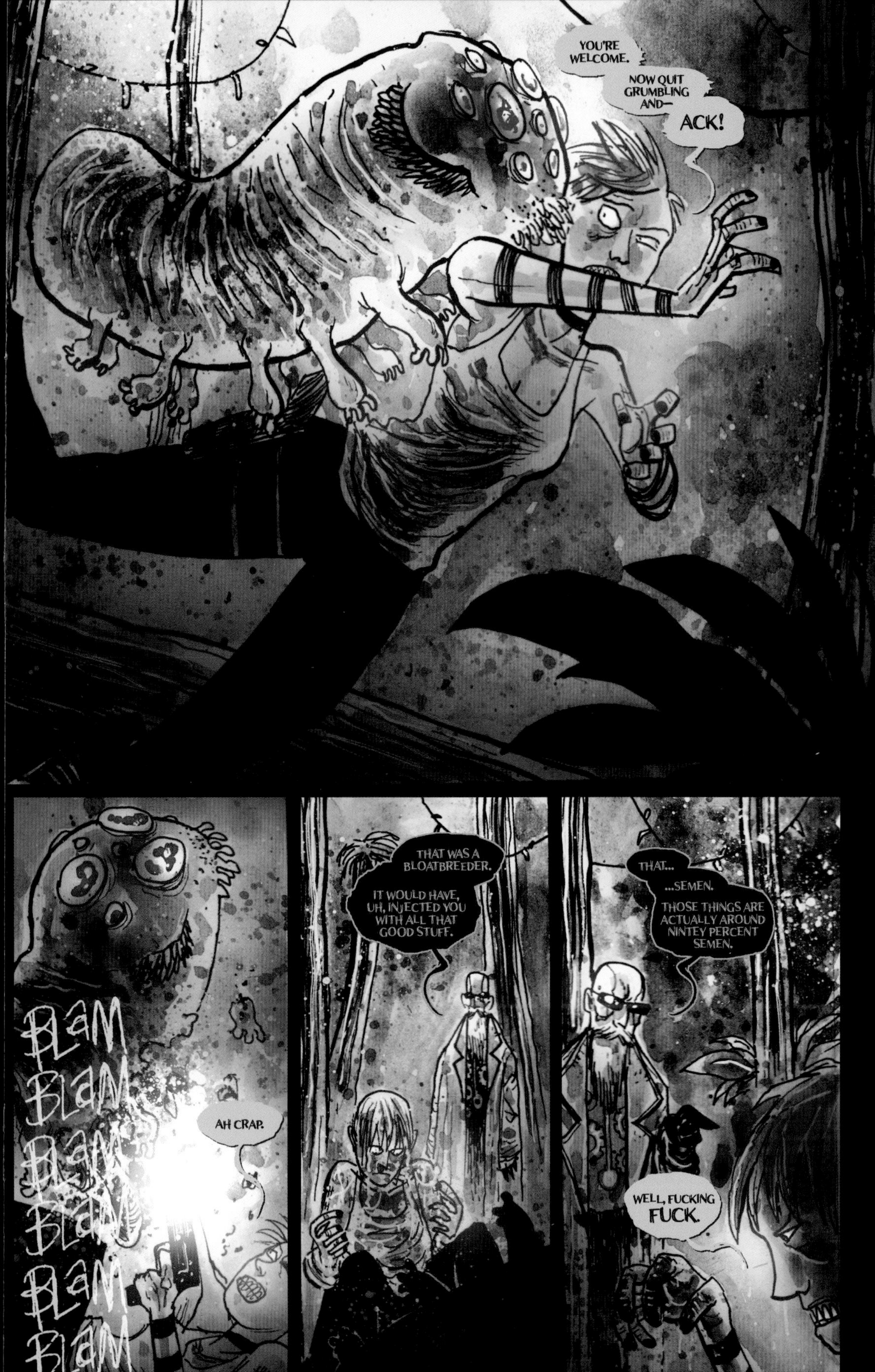
YOU'RE WELCOME.
NOW QUIT GRUMBLING AND—
ACK!
BLAM BLAM BLAM BLAM BLAM BLAM BLAM
AH CRAP.
THAT WAS A BLOATBREEDER.
IT WOULD HAVE, UH, INJECTED YOU WITH ALL THAT GOOD STUFF.
THAT...
...SEMEN.
THOSE THINGS ARE ACTUALLY AROUND NINTEY PERCENT SEMEN.
WELL, FUCKING FUCK.

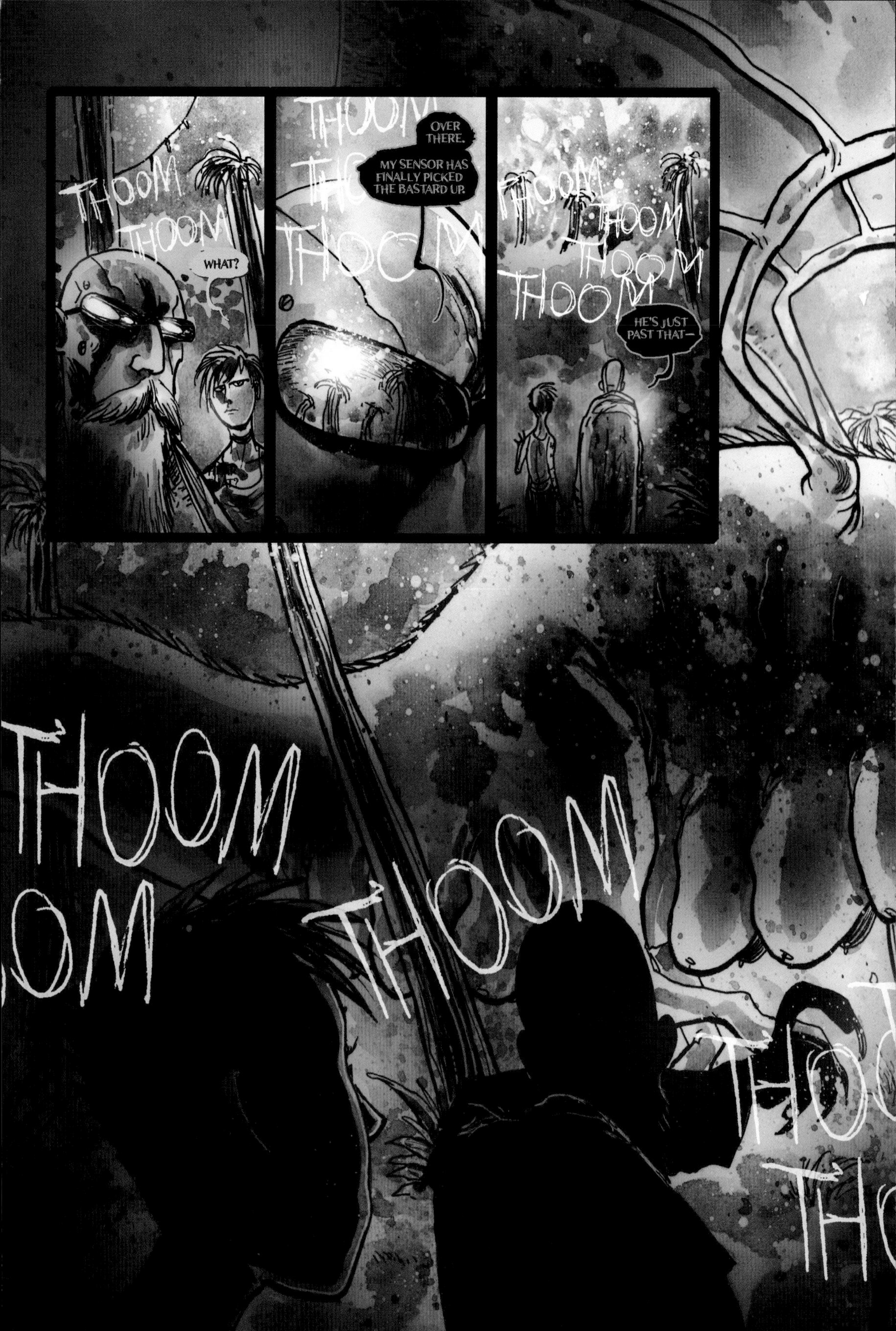
THOOM
THOOM
WHAT?
THOOM
THOOM
THOOM
OVER THERE.
MY SENSOR HAS FINALLY PICKED THE BASTARD UP.
THOOM
THOOM
THOOM
THOOM
HE'S JUST PAST THAT—
THOOM
OOM
THOOM
THO
THO

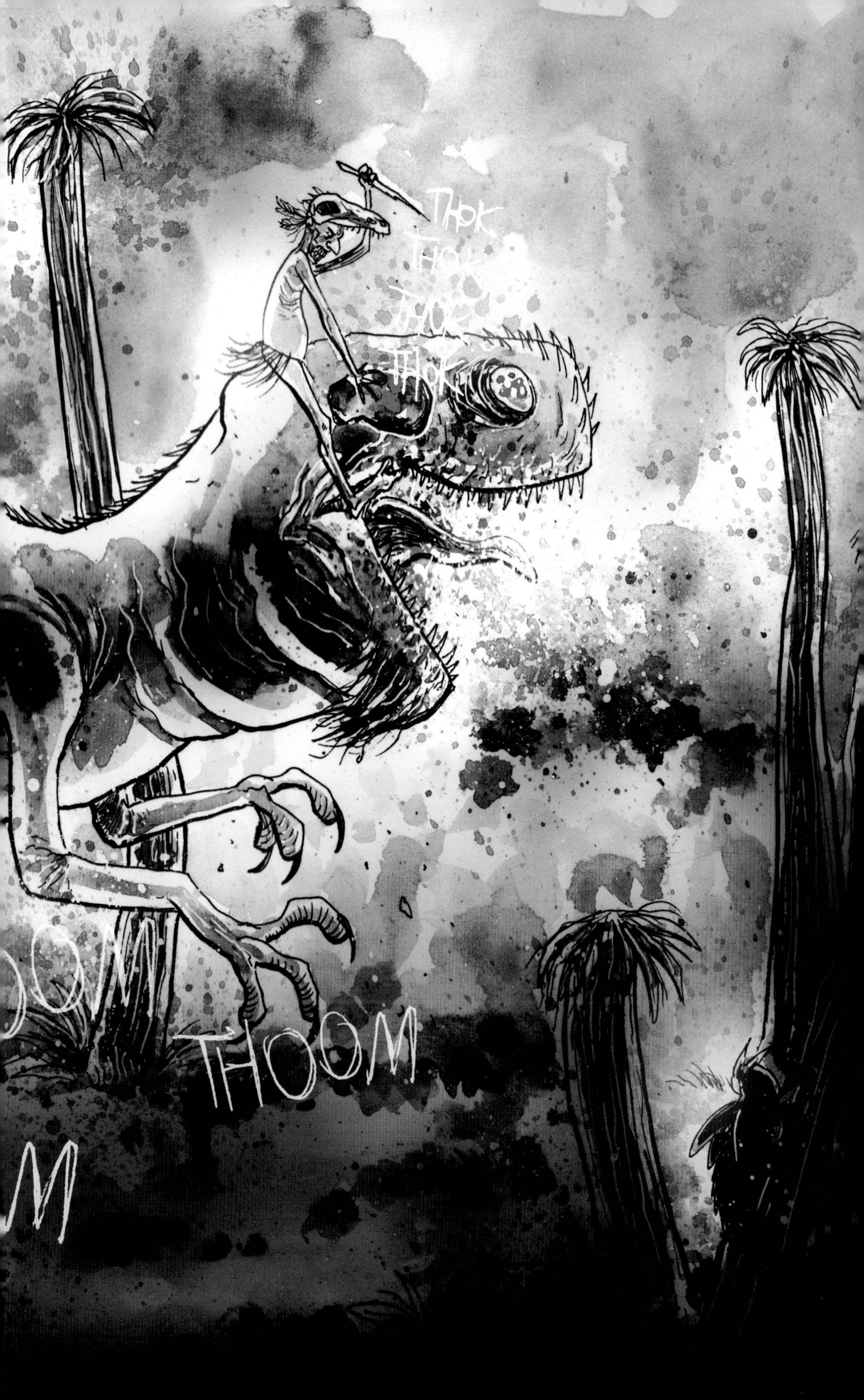
THOK
THOK
THOK
THOK
THOOM

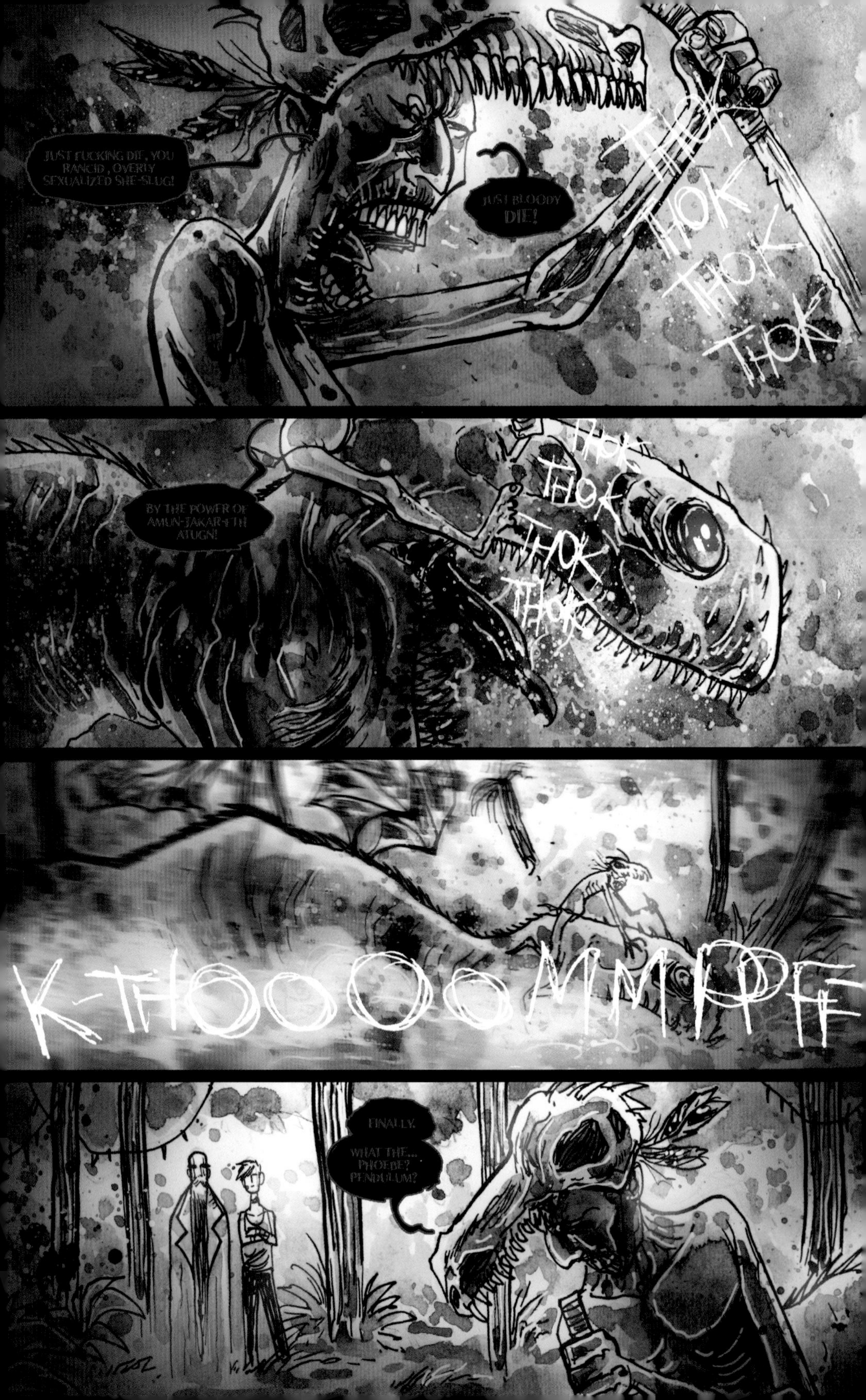
JUST FUCKING DIE, YOU RANCID, OVERLY SEXUALIZED SHE-SLUG!
JUST BLOODY DIE!
THOK THOK THOK THOK
BY THE POWER OF AMUN-JAKAR-ETH ATUGN!
THOK THOK THOK THOK
K-THOOOOOMMPFF
FINALLY.
WHAT THE... PHOEBE? PENDULUM?

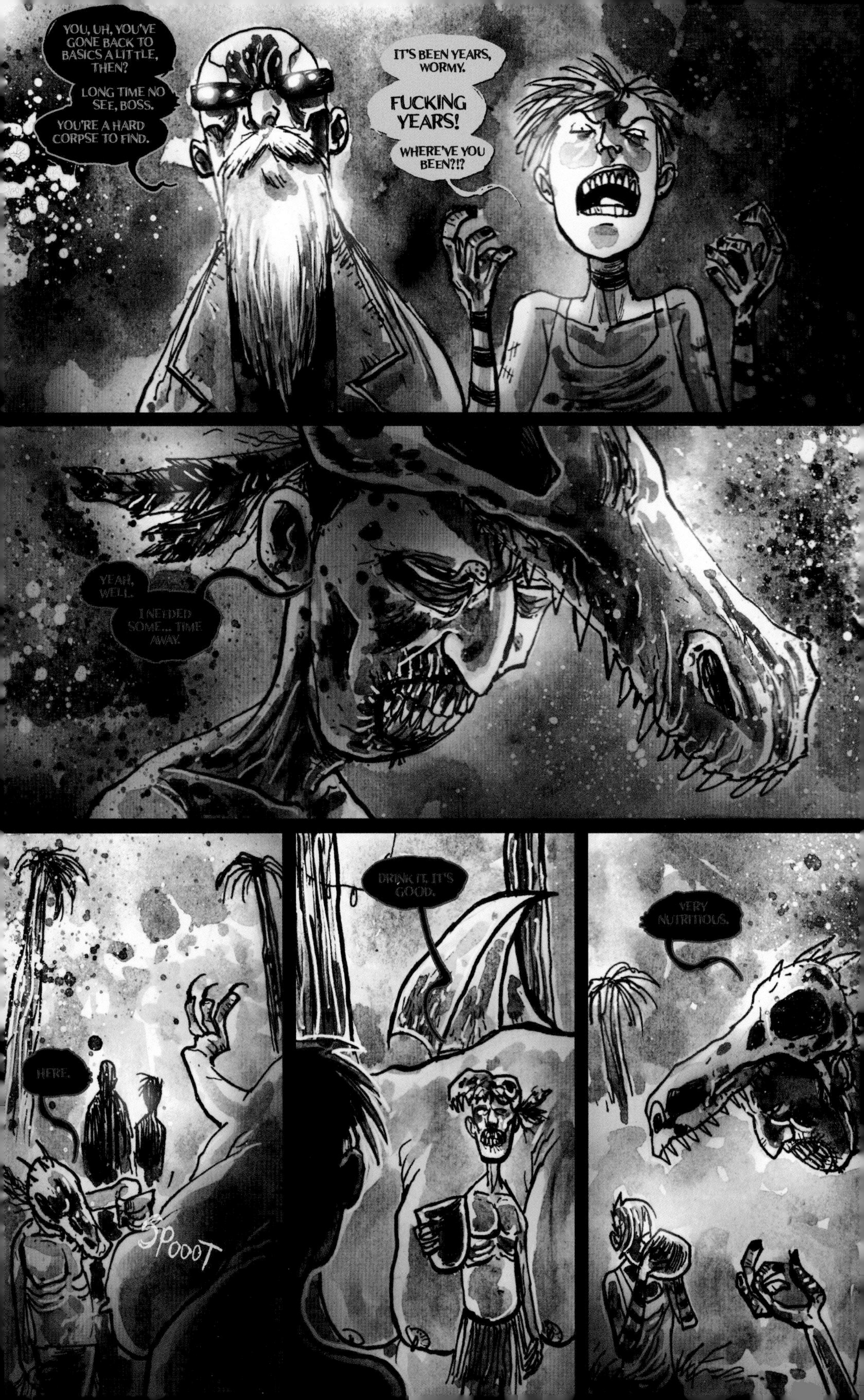
YOU, UH, YOU'VE GONE BACK TO BASICS A LITTLE, THEN?
LONG TIME NO SEE, BOSS.
YOU'RE A HARD CORPSE TO FIND.
IT'S BEEN YEARS, WORMY.
FUCKING YEARS!
WHERE'VE YOU BEEN?!?
YEAH, WELL.
I NEEDED SOME... TIME AWAY.
HERE.
SPOOOT
DRINK IT. IT'S GOOD.
VERY NUTRITIOUS.

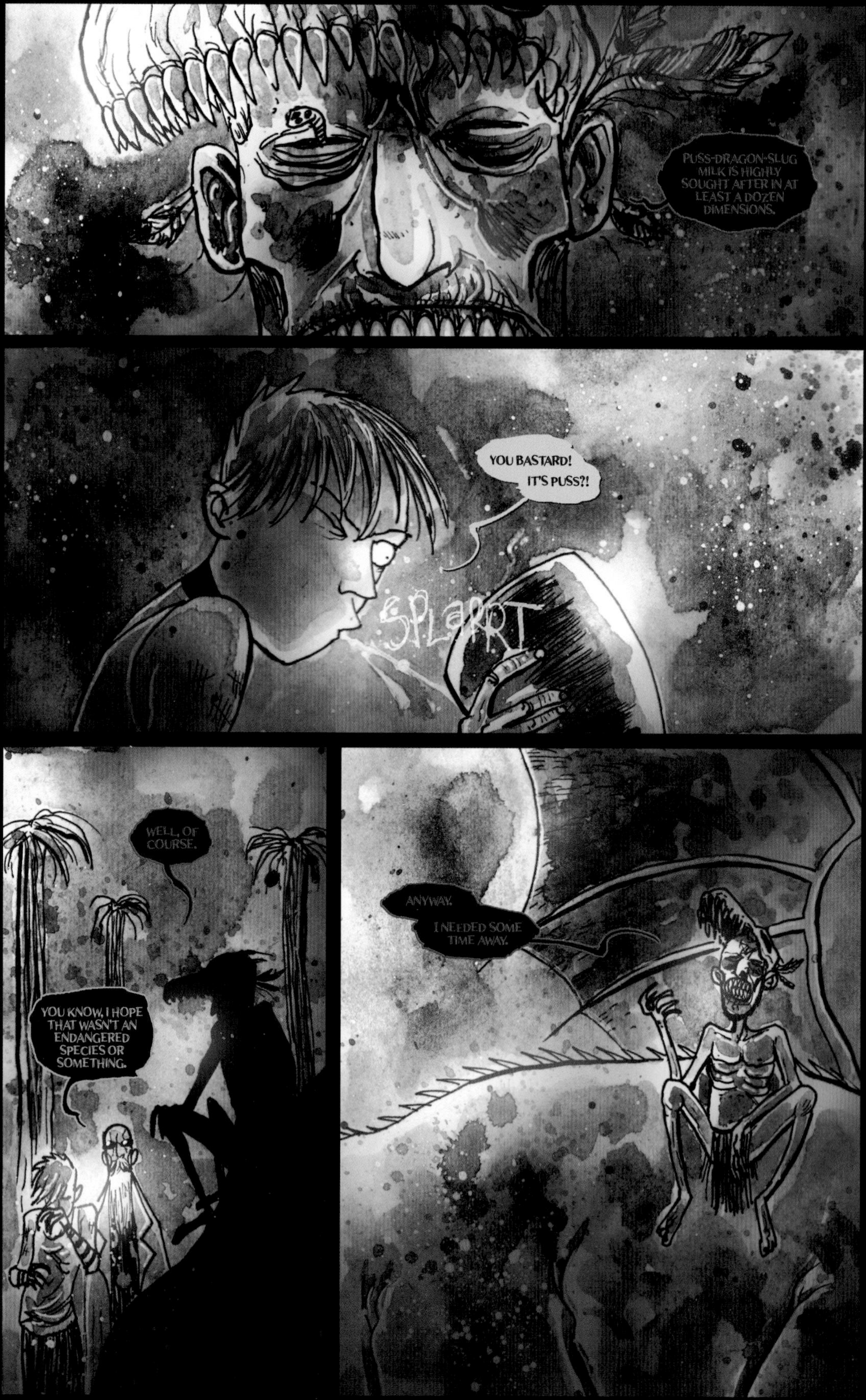
PUSS-DRAGON-SLUG MILK IS HIGHLY SOUGHT AFTER IN AT LEAST A DOZEN DIMENSIONS.
YOU BASTARD!
IT'S PUSS?!
SPLARRT
WELL, OF COURSE.
YOU KNOW, I HOPE THAT WASN'T AN ENDANGERED SPECIES OR SOMETHING.
ANYWAY.
I NEEDED SOME TIME AWAY.

LIKE I SAID.

I NEEDED SOME TIME AWAY.

AFTER I SAVED THE WORLD... AGAIN, I MIGHT ADD, AND FOR FREE- I HOOKED UP WITH THAT CRAZY WITCH WOMAN—

OH, YEAH, WHAT WAS HER NAME?

BAH, IT'S NOT EVEN WORTH REMEMBERING NOW.

BUT SHE WAS ABSOLUTELY INSANE, QUITE LITERALLY, AS IT TURNED OUT.

ONE OF THE MOST MANIPULATIVE LIARS I'VE EVER KNOWN.

AND REMEMBER, I USED TO HAGGLE IN THE MARKETS IN BABYLON, SO I KNOW A THING OR TWO.

TOOK ME FOR ALL THE MONEY I HAD, SOLD THE BLOODY HOUSE, ALIENATED ME FROM YOU GUYS... SHE TOOK OVER MY LIFE.

ONCE THE HONEYMOON WAS OVER... I CAN'T BELIEVE I GOT SUCKED IN.

SHE WAS AS DUMB AS A BAG OF HAMMERS.

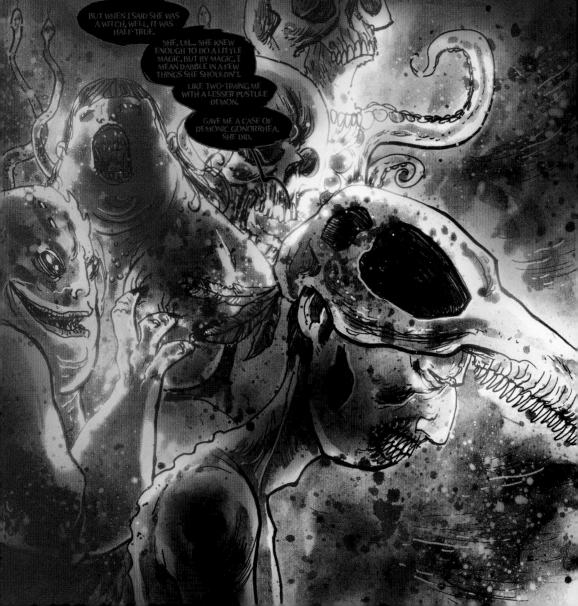

BUT WHEN I SAID SHE WAS A WITCH, WELL, IT WAS HALF-TRUE.

SHE, UH... SHE KNEW ENOUGH TO DO A LITTLE MAGIC, BUT BY MAGIC, I MEAN DABBLE IN A FEW THINGS SHE SHOULDN'T.

LIKE TWO-TIMING ME WITH A LESSER PUSTULE DEMON.

GAVE ME A CASE OF DEMONIC GONORRHEA, SHE DID.

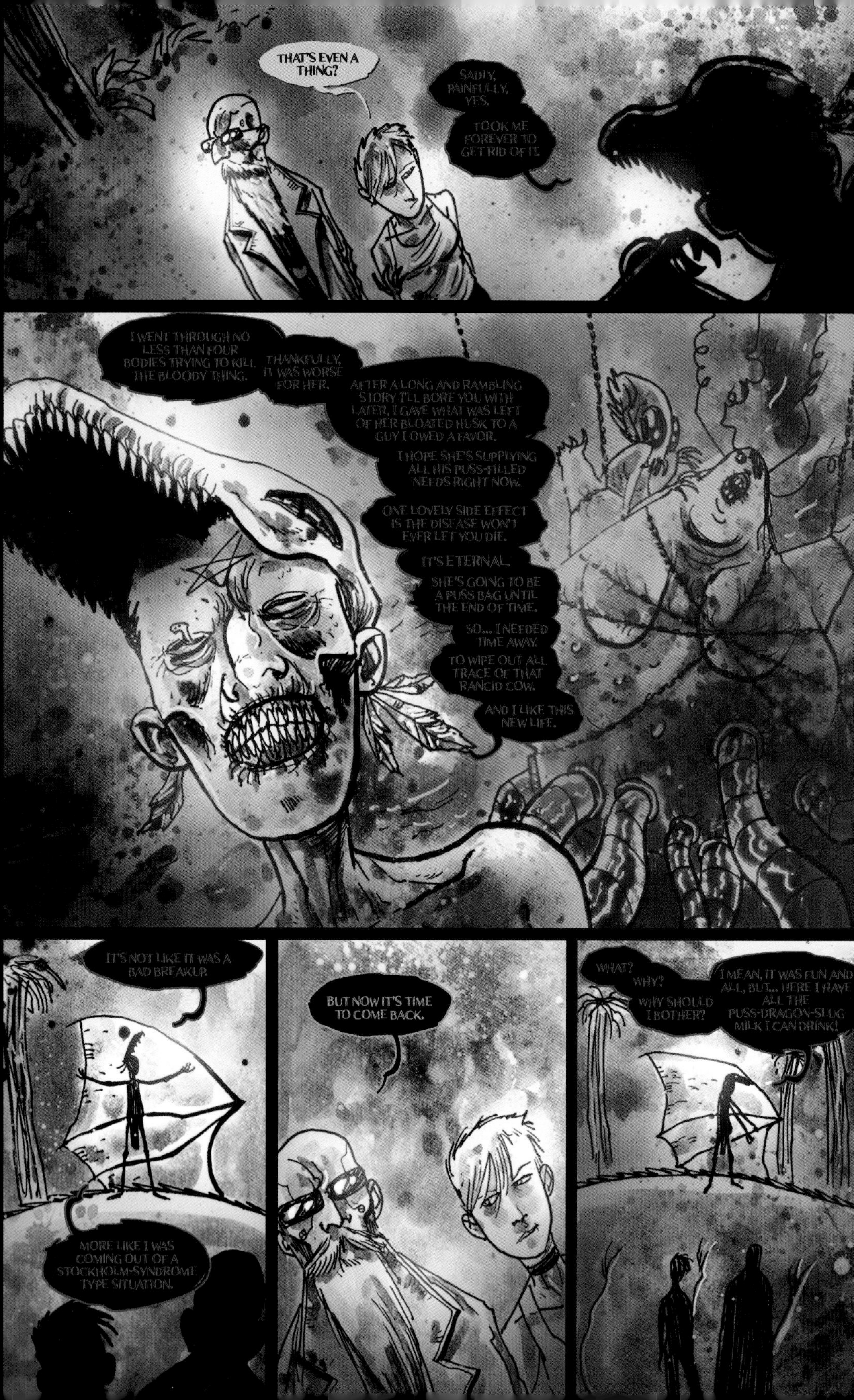
THAT'S EVEN A THING?
SADLY, PAINFULLY, YES.
TOOK ME FOREVER TO GET RID OF IT.
I WENT THROUGH NO LESS THAN FOUR BODIES TRYING TO KILL THE BLOODY THING.
THANKFULLY, IT WAS WORSE FOR HER.
AFTER A LONG AND RAMBLING STORY I'LL BORE YOU WITH LATER, I GAVE WHAT WAS LEFT OF HER BLOATED HUSK TO A GUY I OWED A FAVOR.
I HOPE SHE'S SUPPLYING ALL HIS PUSS-FILLED NEEDS RIGHT NOW.
ONE LOVELY SIDE EFFECT IS THE DISEASE WON'T EVER LET YOU DIE.
IT'S ETERNAL.
SHE'S GOING TO BE A PUSS BAG UNTIL THE END OF TIME.
SO... I NEEDED TIME AWAY.
TO WIPE OUT ALL TRACE OF THAT RANCID COW.
AND I LIKE THIS NEW LIFE.
IT'S NOT LIKE IT WAS A BAD BREAKUP.
MORE LIKE I WAS COMING OUT OF A STOCKHOLM-SYNDROME TYPE SITUATION.
BUT NOW IT'S TIME TO COME BACK.
WHAT? WHY? WHY SHOULD I BOTHER?
I MEAN, IT WAS FUN AND ALL, BUT... HERE I HAVE ALL THE PUSS-DRAGON-SLUG MILK I CAN DRINK!

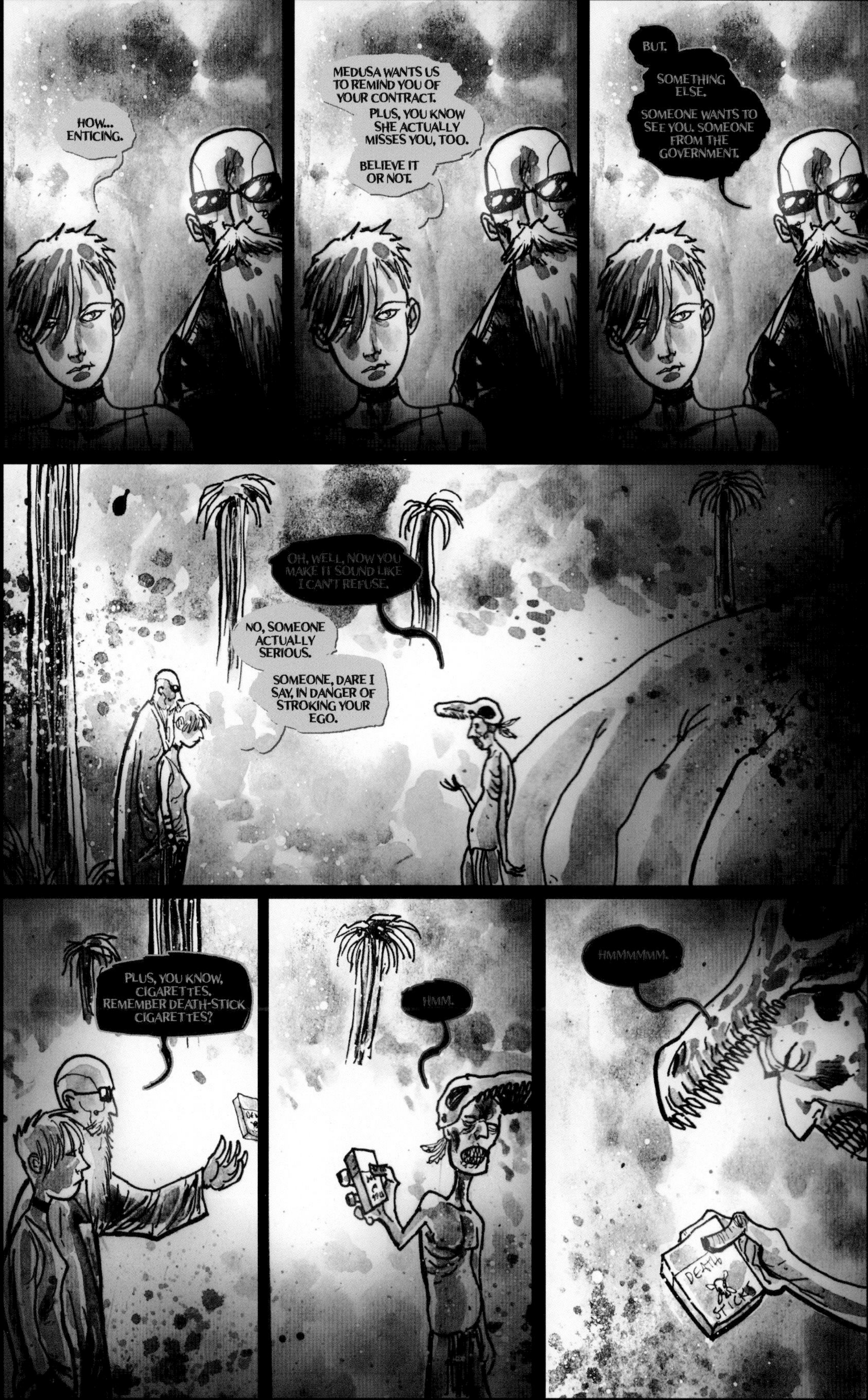
HOW... ENTICING.
MEDUSA WANTS US TO REMIND YOU OF YOUR CONTRACT.
PLUS, YOU KNOW SHE ACTUALLY MISSES YOU, TOO.
BELIEVE IT OR NOT.
BUT.
SOMETHING ELSE.
SOMEONE WANTS TO SEE YOU. SOMEONE FROM THE GOVERNMENT.
OH, WELL, NOW YOU MAKE IT SOUND LIKE I CAN'T REFUSE.
NO, SOMEONE ACTUALLY SERIOUS.
SOMEONE, DARE I SAY, IN DANGER OF STROKING YOUR EGO.
PLUS, YOU KNOW, CIGARETTES. REMEMBER DEATH-STICK CIGARETTES?
HMM.
HMMMMMM.
DEATH STICKS

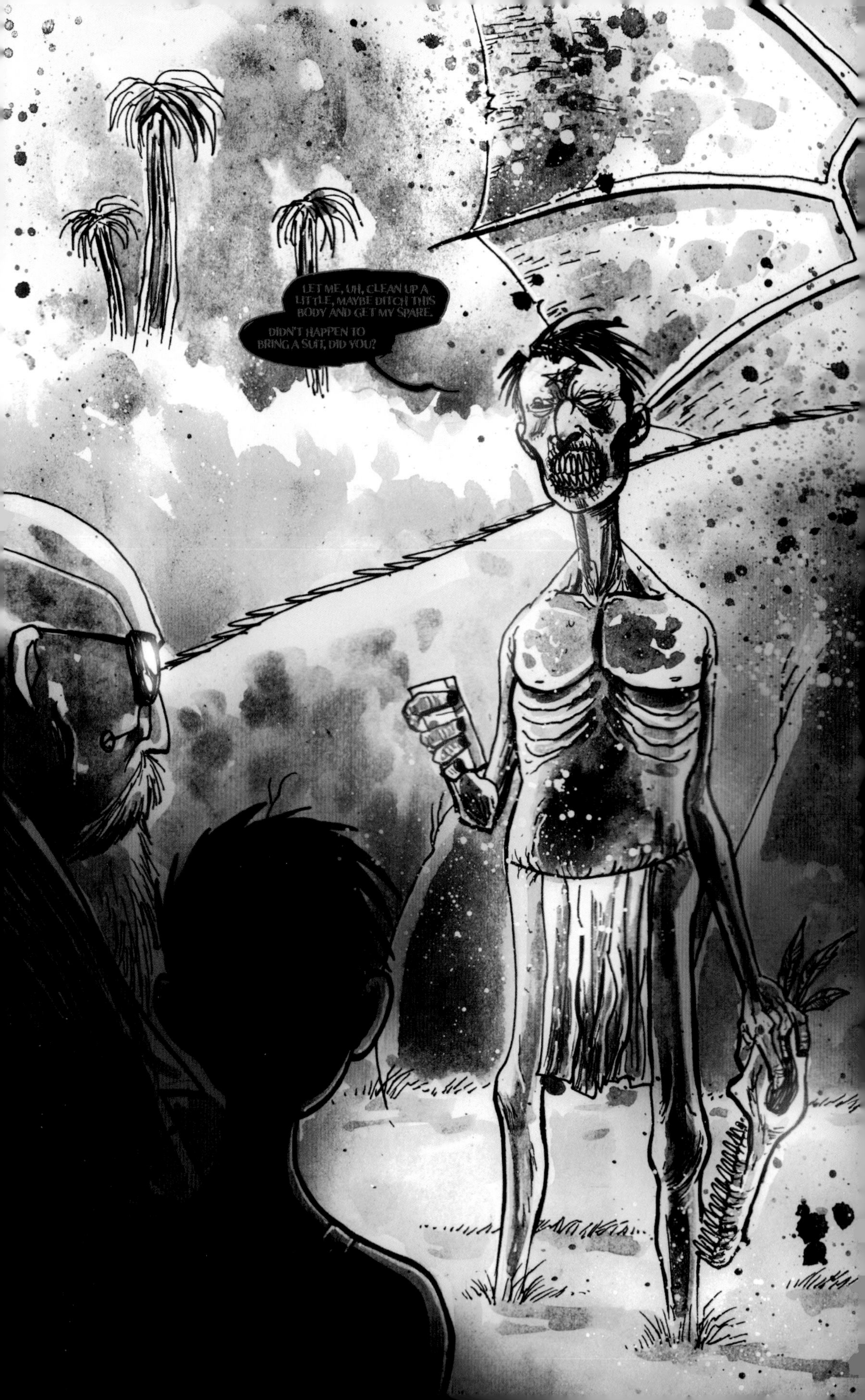
LET ME, UH, CLEAN UP A LITTLE, MAYBE DITCH THIS BODY AND GET MY SPARE.
DIDN'T HAPPEN TO BRING A SUIT, DID YOU?

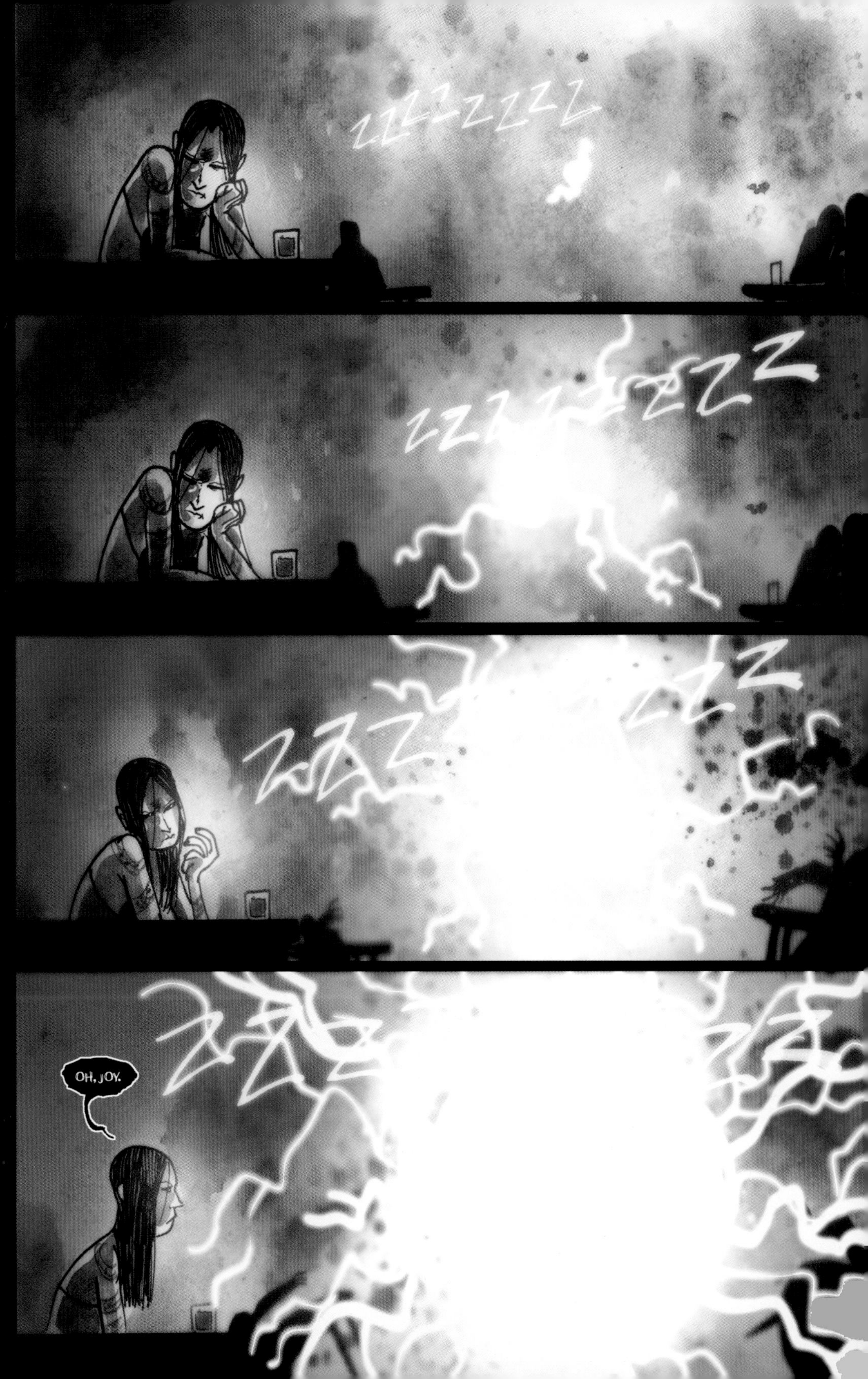
OH, JOY.

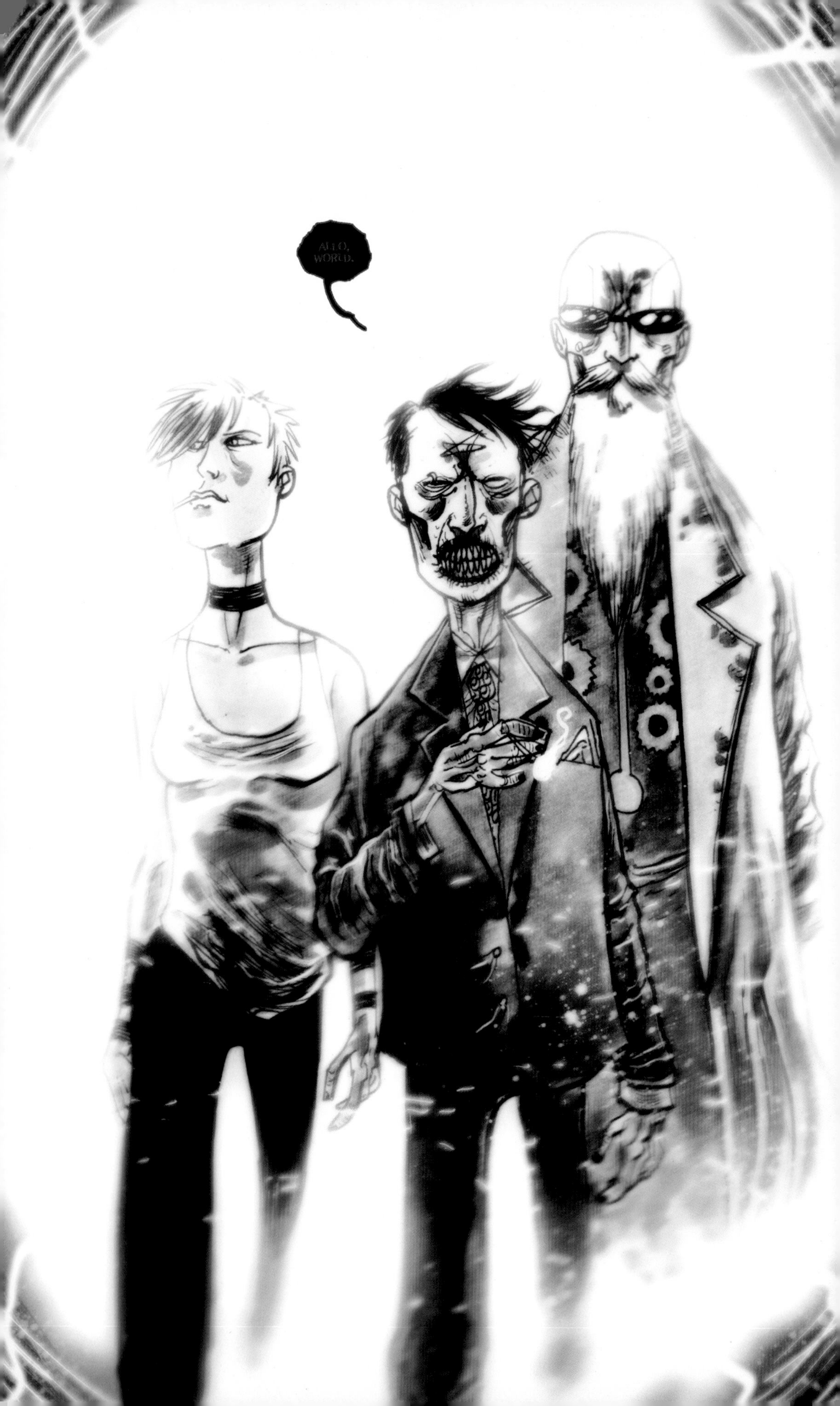
ALLO, WORLD.

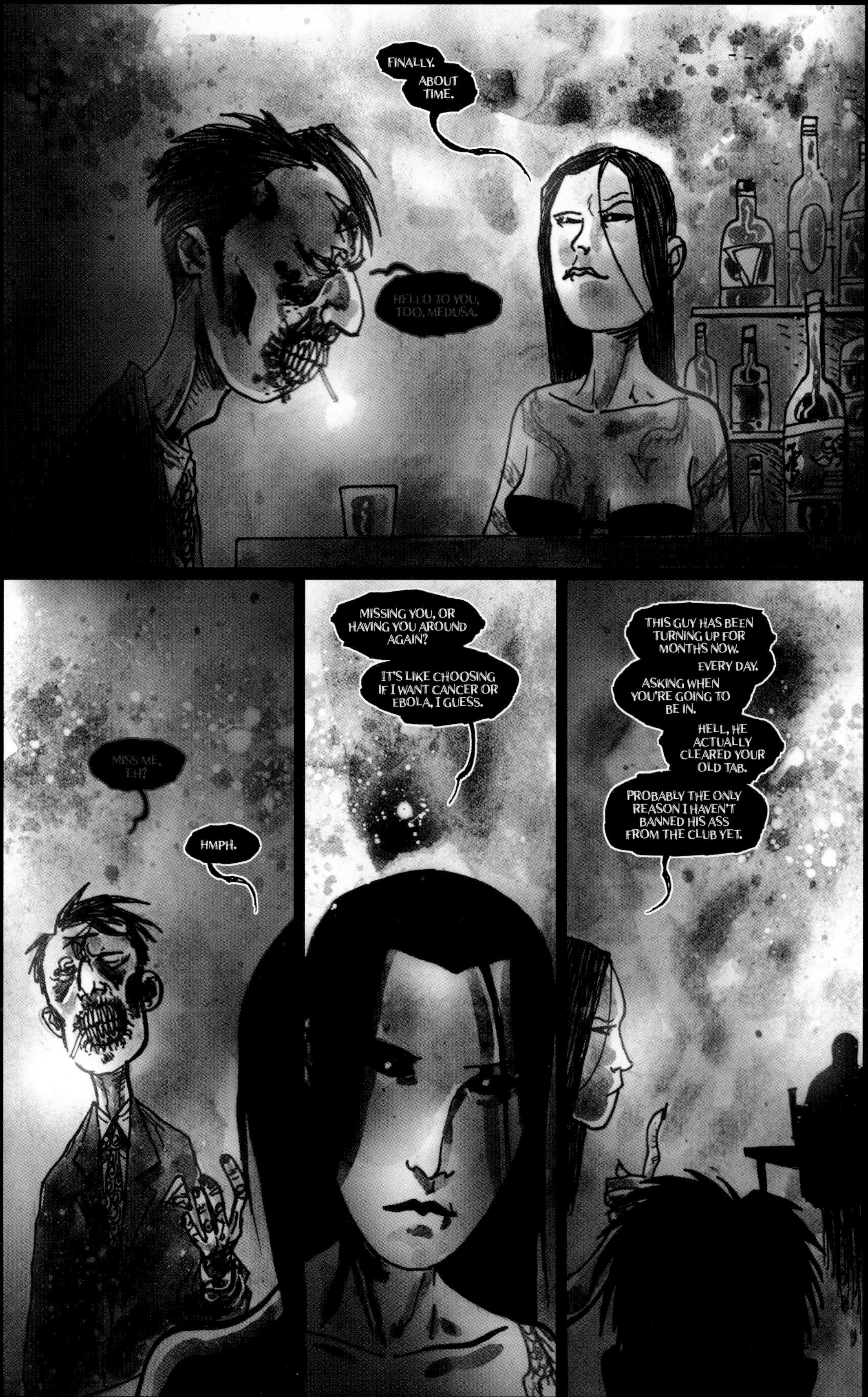

FINALLY.
ABOUT TIME.
HELLO TO YOU, TOO, MEDUSA.
MISS ME, EH?
HMPH.
MISSING YOU, OR HAVING YOU AROUND AGAIN?
IT'S LIKE CHOOSING IF I WANT CANCER OR EBOLA, I GUESS.
THIS GUY HAS BEEN TURNING UP FOR MONTHS NOW.
EVERY DAY.
ASKING WHEN YOU'RE GOING TO BE IN.
HELL, HE ACTUALLY CLEARED YOUR OLD TAB.
PROBABLY THE ONLY REASON I HAVEN'T BANNED HIS ASS FROM THE CLUB YET.

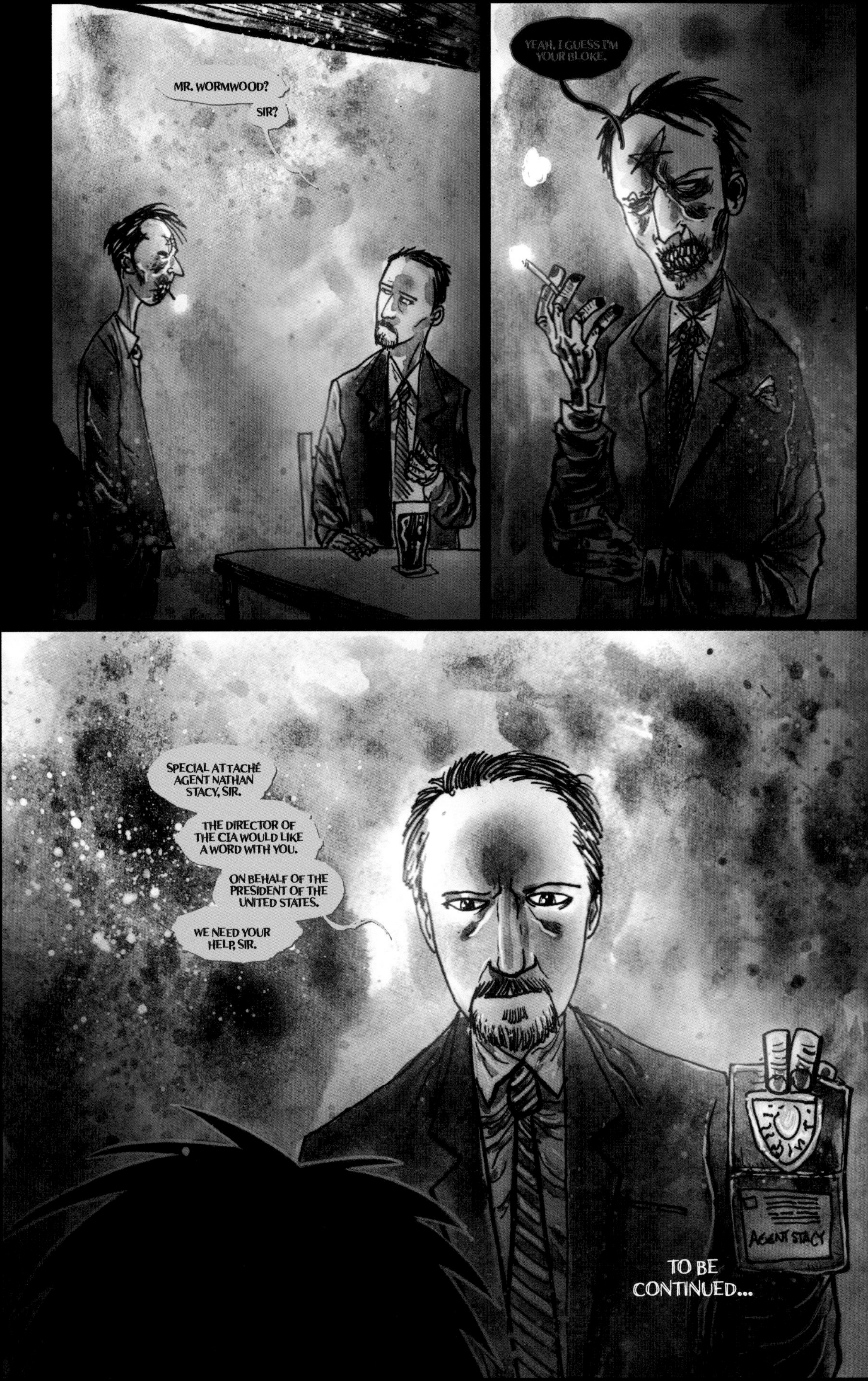
MR. WORMWOOD?
SIR?
YEAH, I GUESS I'M YOUR BLOKE.
SPECIAL ATTACHÉ AGENT NATHAN STACY, SIR.
THE DIRECTOR OF THE CIA WOULD LIKE A WORD WITH YOU.
ON BEHALF OF THE PRESIDENT OF THE UNITED STATES.
WE NEED YOUR HELP, SIR.
AGENT STACY
TO BE CONTINUED...

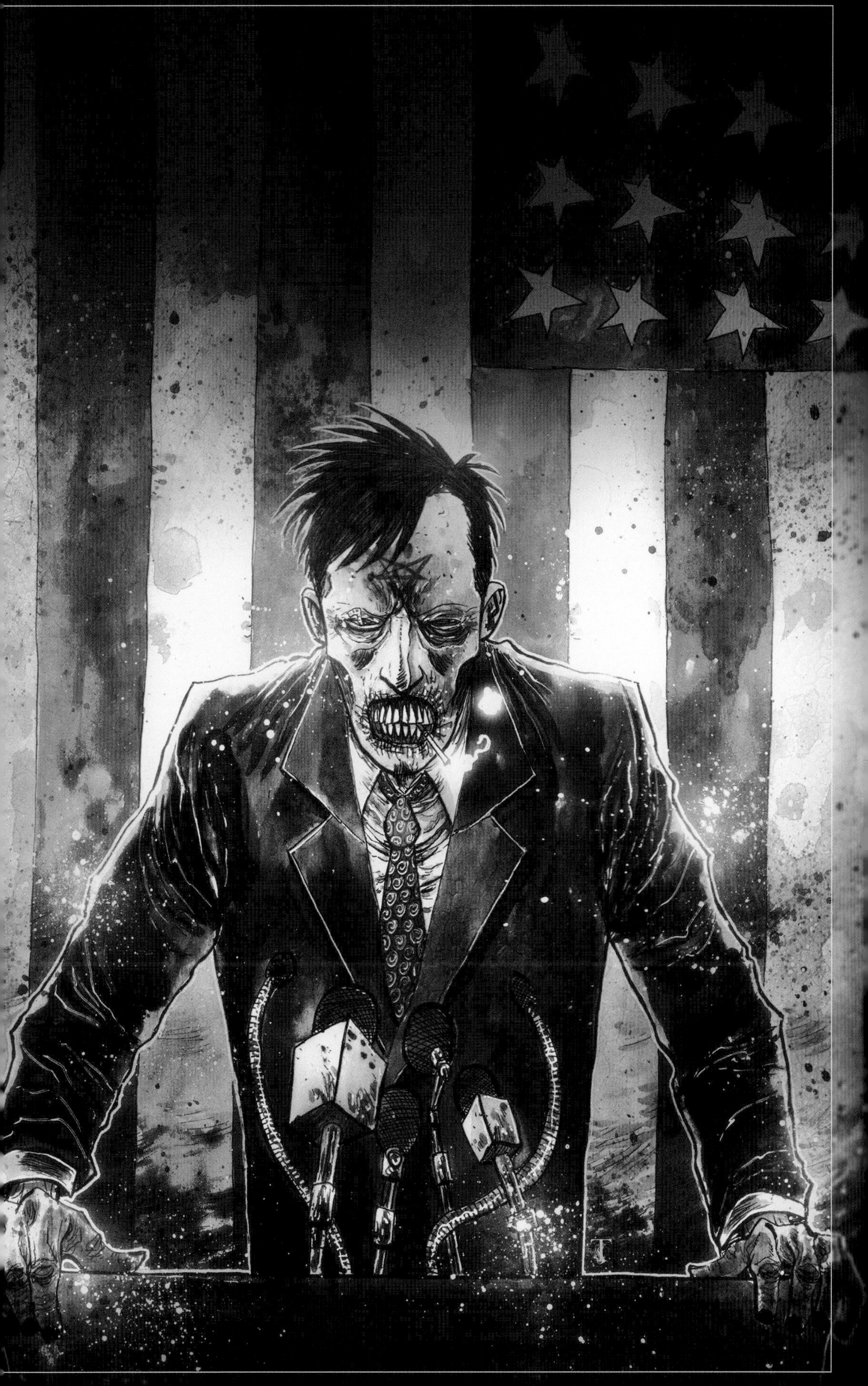

2

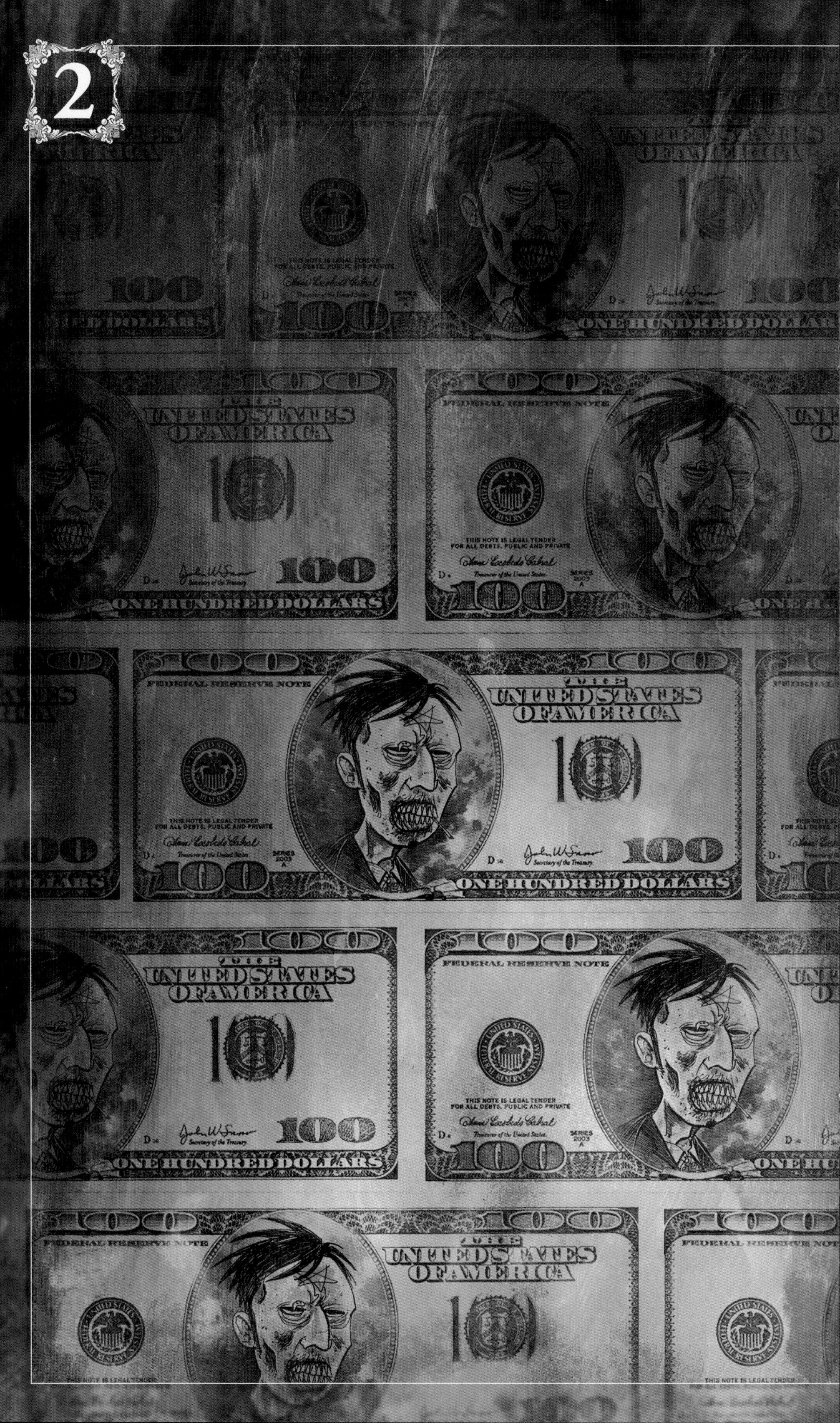
FEDERAL RESERVE NOTE
THE UNITED STATES OF AMERICA
THIS NOTE IS LEGAL TENDER FOR ALL DEBTS, PUBLIC AND PRIVATE
Treasurer of the United States
Secretary of the Treasury
SERIES 2003 A
100
ONE HUNDRED DOLLARS

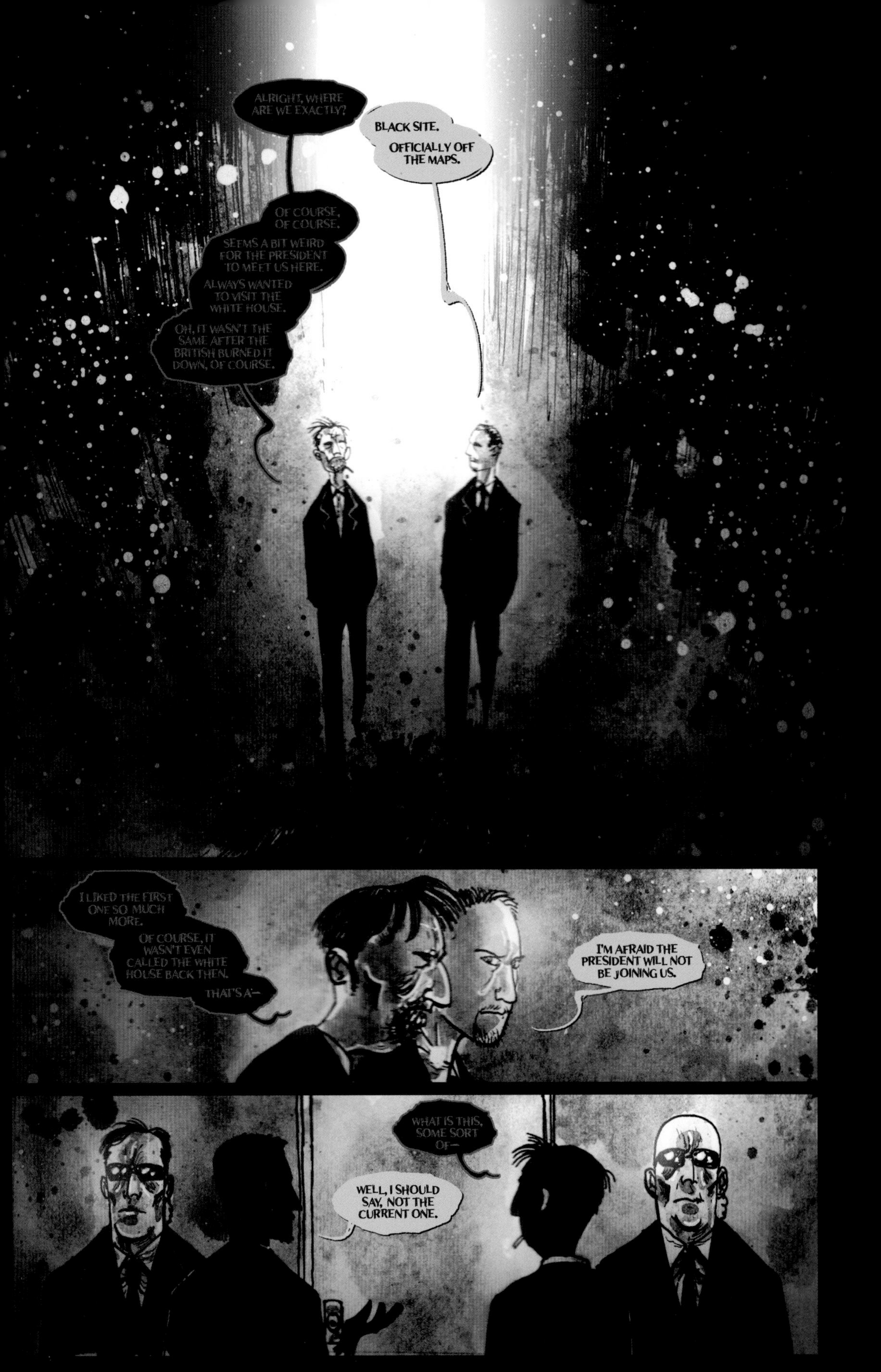
ALRIGHT, WHERE ARE WE EXACTLY?
BLACK SITE.
OFFICIALLY OFF THE MAPS.
OF COURSE, OF COURSE.
SEEMS A BIT WEIRD FOR THE PRESIDENT TO MEET US HERE.
ALWAYS WANTED TO VISIT THE WHITE HOUSE.
OH, IT WASN'T THE SAME AFTER THE BRITISH BURNED IT DOWN, OF COURSE.
I LIKED THE FIRST ONE SO MUCH MORE.
OF COURSE, IT WASN'T EVEN CALLED THE WHITE HOUSE BACK THEN.
THAT'S A—
I'M AFRAID THE PRESIDENT WILL NOT BE JOINING US.
WHAT IS THIS, SOME SORT OF—
WELL, I SHOULD SAY, NOT THE CURRENT ONE.

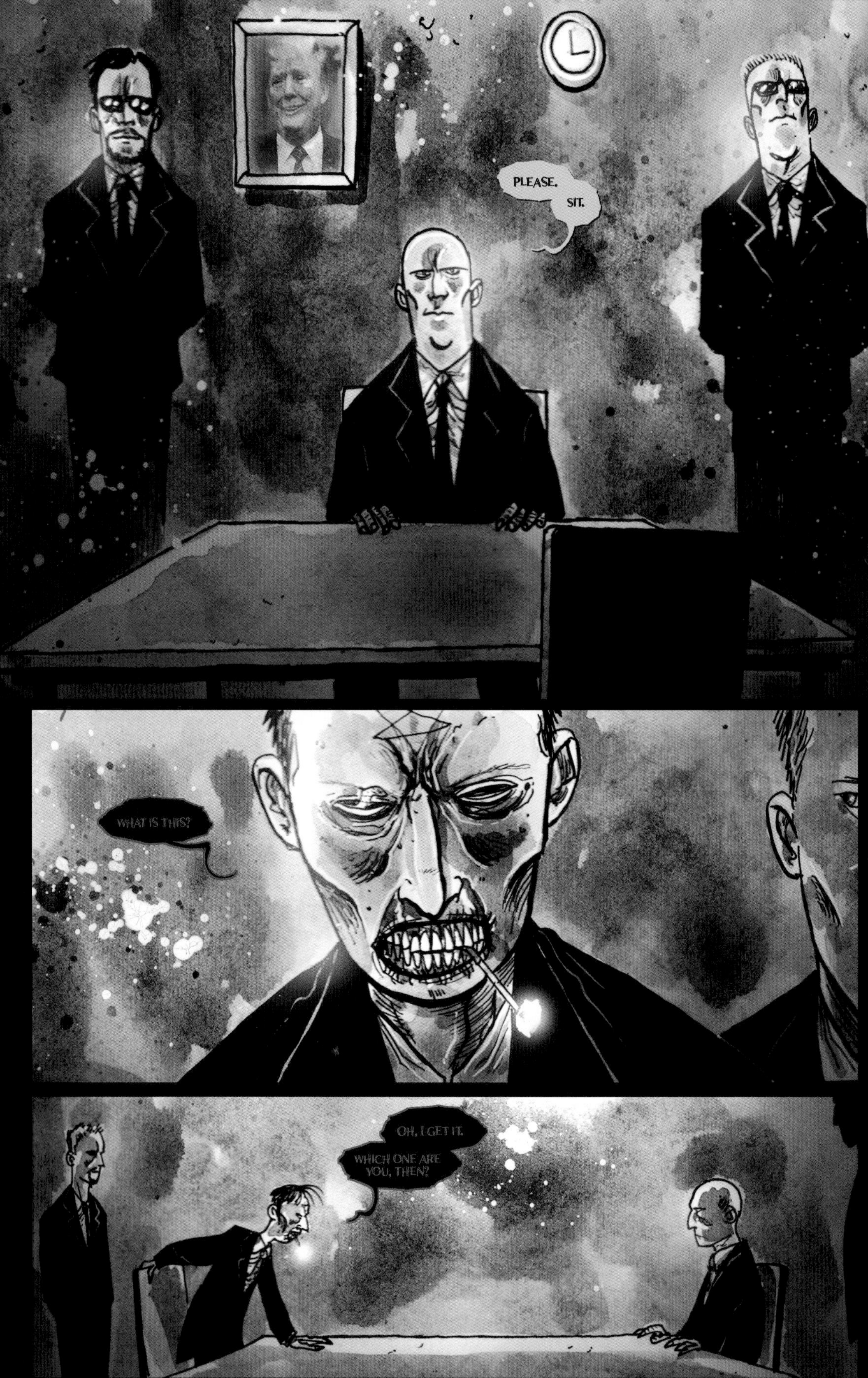
PLEASE.
SIT.
WHAT IS THIS?
OH, I GET IT.
WHICH ONE ARE YOU, THEN?

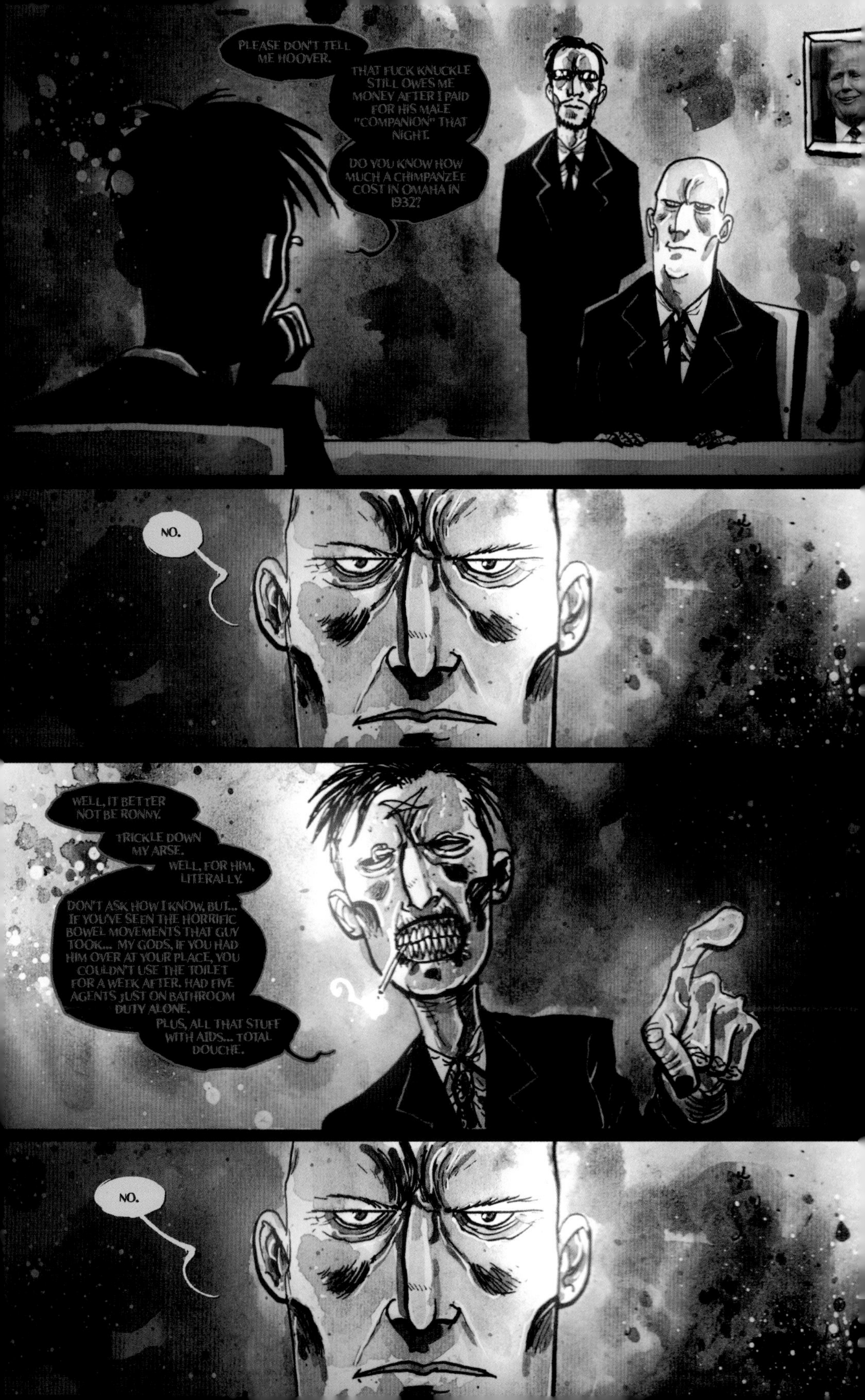
PLEASE DON'T TELL ME HOOVER.
THAT FUCK KNUCKLE STILL OWES ME MONEY AFTER I PAID FOR HIS MALE "COMPANION" THAT NIGHT.
DO YOU KNOW HOW MUCH A CHIMPANZEE COST IN OMAHA IN 1932?
NO.
WELL, IT BETTER NOT BE RONNY.
TRICKLE DOWN MY ARSE.
WELL, FOR HIM, LITERALLY.
DON'T ASK HOW I KNOW, BUT... IF YOU'VE SEEN THE HORRIFIC BOWEL MOVEMENTS THAT GUY TOOK... MY GODS, IF YOU HAD HIM OVER AT YOUR PLACE, YOU COULDN'T USE THE TOILET FOR A WEEK AFTER. HAD FIVE AGENTS JUST ON BATHROOM DUTY ALONE.
PLUS, ALL THAT STUFF WITH AIDS... TOTAL DOUCHE.
NO.

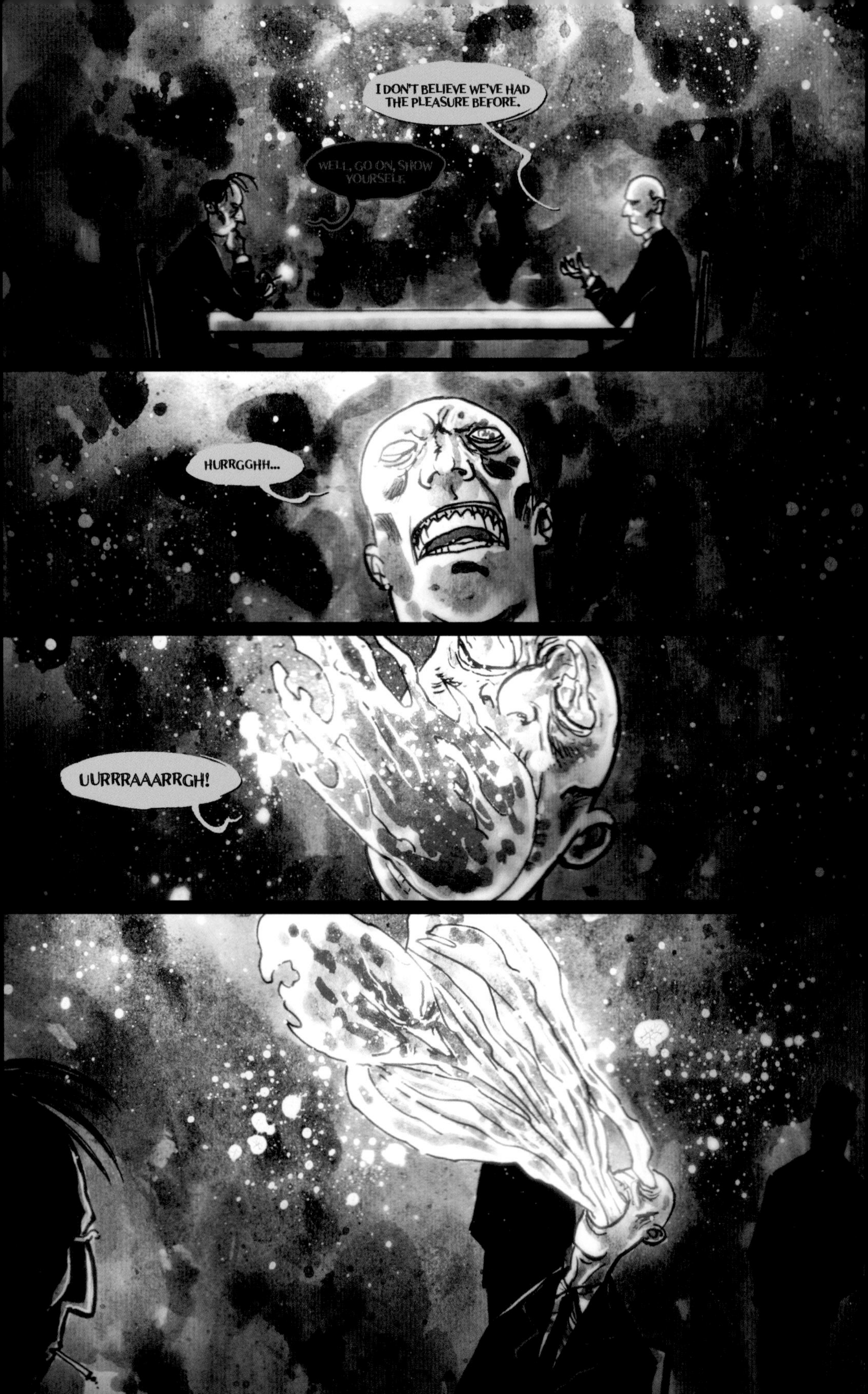
I DON'T BELIEVE WE'VE HAD THE PLEASURE BEFORE.
WELL, GO ON, SHOW YOURSELF.
HURRGGHH...
UURRRAAARRGH!

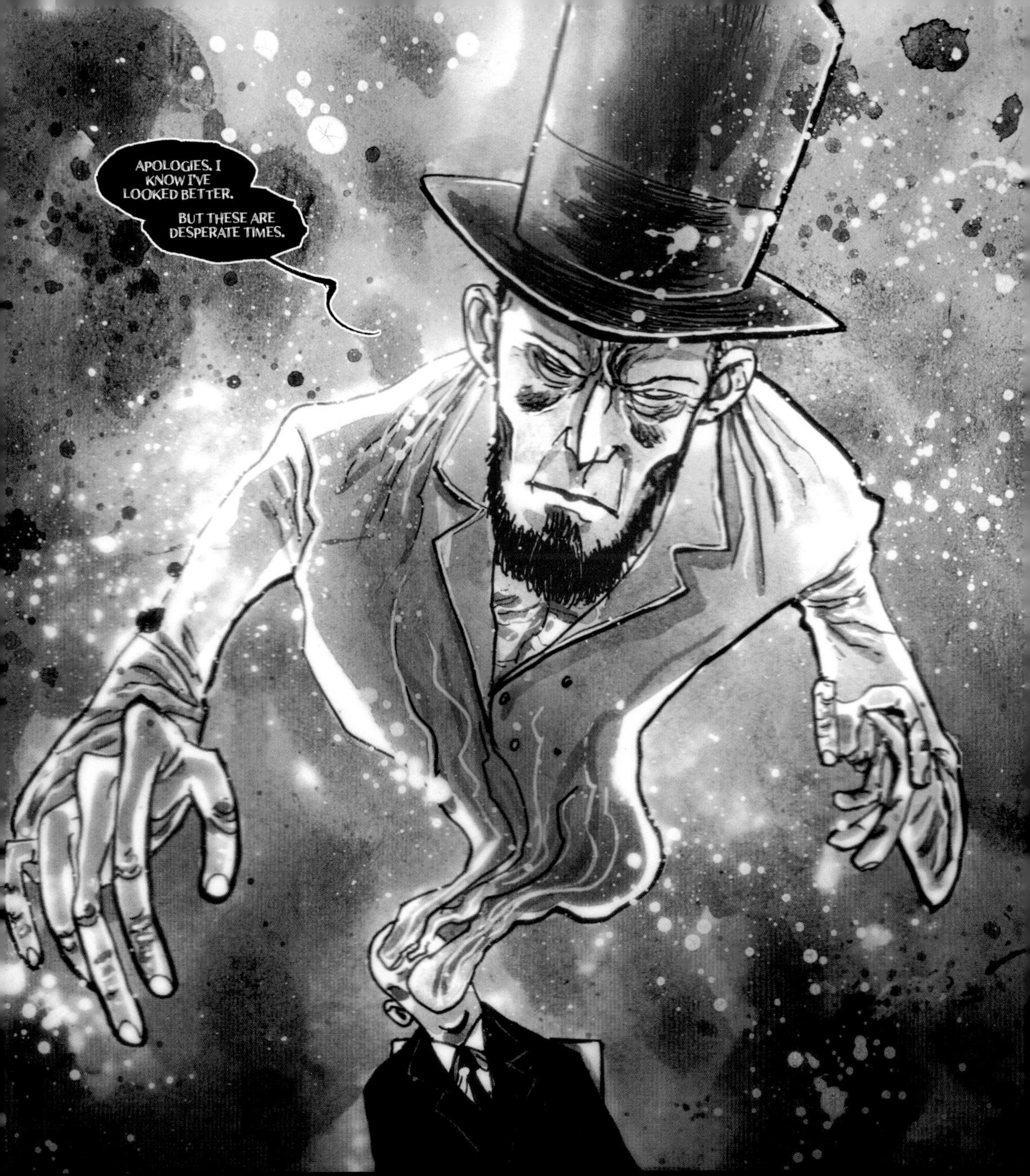
APOLOGIES. I KNOW I'VE LOOKED BETTER.
BUT THESE ARE DESPERATE TIMES.

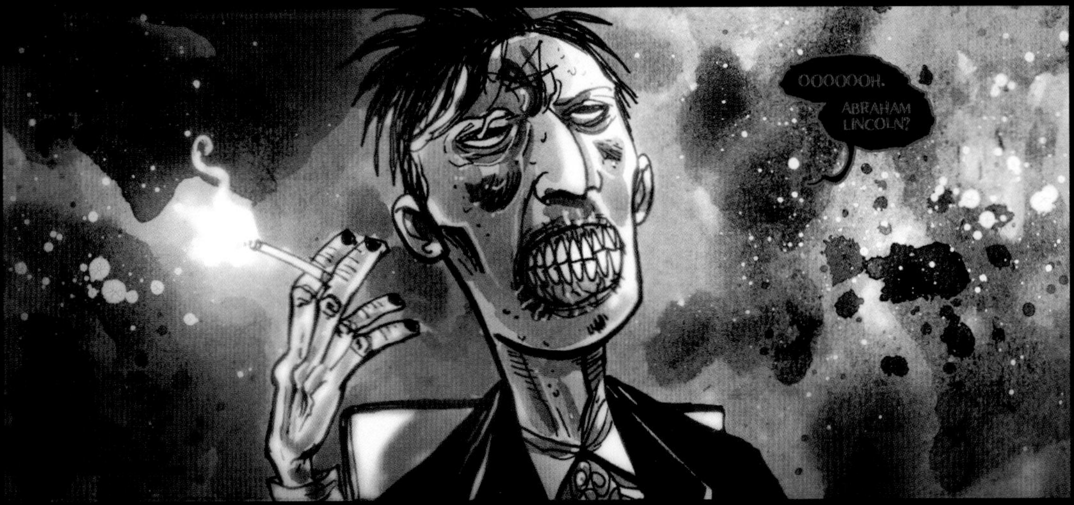
OOOOOOH.
ABRAHAM LINCOLN?

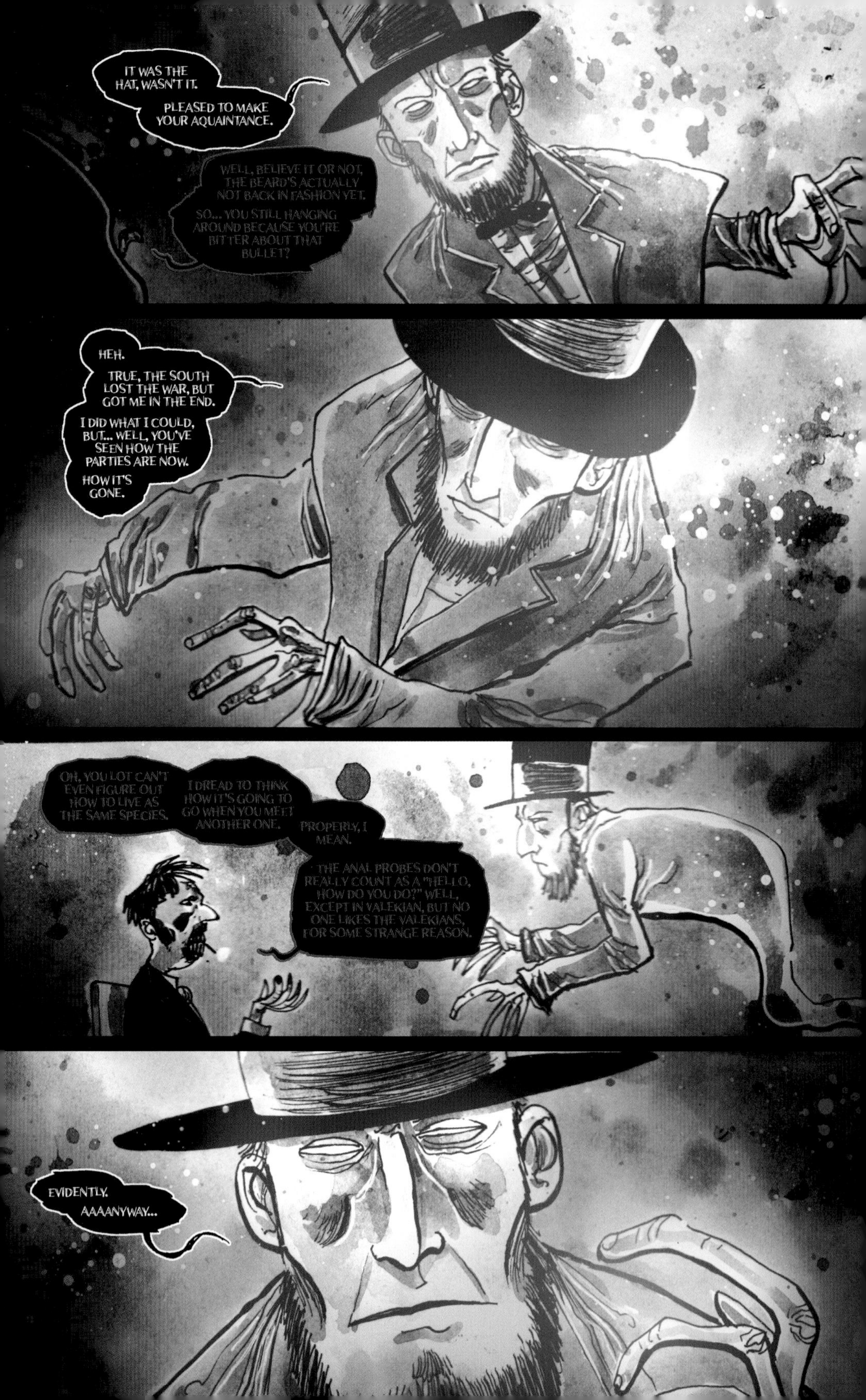
IT WAS THE HAT, WASN'T IT.
PLEASED TO MAKE YOUR AQUAINTANCE.
WELL, BELIEVE IT OR NOT, THE BEARD'S ACTUALLY NOT BACK IN FASHION YET.
SO... YOU STILL HANGING AROUND BECAUSE YOU'RE BITTER ABOUT THAT BULLET?
HEH.
TRUE, THE SOUTH LOST THE WAR, BUT GOT ME IN THE END.
I DID WHAT I COULD, BUT... WELL, YOU'VE SEEN HOW THE PARTIES ARE NOW.
HOW IT'S GONE.
OH, YOU LOT CAN'T EVEN FIGURE OUT HOW TO LIVE AS THE SAME SPECIES.
I DREAD TO THINK HOW IT'S GOING TO GO WHEN YOU MEET ANOTHER ONE.
PROPERLY, I MEAN.
THE ANAL PROBES DON'T REALLY COUNT AS A "HELLO, HOW DO YOU DO?" WELL, EXCEPT IN VALEKIAN, BUT NO ONE LIKES THE VALEKIANS, FOR SOME STRANGE REASON.
EVIDENTLY.
AAAANYWAY...

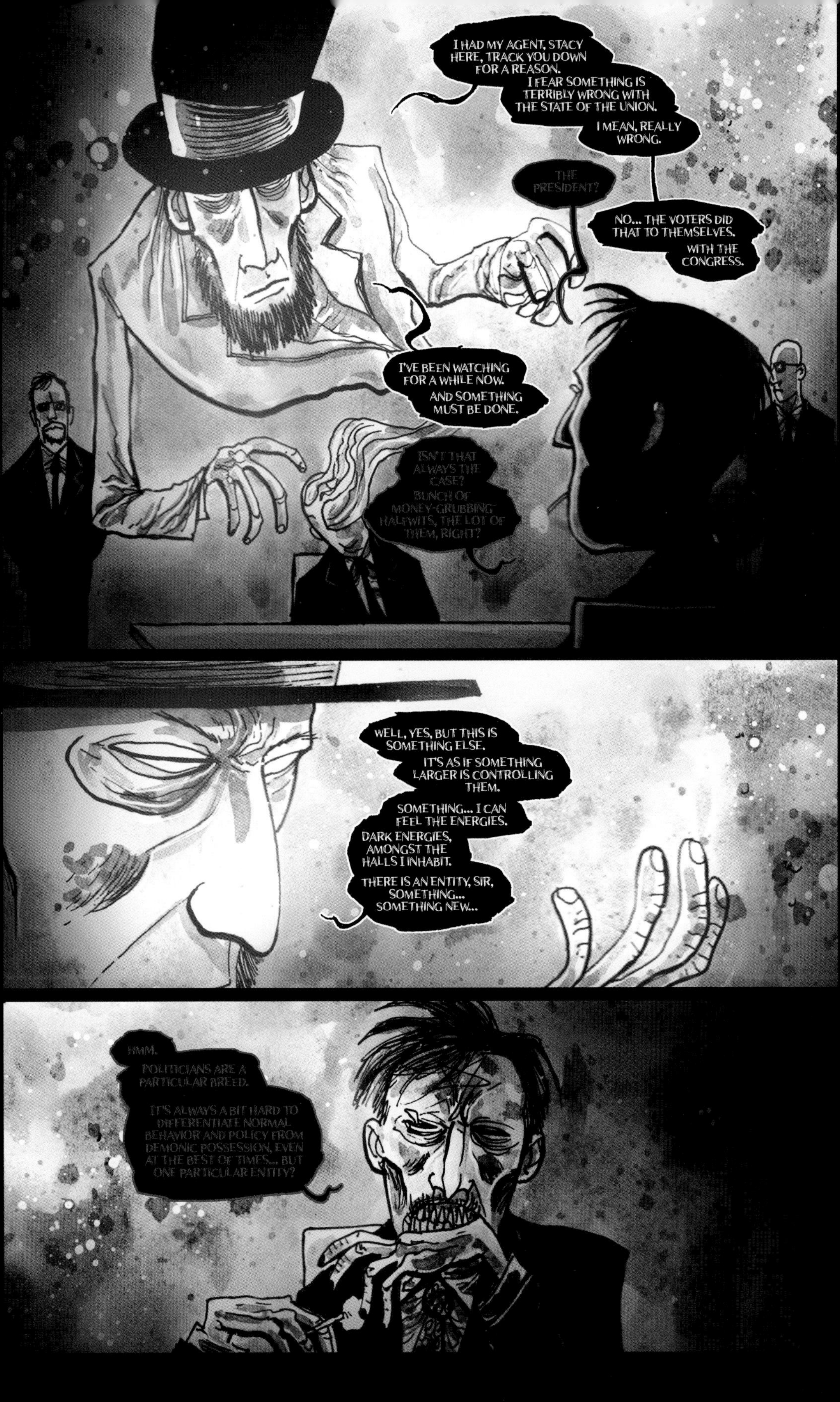

I HAD MY AGENT, STACY HERE, TRACK YOU DOWN FOR A REASON.
I FEAR SOMETHING IS TERRIBLY WRONG WITH THE STATE OF THE UNION.
I MEAN, REALLY WRONG.
THE PRESIDENT?
NO... THE VOTERS DID THAT TO THEMSELVES.
WITH THE CONGRESS.
I'VE BEEN WATCHING FOR A WHILE NOW.
AND SOMETHING MUST BE DONE.
ISN'T THAT ALWAYS THE CASE?
BUNCH OF MONEY-GRUBBING HALFWITS, THE LOT OF THEM, RIGHT?
WELL, YES, BUT THIS IS SOMETHING ELSE.
IT'S AS IF SOMETHING LARGER IS CONTROLLING THEM.
SOMETHING... I CAN FEEL THE ENERGIES.
DARK ENERGIES, AMONGST THE HALLS I INHABIT.
THERE IS AN ENTITY, SIR, SOMETHING... SOMETHING NEW...
HMM.
POLITICIANS ARE A PARTICULAR BREED.
IT'S ALWAYS A BIT HARD TO DIFFERENTIATE NORMAL BEHAVIOR AND POLICY FROM DEMONIC POSSESSION, EVEN AT THE BEST OF TIMES... BUT ONE PARTICULAR ENTITY?

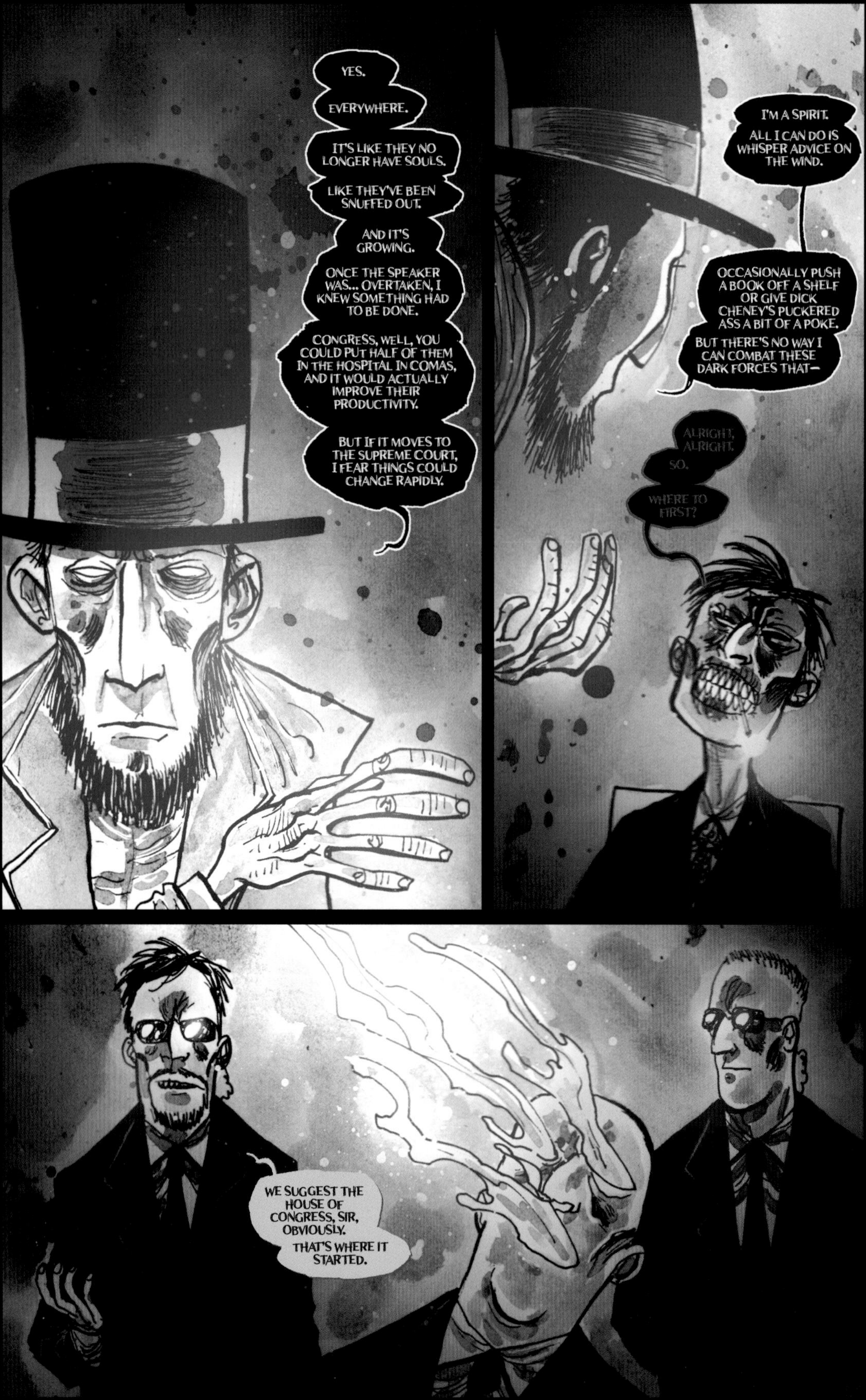
YES.
EVERYWHERE.
IT'S LIKE THEY NO LONGER HAVE SOULS.
LIKE THEY'VE BEEN SNUFFED OUT.
AND IT'S GROWING.
ONCE THE SPEAKER WAS... OVERTAKEN, I KNEW SOMETHING HAD TO BE DONE.
CONGRESS, WELL, YOU COULD PUT HALF OF THEM IN THE HOSPITAL IN COMAS, AND IT WOULD ACTUALLY IMPROVE THEIR PRODUCTIVITY.
BUT IF IT MOVES TO THE SUPREME COURT, I FEAR THINGS COULD CHANGE RAPIDLY.
I'M A SPIRIT.
ALL I CAN DO IS WHISPER ADVICE ON THE WIND.
OCCASIONALLY PUSH A BOOK OFF A SHELF OR GIVE DICK CHENEY'S PUCKERED ASS A BIT OF A POKE.
BUT THERE'S NO WAY I CAN COMBAT THESE DARK FORCES THAT—
ALRIGHT, ALRIGHT.
SO.
WHERE TO FIRST?
WE SUGGEST THE HOUSE OF CONGRESS, SIR, OBVIOUSLY.
THAT'S WHERE IT STARTED.

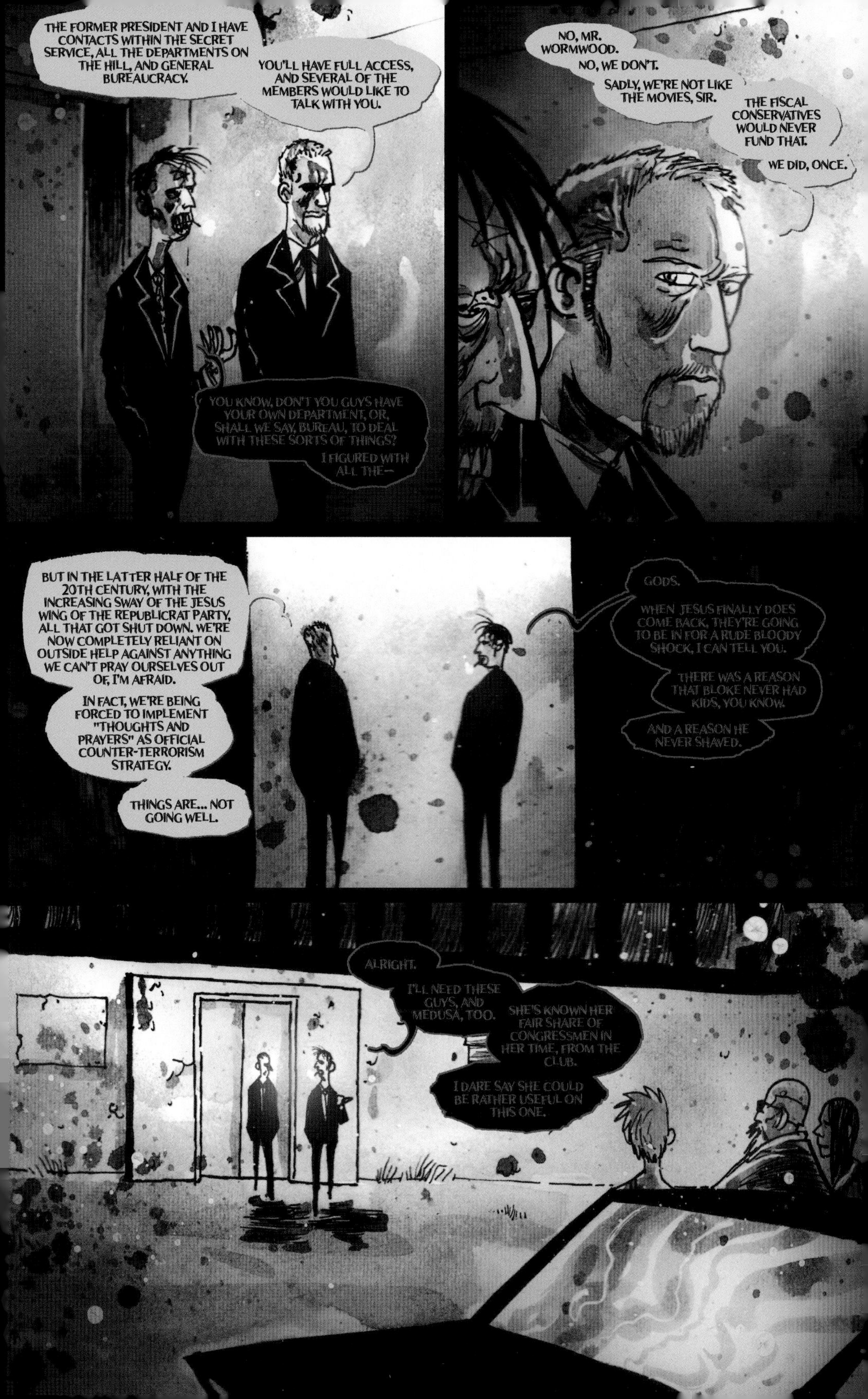
THE FORMER PRESIDENT AND I HAVE CONTACTS WITHIN THE SECRET SERVICE, ALL THE DEPARTMENTS ON THE HILL, AND GENERAL BUREAUCRACY.
YOU'LL HAVE FULL ACCESS, AND SEVERAL OF THE MEMBERS WOULD LIKE TO TALK WITH YOU.
YOU KNOW, DON'T YOU GUYS HAVE YOUR OWN DEPARTMENT, OR, SHALL WE SAY, BUREAU, TO DEAL WITH THESE SORTS OF THINGS?
I FIGURED WITH ALL THE—
NO, MR. WORMWOOD.
NO, WE DON'T.
SADLY, WE'RE NOT LIKE THE MOVIES, SIR.
THE FISCAL CONSERVATIVES WOULD NEVER FUND THAT.
WE DID, ONCE.
BUT IN THE LATTER HALF OF THE 20TH CENTURY, WITH THE INCREASING SWAY OF THE JESUS WING OF THE REPUBLICRAT PARTY, ALL THAT GOT SHUT DOWN. WE'RE NOW COMPLETELY RELIANT ON OUTSIDE HELP AGAINST ANYTHING WE CAN'T PRAY OURSELVES OUT OF, I'M AFRAID.
IN FACT, WE'RE BEING FORCED TO IMPLEMENT "THOUGHTS AND PRAYERS" AS OFFICIAL COUNTER-TERRORISM STRATEGY.
THINGS ARE... NOT GOING WELL.
GODS.
WHEN JESUS FINALLY DOES COME BACK, THEY'RE GOING TO BE IN FOR A RUDE BLOODY SHOCK, I CAN TELL YOU.
THERE WAS A REASON THAT BLOKE NEVER HAD KIDS, YOU KNOW.
AND A REASON HE NEVER SHAVED.
ALRIGHT.
I'LL NEED THESE GUYS, AND MEDUSA, TOO.
SHE'S KNOWN HER FAIR SHARE OF CONGRESSMEN IN HER TIME, FROM THE CLUB.
I DARE SAY SHE COULD BE RATHER USEFUL ON THIS ONE.

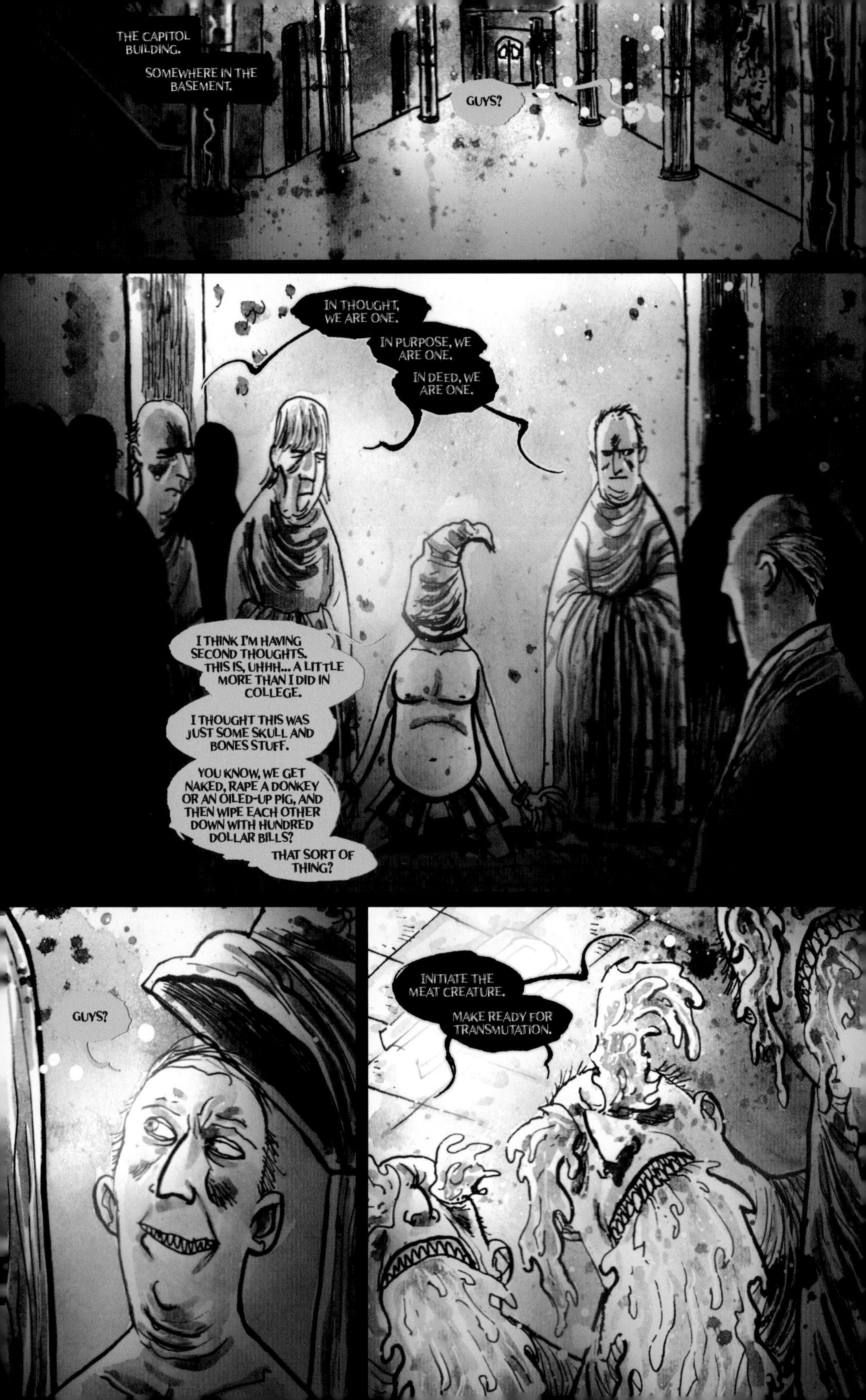
THE CAPITOL BUILDING.
SOMEWHERE IN THE BASEMENT.
GUYS?
IN THOUGHT, WE ARE ONE.
IN PURPOSE, WE ARE ONE.
IN DEED, WE ARE ONE.
I THINK I'M HAVING SECOND THOUGHTS. THIS IS, UHHH... A LITTLE MORE THAN I DID IN COLLEGE.
I THOUGHT THIS WAS JUST SOME SKULL AND BONES STUFF.
YOU KNOW, WE GET NAKED, RAPE A DONKEY OR AN OILED-UP PIG, AND THEN WIPE EACH OTHER DOWN WITH HUNDRED DOLLAR BILLS?
THAT SORT OF THING?
GUYS?
INITIATE THE MEAT CREATURE.
MAKE READY FOR TRANSMUTATION.

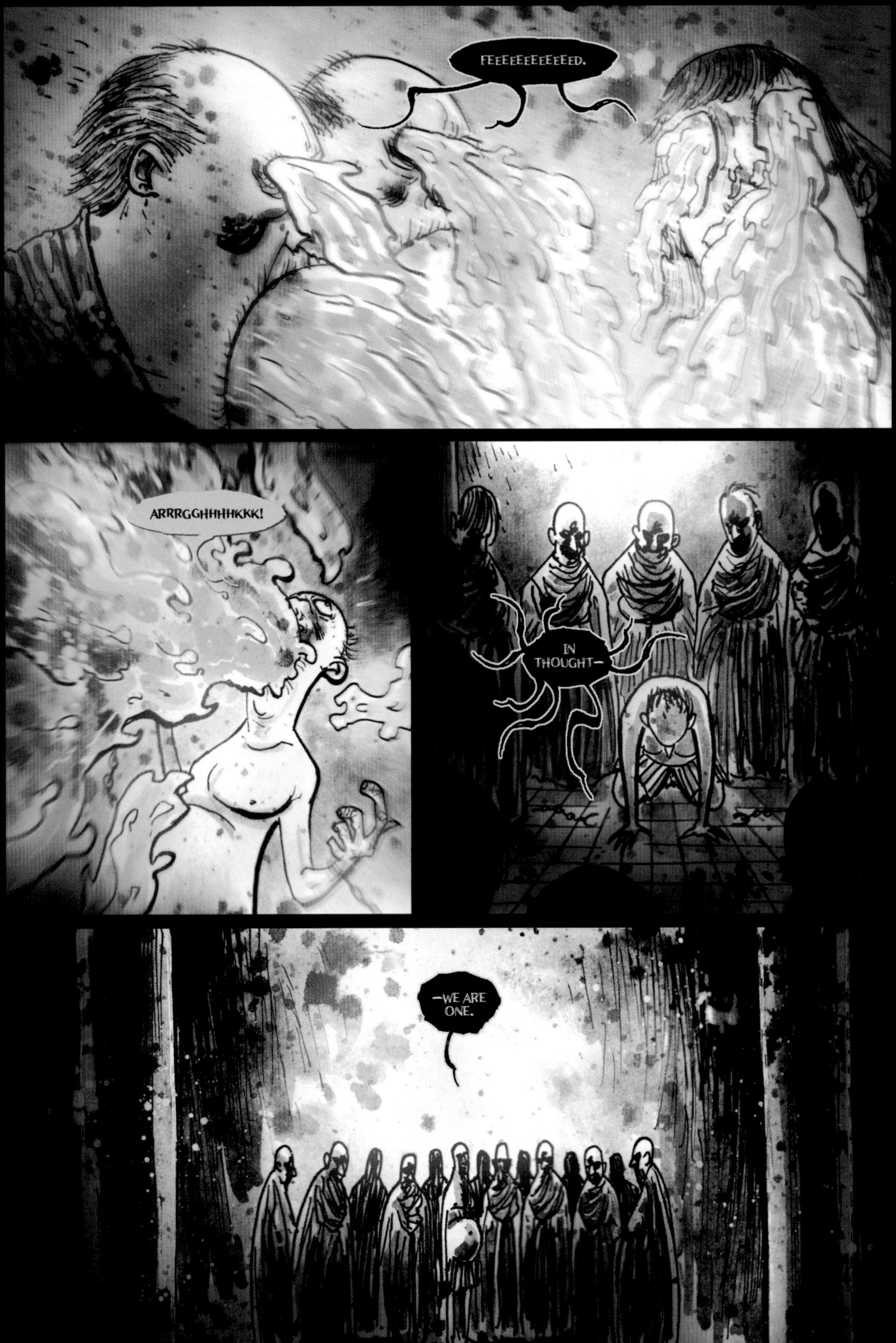
FEEEEEEEEEEEED.
ARRRGGHHHHKKK!
IN THOUGHT—
—WE ARE ONE.

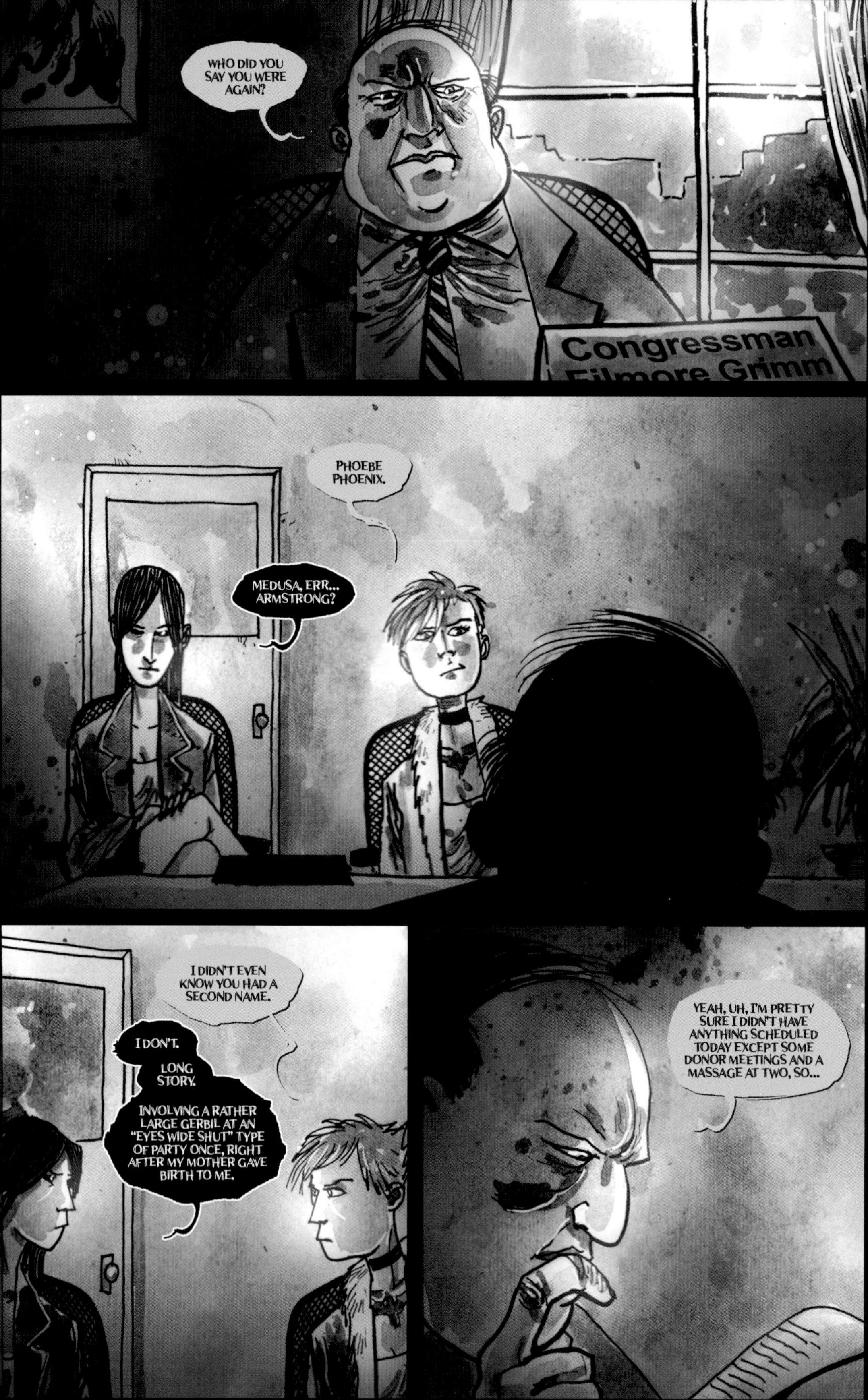
WHO DID YOU SAY YOU WERE AGAIN?
Congressman Filmore Grimm
PHOEBE PHOENIX.
MEDUSA, ERR... ARMSTRONG?
I DIDN'T EVEN KNOW YOU HAD A SECOND NAME.
I DON'T.
LONG STORY.
INVOLVING A RATHER LARGE GERBIL AT AN "EYES WIDE SHUT" TYPE OF PARTY ONCE, RIGHT AFTER MY MOTHER GAVE BIRTH TO ME.
YEAH, UH, I'M PRETTY SURE I DIDN'T HAVE ANYTHING SCHEDULED TODAY EXCEPT SOME DONOR MEETINGS AND A MASSAGE AT TWO, SO...

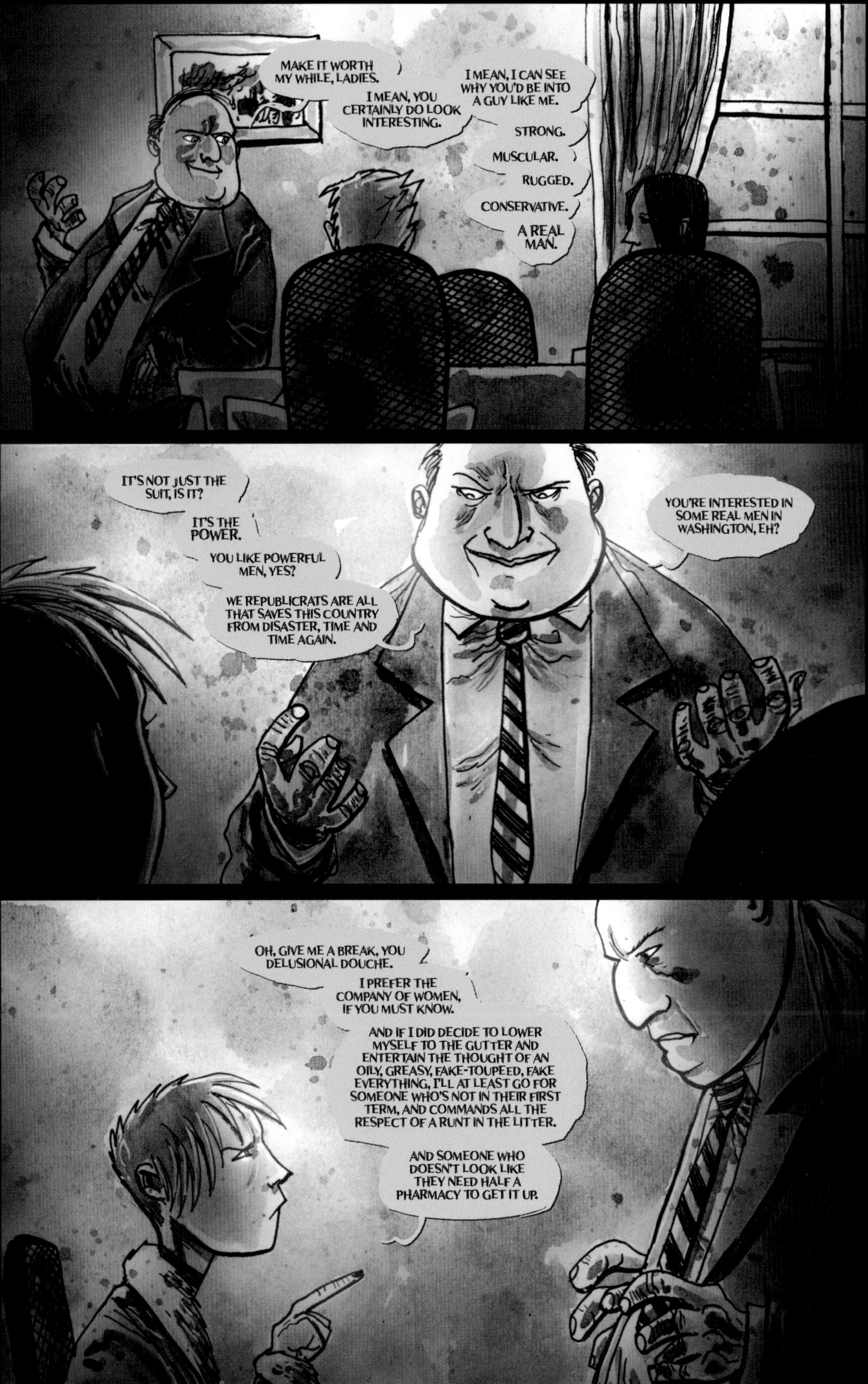
MAKE IT WORTH MY WHILE, LADIES.
I MEAN, YOU CERTAINLY DO LOOK INTERESTING.
I MEAN, I CAN SEE WHY YOU'D BE INTO A GUY LIKE ME.
STRONG.
MUSCULAR.
RUGGED.
CONSERVATIVE.
A REAL MAN.
IT'S NOT JUST THE SUIT, IS IT?
IT'S THE POWER.
YOU LIKE POWERFUL MEN, YES?
WE REPUBLICRATS ARE ALL THAT SAVES THIS COUNTRY FROM DISASTER, TIME AND TIME AGAIN.
YOU'RE INTERESTED IN SOME REAL MEN IN WASHINGTON, EH?
OH, GIVE ME A BREAK, YOU DELUSIONAL DOUCHE.
I PREFER THE COMPANY OF WOMEN, IF YOU MUST KNOW.
AND IF I DID DECIDE TO LOWER MYSELF TO THE GUTTER AND ENTERTAIN THE THOUGHT OF AN OILY, GREASY, FAKE-TOUPEED, FAKE EVERYTHING, I'LL AT LEAST GO FOR SOMEONE WHO'S NOT IN THEIR FIRST TERM, AND COMMANDS ALL THE RESPECT OF A RUNT IN THE LITTER.
AND SOMEONE WHO DOESN'T LOOK LIKE THEY NEED HALF A PHARMACY TO GET IT UP.

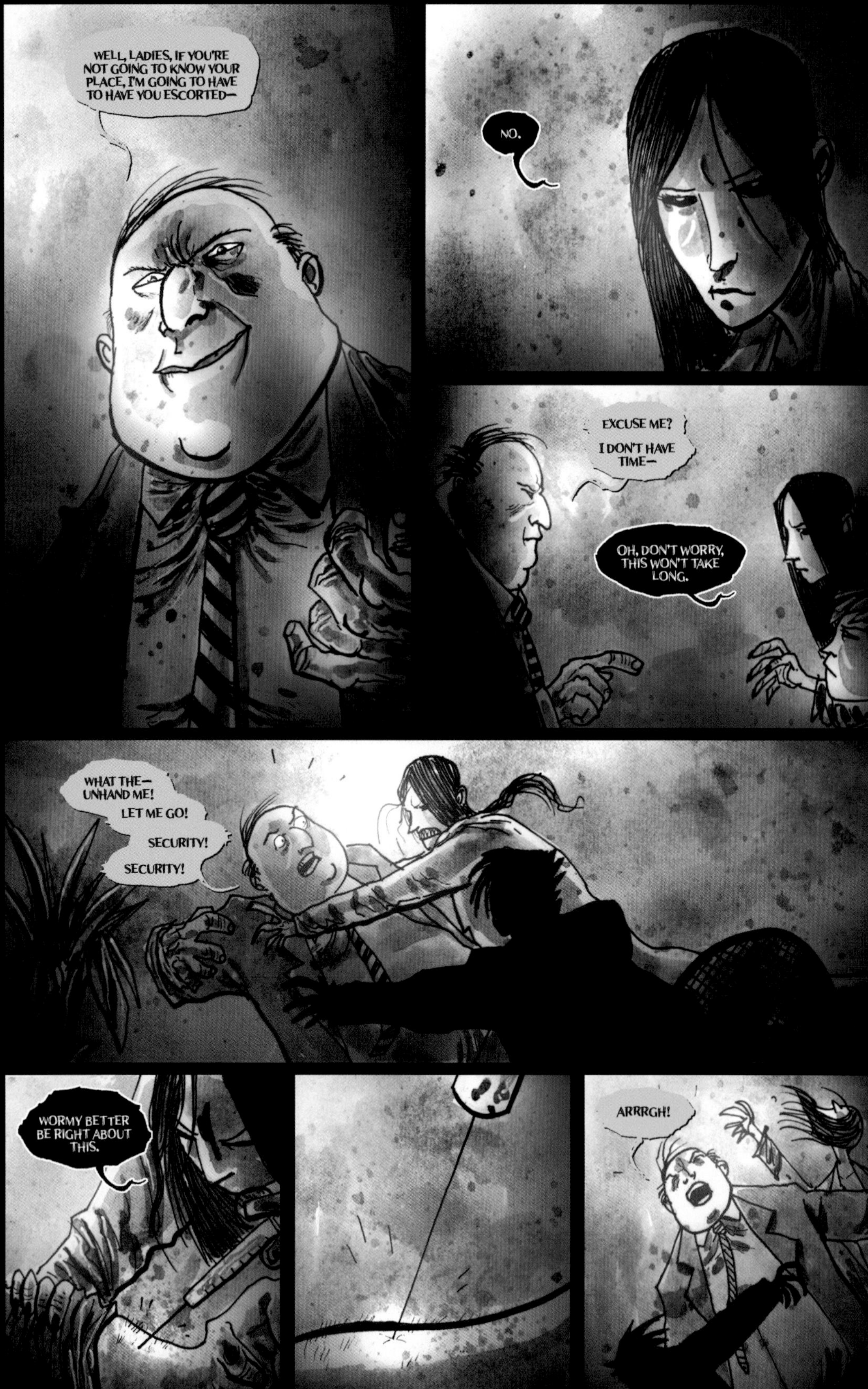
WELL, LADIES, IF YOU'RE NOT GOING TO KNOW YOUR PLACE, I'M GOING TO HAVE TO HAVE YOU ESCORTED—
NO.
EXCUSE ME?
I DON'T HAVE TIME—
OH, DON'T WORRY, THIS WON'T TAKE LONG.
WHAT THE—
UNHAND ME!
LET ME GO!
SECURITY!
SECURITY!
WORMY BETTER BE RIGHT ABOUT THIS.
ARRRGH!

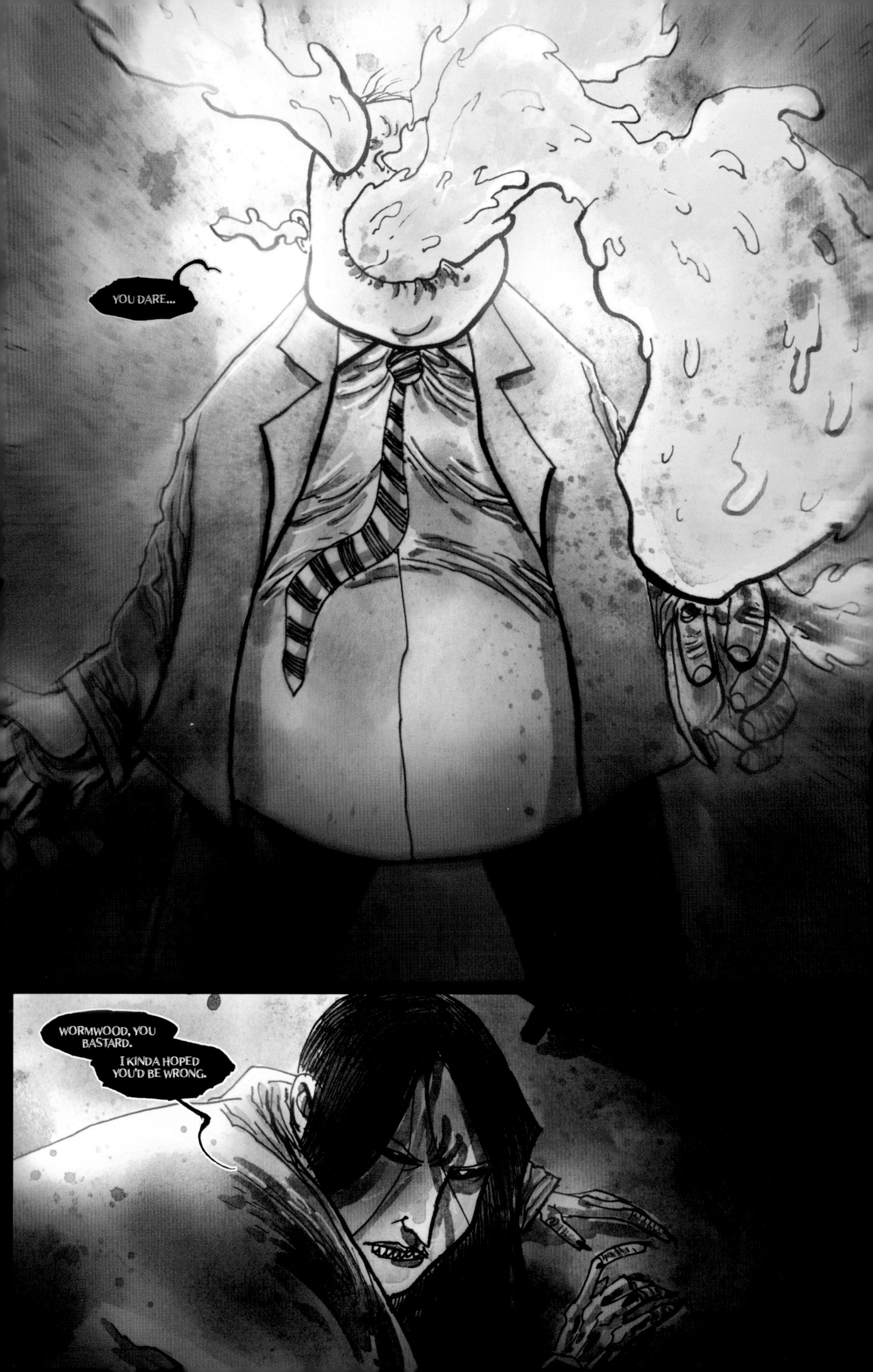
YOU DARE...
WORMWOOD, YOU BASTARD.
I KINDA HOPED YOU'D BE WRONG.

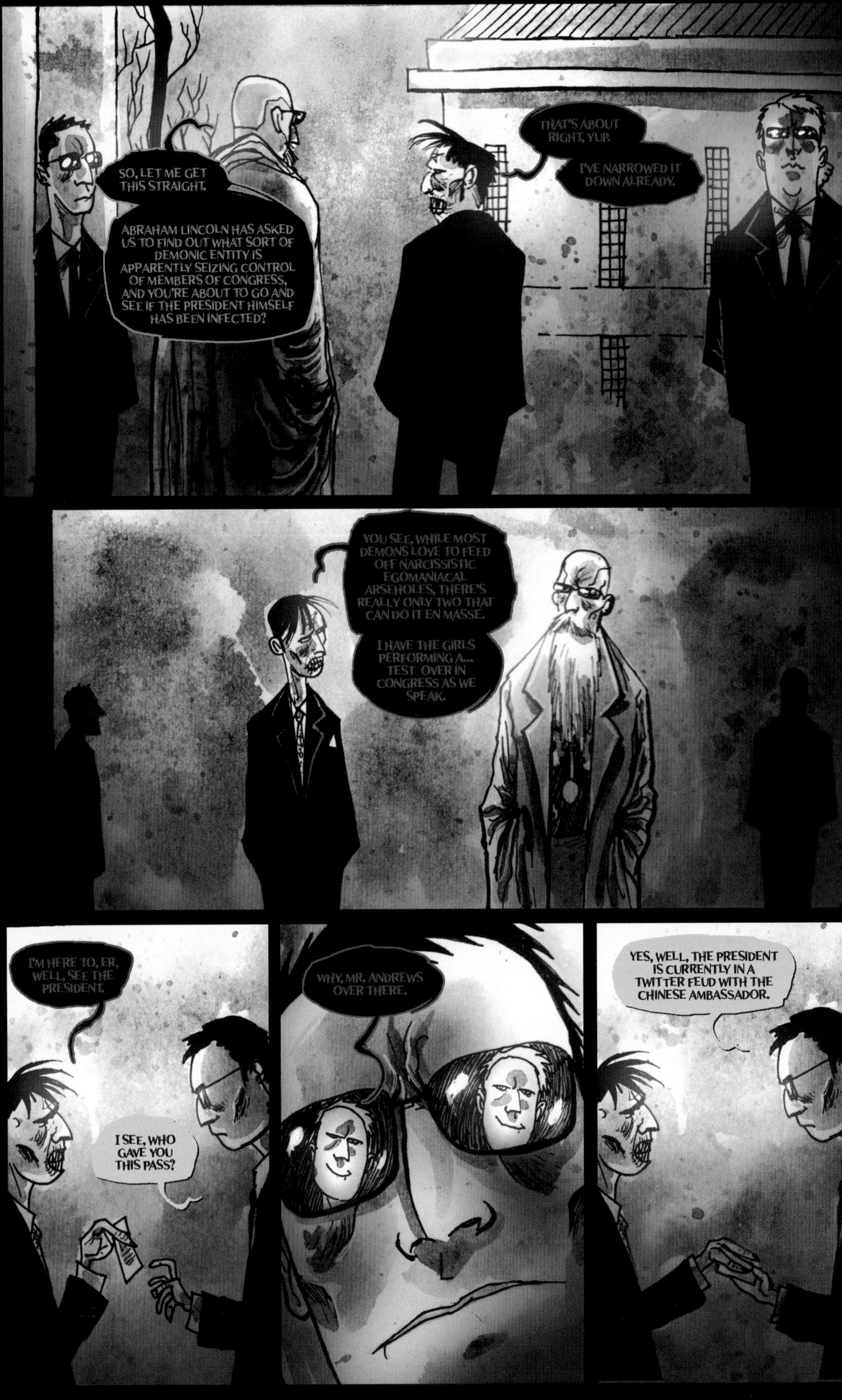

SO, LET ME GET THIS STRAIGHT.
ABRAHAM LINCOLN HAS ASKED US TO FIND OUT WHAT SORT OF DEMONIC ENTITY IS APPARENTLY SEIZING CONTROL OF MEMBERS OF CONGRESS, AND YOU'RE ABOUT TO GO AND SEE IF THE PRESIDENT HIMSELF HAS BEEN INFECTED?
THAT'S ABOUT RIGHT, YUP.
I'VE NARROWED IT DOWN ALREADY.
YOU SEE, WHILE MOST DEMONS LOVE TO FEED OFF NARCISSISTIC EGOMANIACAL ARSEHOLES, THERE'S REALLY ONLY TWO THAT CAN DO IT EN MASSE.
I HAVE THE GIRLS PERFORMING A... TEST OVER IN CONGRESS AS WE SPEAK.
I'M HERE TO, ER, WELL, SEE THE PRESIDENT.
I SEE, WHO GAVE YOU THIS PASS?
WHY, MR. ANDREWS OVER THERE.
YES, WELL, THE PRESIDENT IS CURRENTLY IN A TWITTER FEUD WITH THE CHINESE AMBASSADOR.

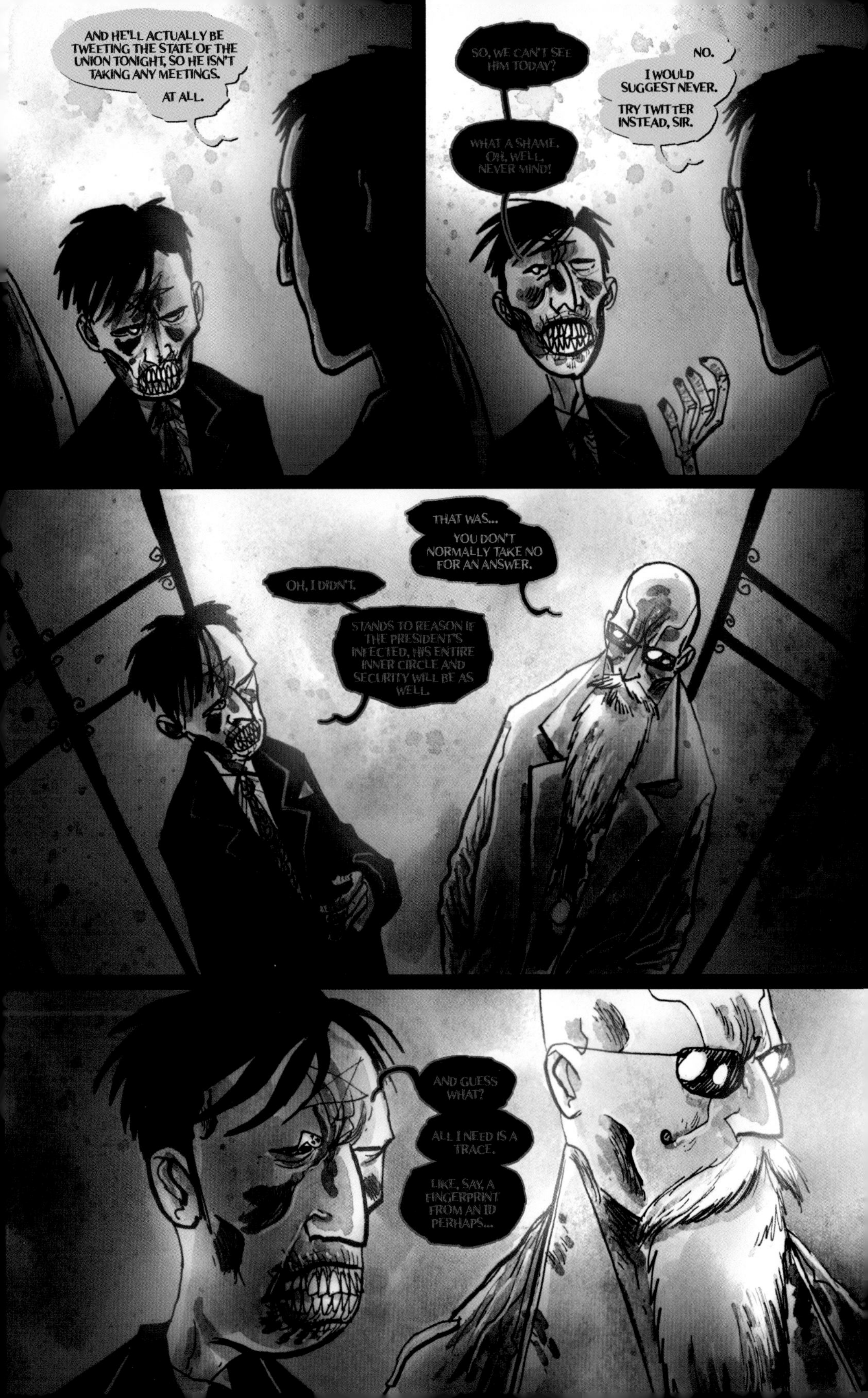
AND HE'LL ACTUALLY BE TWEETING THE STATE OF THE UNION TONIGHT, SO HE ISN'T TAKING ANY MEETINGS.
AT ALL.
SO, WE CAN'T SEE HIM TODAY?
NO.
I WOULD SUGGEST NEVER.
TRY TWITTER INSTEAD, SIR.
WHAT A SHAME. OH, WELL, NEVER MIND!
THAT WAS...
YOU DON'T NORMALLY TAKE NO FOR AN ANSWER.
OH, I DIDN'T.
STANDS TO REASON IF THE PRESIDENT'S INFECTED, HIS ENTIRE INNER CIRCLE AND SECURITY WILL BE AS WELL.
AND GUESS WHAT?
ALL I NEED IS A TRACE.
LIKE, SAY, A FINGERPRINT FROM AN ID PERHAPS...

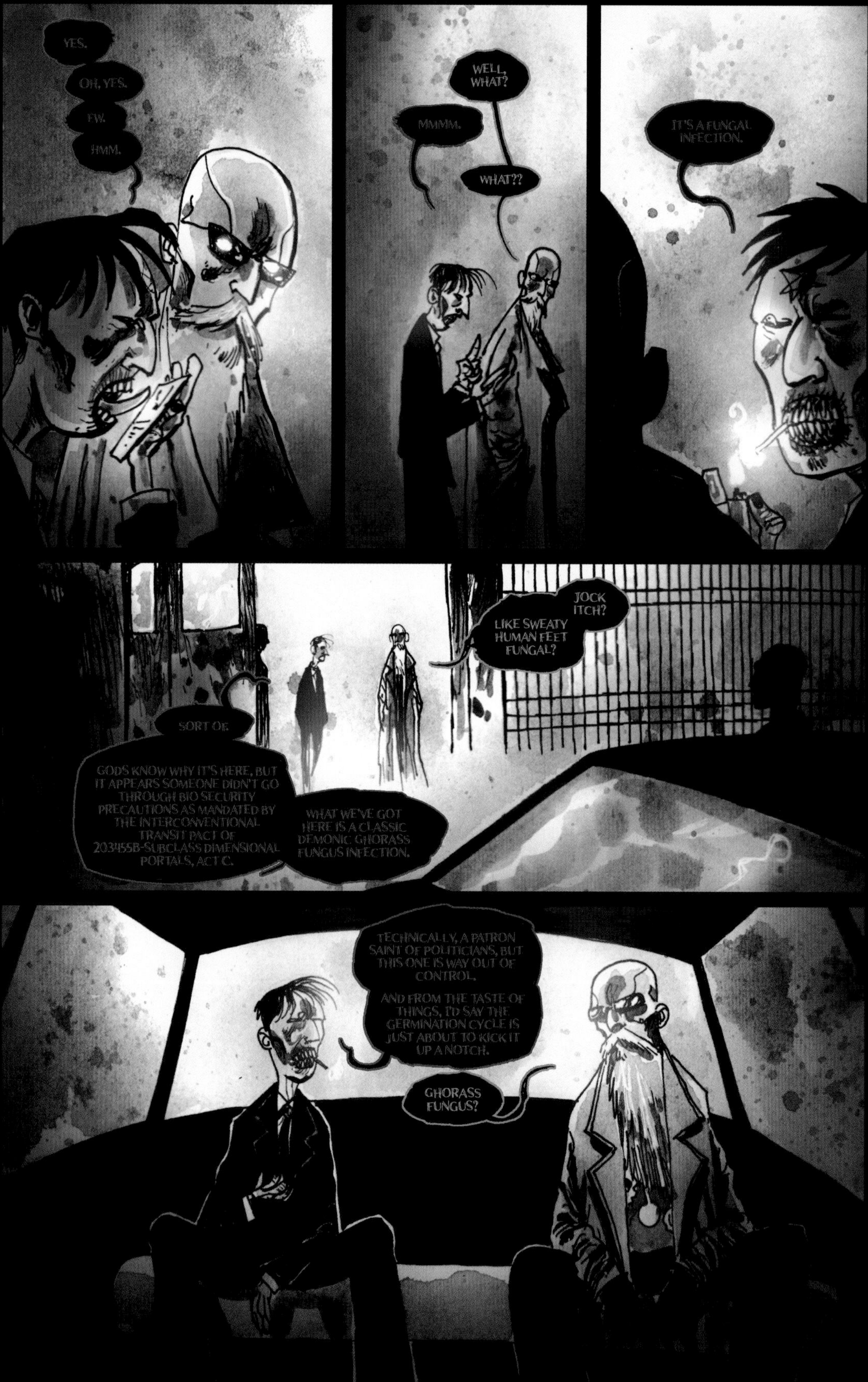

YES.
OH, YES.
EW.
HMM.
WELL, WHAT?
MMMM.
WHAT??
IT'S A FUNGAL INFECTION.
LIKE SWEATY HUMAN FEET FUNGAL?
JOCK ITCH?
SORT OF.
GODS KNOW WHY IT'S HERE, BUT IT APPEARS SOMEONE DIDN'T GO THROUGH BIO SECURITY PRECAUTIONS AS MANDATED BY THE INTERCONVENTIONAL TRANSIT PACT OF 203455B-SUBCLASS DIMENSIONAL PORTALS, ACT C.
WHAT WE'VE GOT HERE IS A CLASSIC DEMONIC GHORASS FUNGUS INFECTION.
GHORASS FUNGUS?
TECHNICALLY, A PATRON SAINT OF POLITICIANS, BUT THIS ONE IS WAY OUT OF CONTROL.
AND FROM THE TASTE OF THINGS, I'D SAY THE GERMINATION CYCLE IS JUST ABOUT TO KICK IT UP A NOTCH.

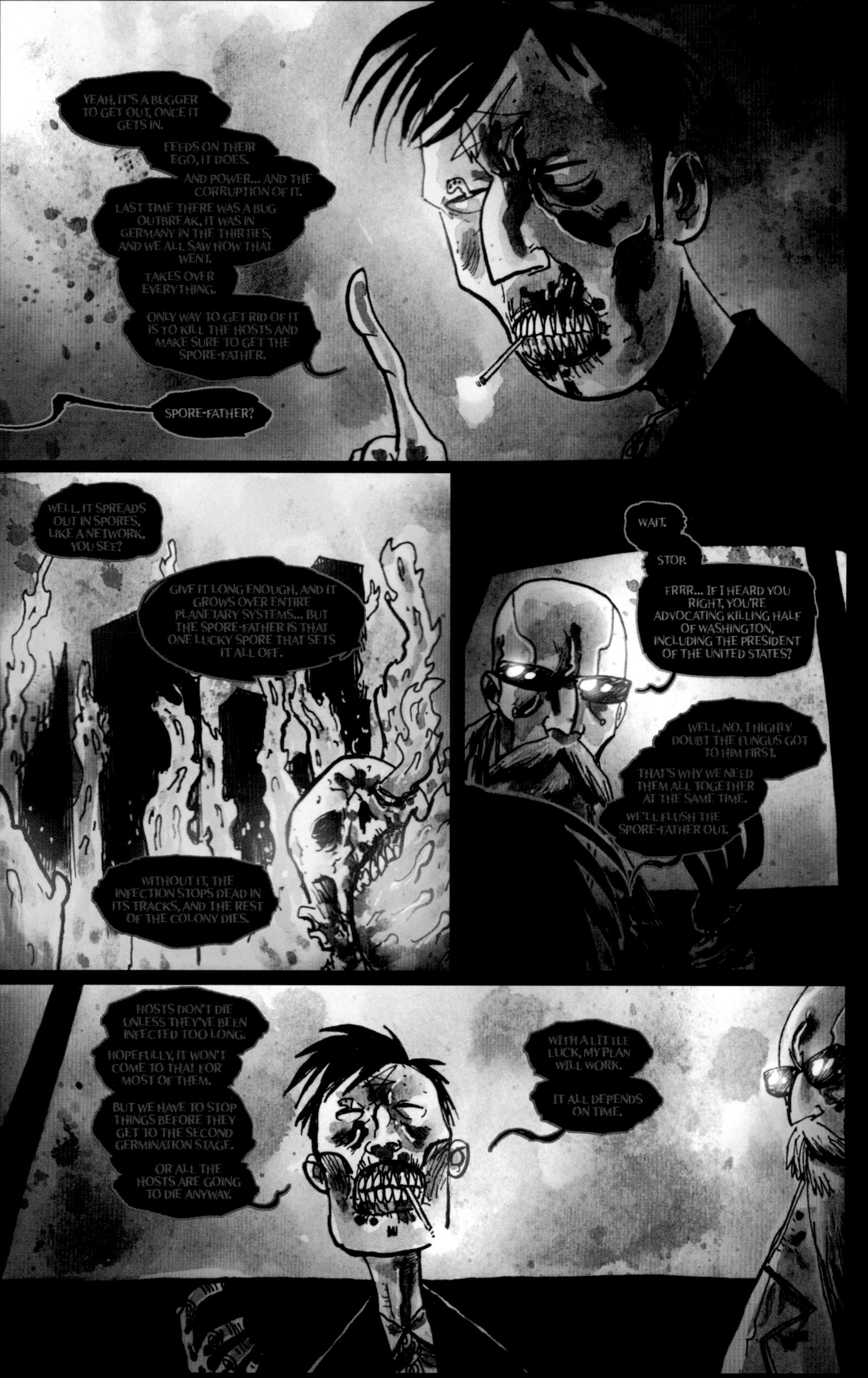
YEAH, IT'S A BUGGER TO GET OUT, ONCE IT GETS IN.
FEEDS ON THEIR EGO, IT DOES.
AND POWER... AND THE CORRUPTION OF IT.
LAST TIME THERE WAS A BUG OUTBREAK, IT WAS IN GERMANY IN THE THIRTIES, AND WE ALL SAW HOW THAT WENT.
TAKES OVER EVERYTHING.
ONLY WAY TO GET RID OF IT IS TO KILL THE HOSTS AND MAKE SURE TO GET THE SPORE-FATHER.
SPORE-FATHER?
WELL, IT SPREADS OUT IN SPORES, LIKE A NETWORK, YOU SEE?
GIVE IT LONG ENOUGH, AND IT GROWS OVER ENTIRE PLANETARY SYSTEMS... BUT THE SPORE-FATHER IS THAT ONE LUCKY SPORE THAT SETS IT ALL OFF.
WITHOUT IT, THE INFECTION STOPS DEAD IN ITS TRACKS, AND THE REST OF THE COLONY DIES.
WAIT.
STOP.
ERRR... IF I HEARD YOU RIGHT, YOU'RE ADVOCATING KILLING HALF OF WASHINGTON, INCLUDING THE PRESIDENT OF THE UNITED STATES?
WELL, NO. I HIGHLY DOUBT THE FUNGUS GOT TO HIM FIRST.
THAT'S WHY WE NEED THEM ALL TOGETHER AT THE SAME TIME.
WE'LL FLUSH THE SPORE-FATHER OUT.
HOSTS DON'T DIE UNLESS THEY'VE BEEN INFECTED TOO LONG.
HOPEFULLY, IT WON'T COME TO THAT FOR MOST OF THEM.
BUT WE HAVE TO STOP THINGS BEFORE THEY GET TO THE SECOND GERMINATION STAGE.
OR ALL THE HOSTS ARE GOING TO DIE ANYWAY.
WITH A LITTLE LUCK, MY PLAN WILL WORK.
IT ALL DEPENDS ON TIME.

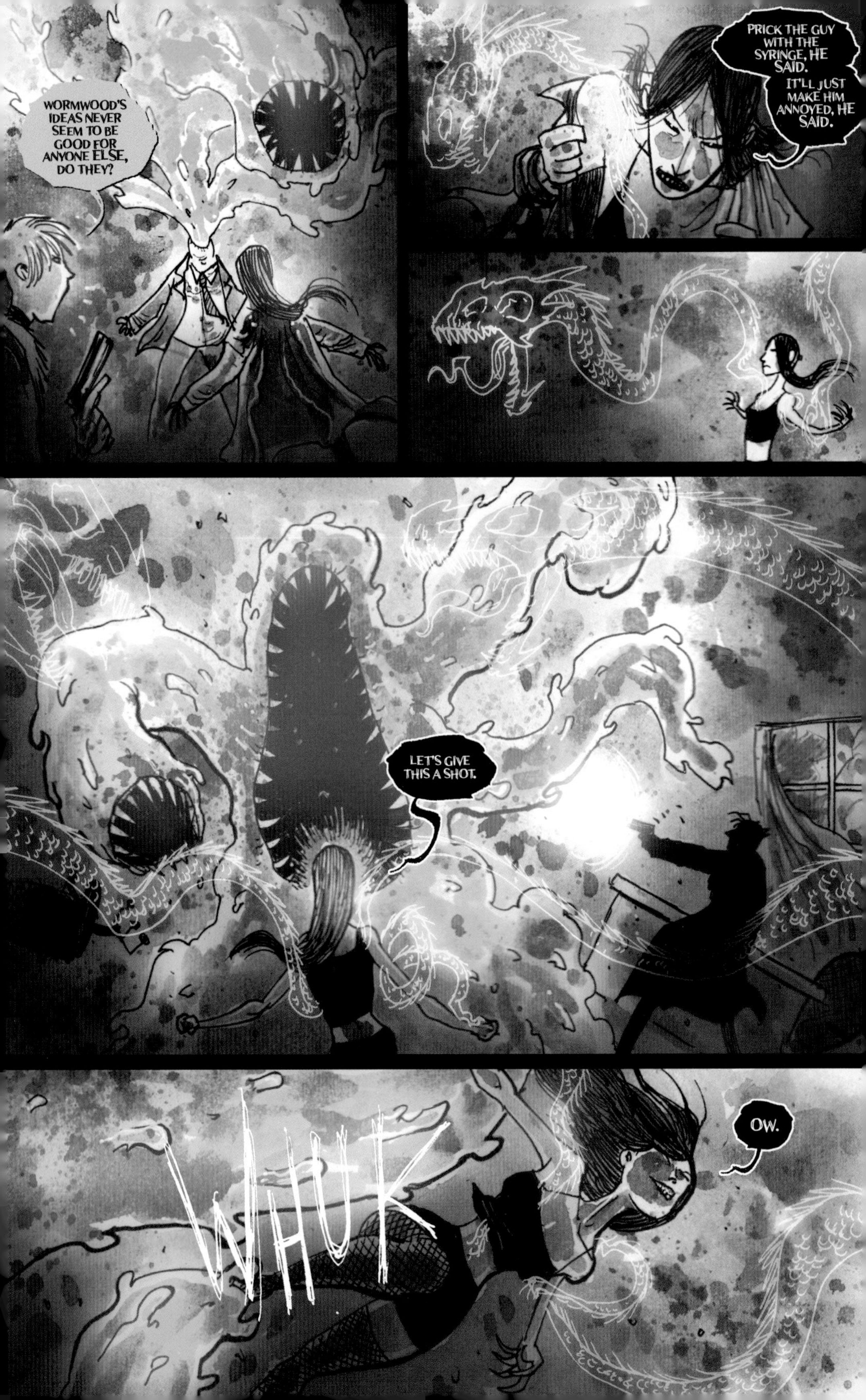
WORMWOOD'S IDEAS NEVER SEEM TO BE GOOD FOR ANYONE ELSE, DO THEY?
PRICK THE GUY WITH THE SYRINGE, HE SAID.
IT'LL JUST MAKE HIM ANNOYED, HE SAID.
LET'S GIVE THIS A SHOT.
WHUK
OW.

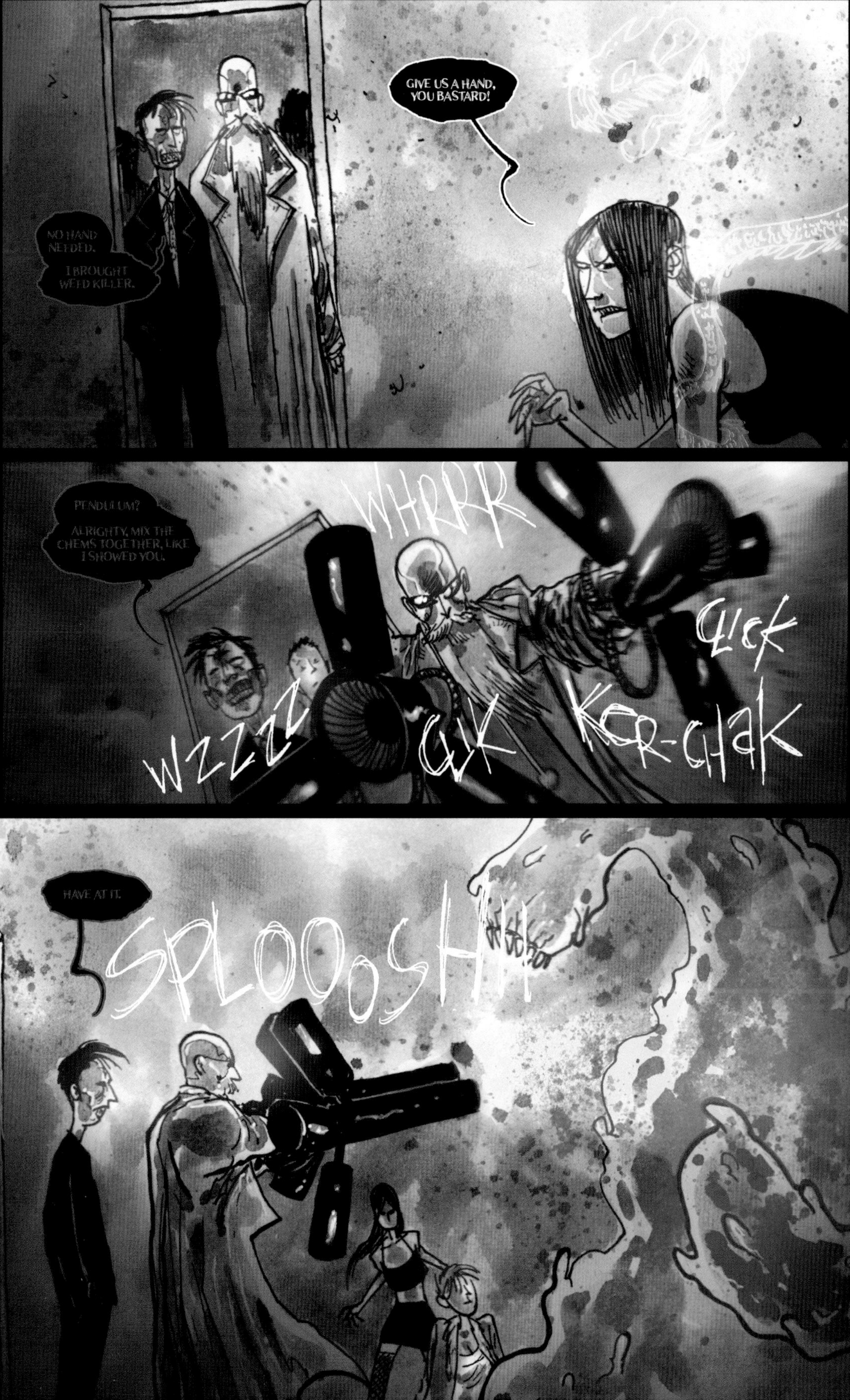
GIVE US A HAND, YOU BASTARD!
NO HAND NEEDED.
I BROUGHT WEED KILLER.
PENDULUM?
ALRIGHTY, MIX THE CHEMS TOGETHER, LIKE I SHOWED YOU.
WHRRR
CLICK
WZZZZ
CLK
KER-CHAK
HAVE AT IT.
SPLOOOSHH

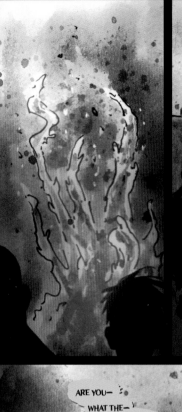

SORTED.

WELL, GEE, WOULDN'T IT HAVE BEEN GREAT IF YOU'D GIVEN US SOME OF THAT?

WELL, I HAD TO FIGURE OUT WHICH SORT OF FUNGUS IT WAS FIRST.

NOW I KNOW WHAT SORT OF BASTARD WE'RE DEALING WITH.

AND JUST WHAT WE NEED TO FIX IT.

ARE YOU—

WHAT THE—

WHAT THE HELL ARE YOU DOING TO HIS GENITALS??

RELAX. NOT LIKE HE NEEDS THEM ANYMORE.

DAMN. IT'S A BUGGER OF A JOB TO FIND THEM THOUGH.

KSHK

SHRRK

RIIIPP

AH, HERE WE GO.

JUST WHAT WE WANT.

WHAT I WANT IS A SHOWER AND A GLASS OF WINE AFTER THIS, BUT IF CONGRESSIONAL PENIS FLOATS YOUR BOAT, FAIR ENOUGH.

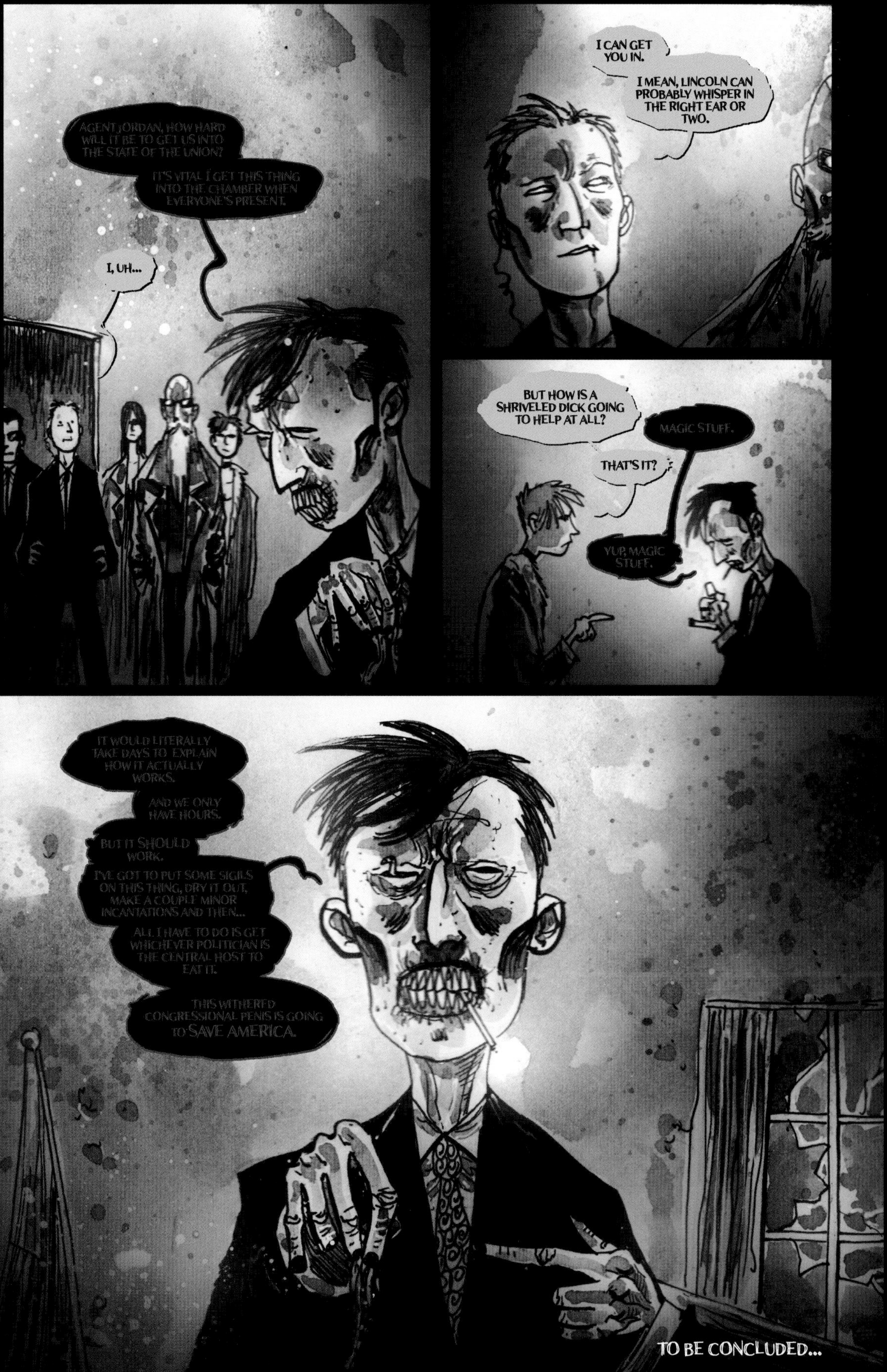

AGENT JORDAN, HOW HARD WILL IT BE TO GET US INTO THE STATE OF THE UNION?
IT'S VITAL I GET THIS THING INTO THE CHAMBER WHEN EVERYONE'S PRESENT.
I, UH...
I CAN GET YOU IN.
I MEAN, LINCOLN CAN PROBABLY WHISPER IN THE RIGHT EAR OR TWO.
BUT HOW IS A SHRIVELED DICK GOING TO HELP AT ALL?
MAGIC STUFF.
THAT'S IT?
YUP, MAGIC STUFF.
IT WOULD LITERALLY TAKE DAYS TO EXPLAIN HOW IT ACTUALLY WORKS.
AND WE ONLY HAVE HOURS.
BUT IT SHOULD WORK.
I'VE GOT TO PUT SOME SIGILS ON THIS THING, DRY IT OUT, MAKE A COUPLE MINOR INCANTATIONS AND THEN...
ALL I HAVE TO DO IS GET WHICHEVER POLITICIAN IS THE CENTRAL HOST TO EAT IT.
THIS WITHERED CONGRESSIONAL PENIS IS GOING TO SAVE AMERICA.
TO BE CONCLUDED...

3

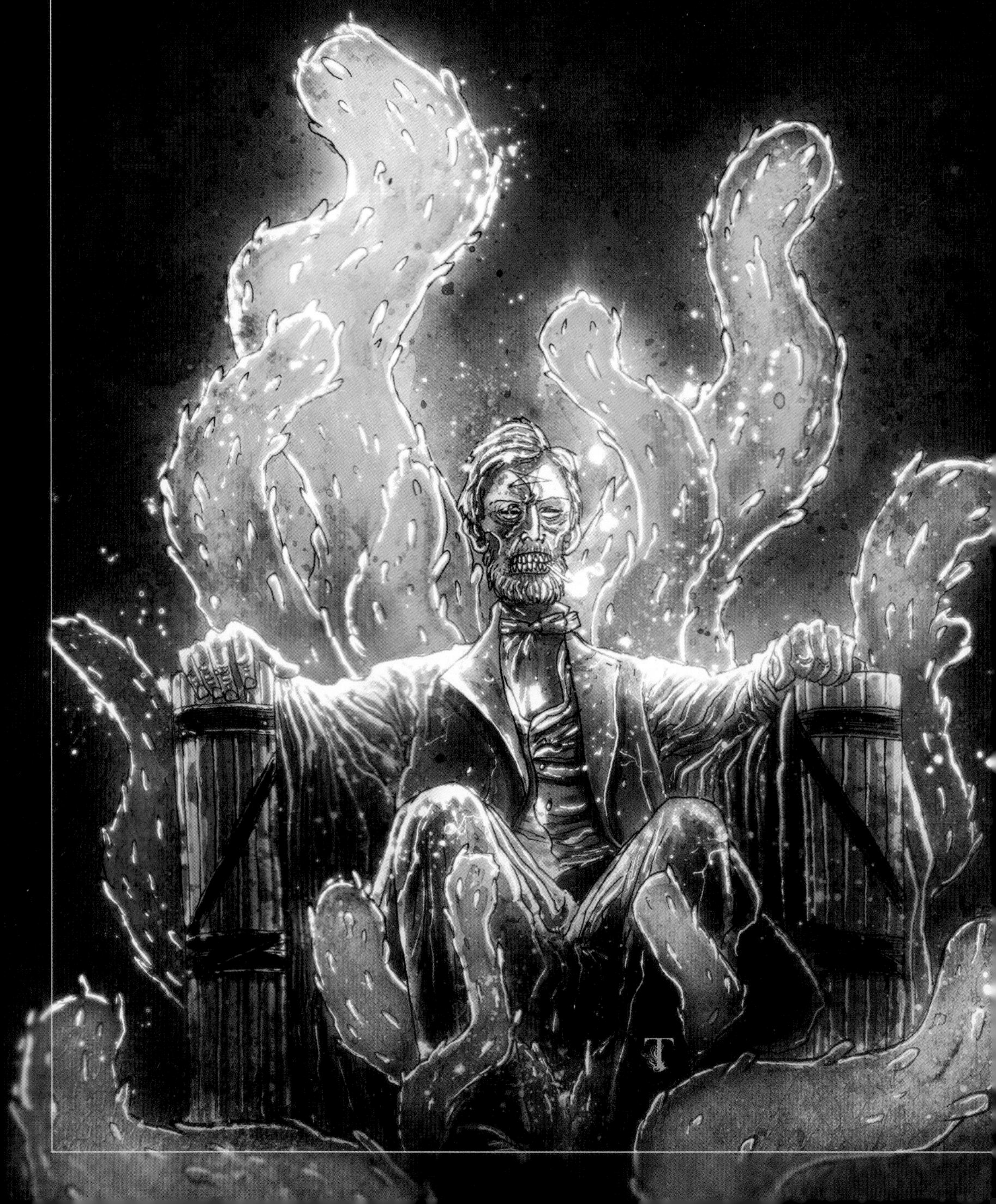

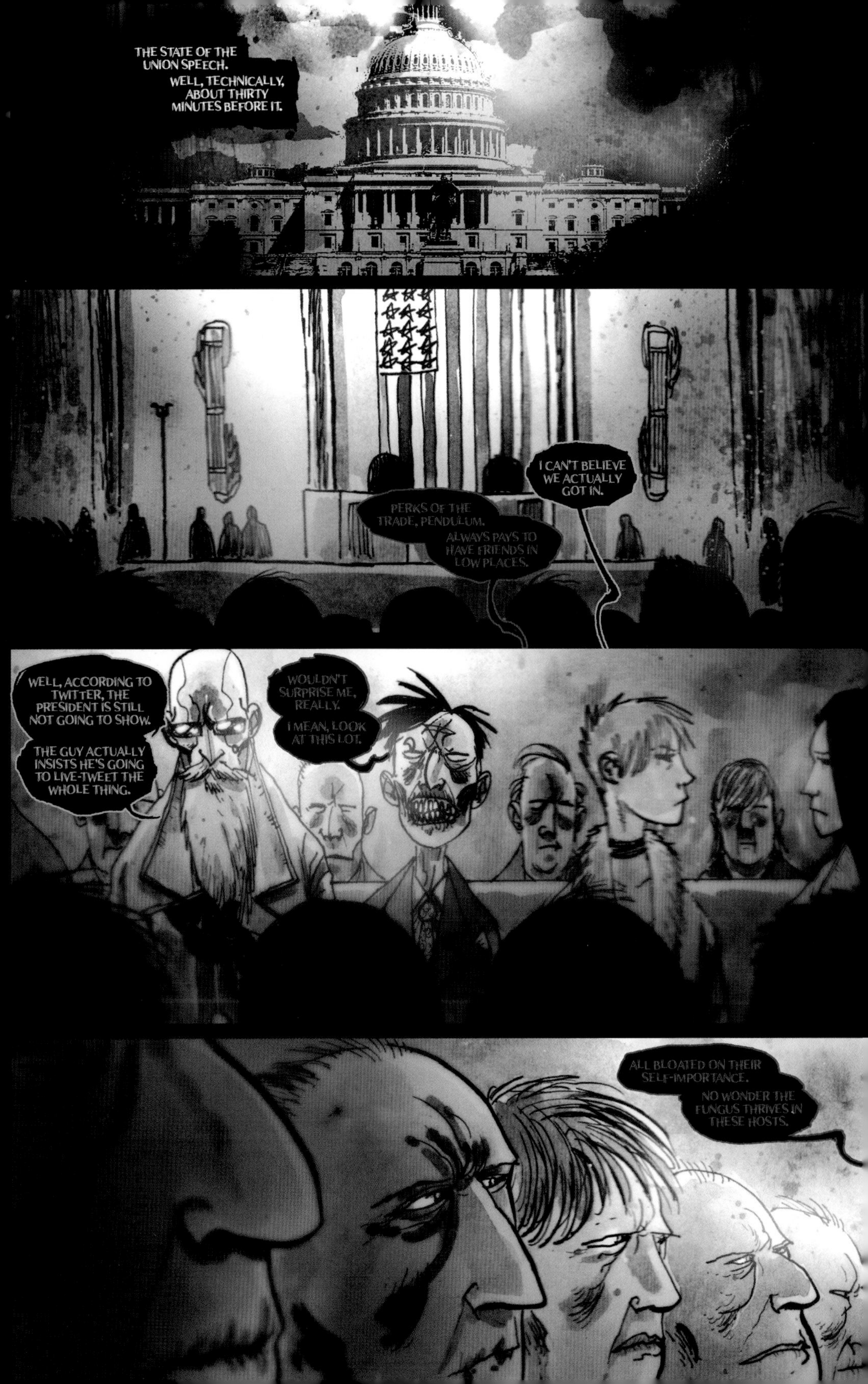
THE STATE OF THE UNION SPEECH.
WELL, TECHNICALLY, ABOUT THIRTY MINUTES BEFORE IT.
I CAN'T BELIEVE WE ACTUALLY GOT IN.
PERKS OF THE TRADE, PENDULUM.
ALWAYS PAYS TO HAVE FRIENDS IN LOW PLACES.
WELL, ACCORDING TO TWITTER, THE PRESIDENT IS STILL NOT GOING TO SHOW.
THE GUY ACTUALLY INSISTS HE'S GOING TO LIVE-TWEET THE WHOLE THING.
WOULDN'T SURPRISE ME, REALLY.
I MEAN, LOOK AT THIS LOT.
ALL BLOATED ON THEIR SELF-IMPORTANCE.
NO WONDER THE FUNGUS THRIVES IN THESE HOSTS.

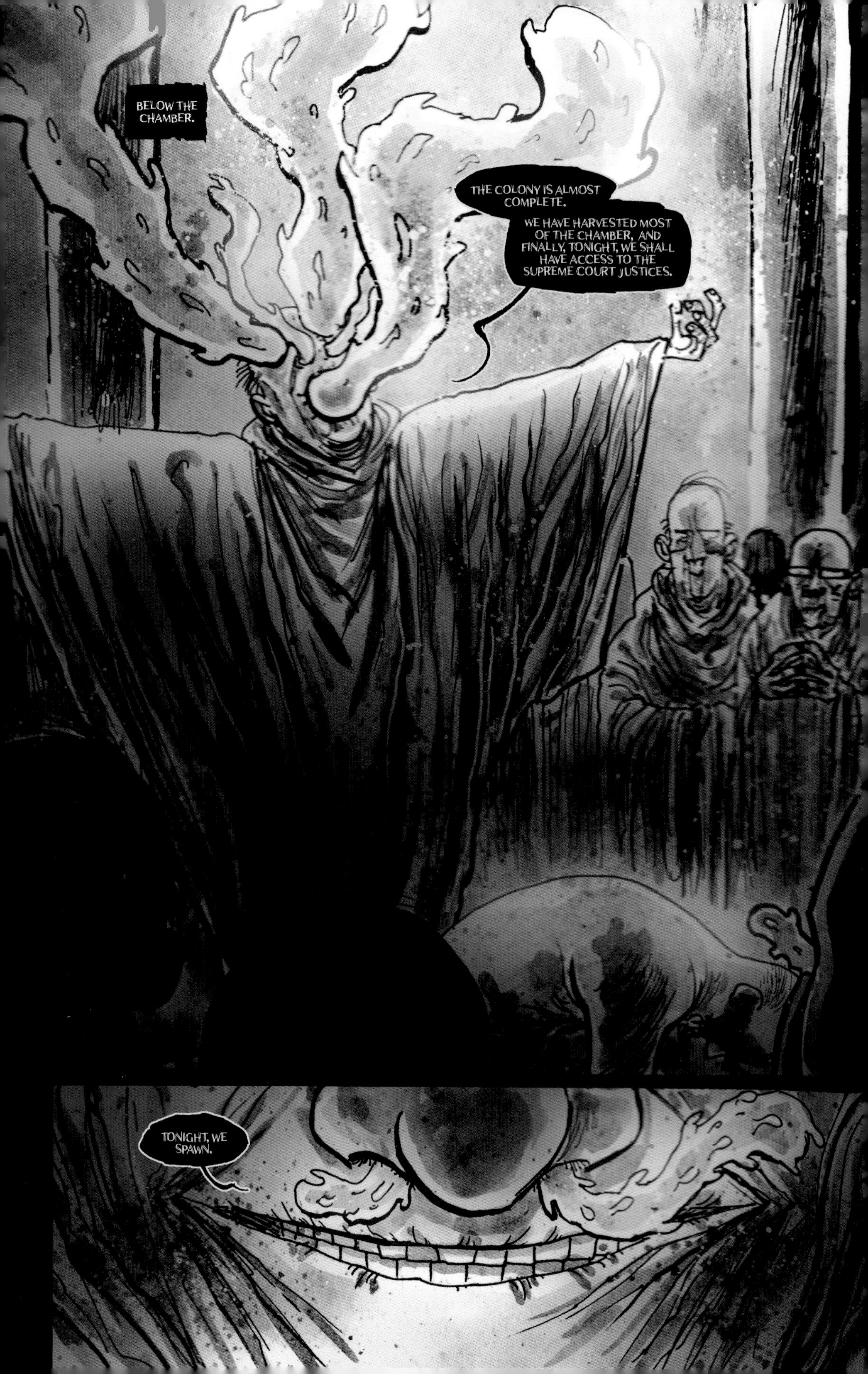
BELOW THE CHAMBER.
THE COLONY IS ALMOST COMPLETE.
WE HAVE HARVESTED MOST OF THE CHAMBER, AND FINALLY, TONIGHT, WE SHALL HAVE ACCESS TO THE SUPREME COURT JUSTICES.
TONIGHT, WE SPAWN.

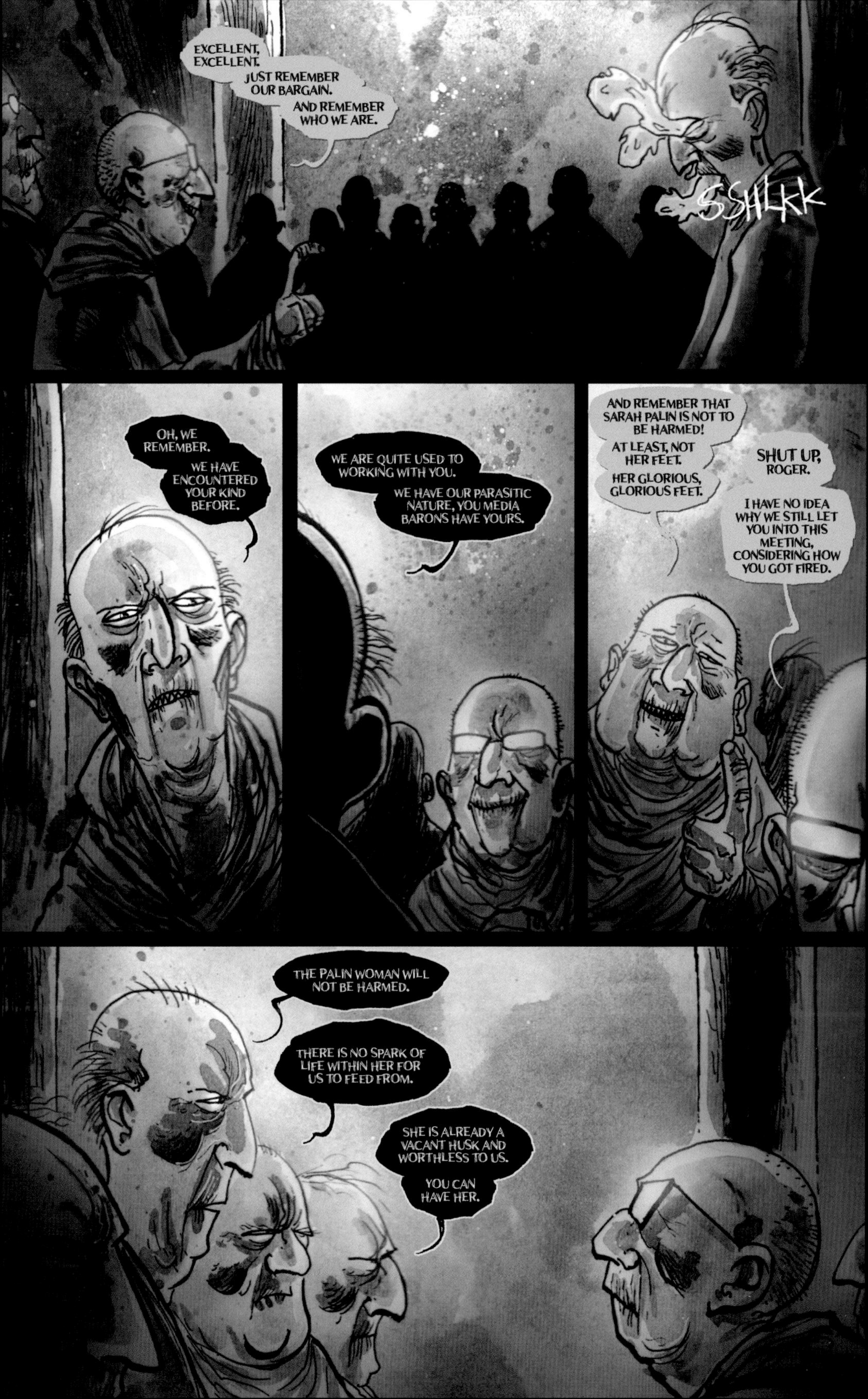
EXCELLENT, EXCELLENT.
JUST REMEMBER OUR BARGAIN.
AND REMEMBER WHO WE ARE.
SSHLKK
OH, WE REMEMBER.
WE HAVE ENCOUNTERED YOUR KIND BEFORE.
WE ARE QUITE USED TO WORKING WITH YOU.
WE HAVE OUR PARASITIC NATURE, YOU MEDIA BARONS HAVE YOURS.
AND REMEMBER THAT SARAH PALIN IS NOT TO BE HARMED!
AT LEAST, NOT HER FEET.
HER GLORIOUS, GLORIOUS FEET.
SHUT UP, ROGER.
I HAVE NO IDEA WHY WE STILL LET YOU INTO THIS MEETING, CONSIDERING HOW YOU GOT FIRED.
THE PALIN WOMAN WILL NOT BE HARMED.
THERE IS NO SPARK OF LIFE WITHIN HER FOR US TO FEED FROM.
SHE IS ALREADY A VACANT HUSK AND WORTHLESS TO US.
YOU CAN HAVE HER.

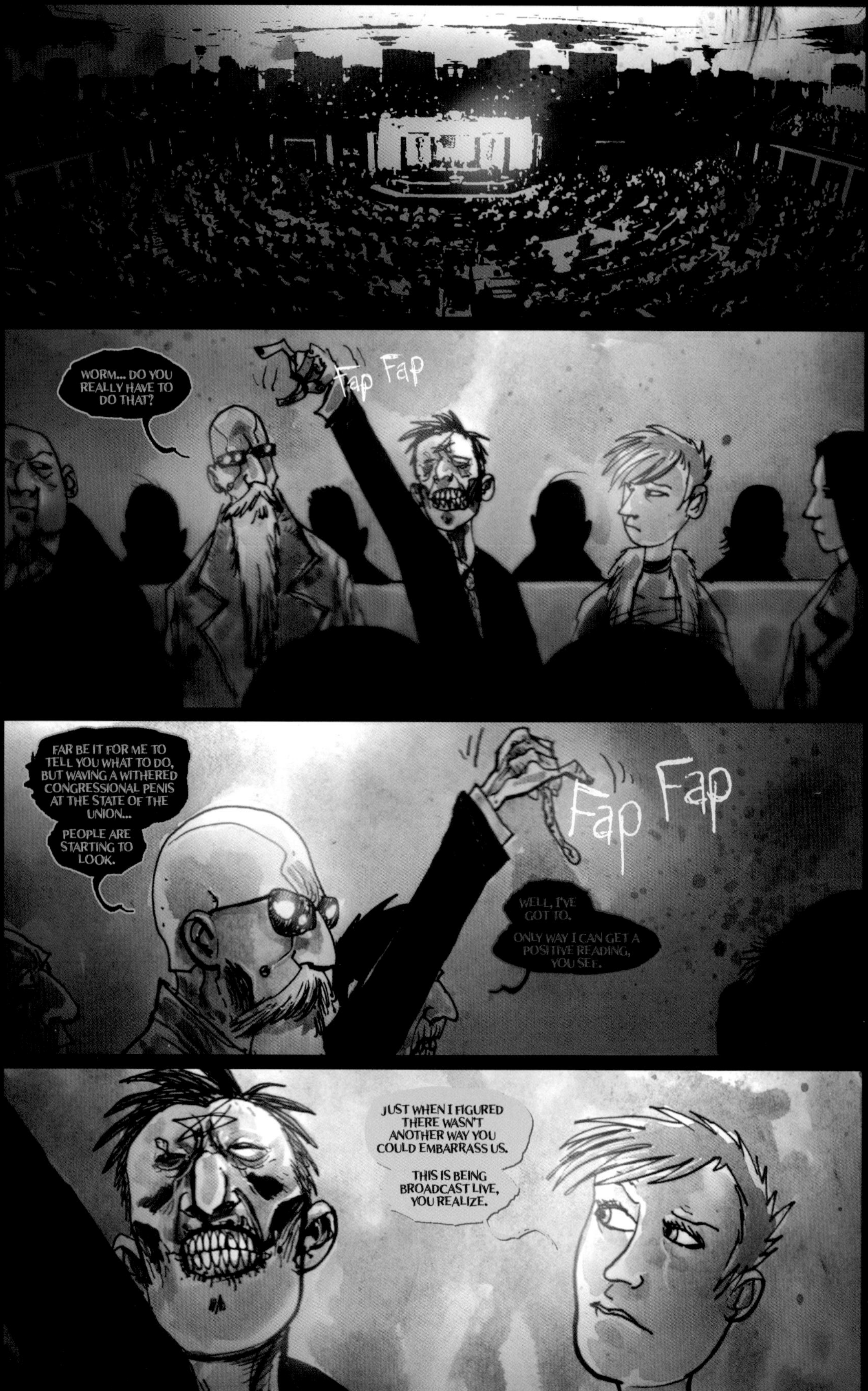
WORM... DO YOU REALLY HAVE TO DO THAT?
Fap Fap
FAR BE IT FOR ME TO TELL YOU WHAT TO DO, BUT WAVING A WITHERED CONGRESSIONAL PENIS AT THE STATE OF THE UNION...
PEOPLE ARE STARTING TO LOOK.
Fap Fap
WELL, I'VE GOT TO.
ONLY WAY I CAN GET A POSITIVE READING, YOU SEE.
JUST WHEN I FIGURED THERE WASN'T ANOTHER WAY YOU COULD EMBARRASS US.
THIS IS BEING BROADCAST LIVE, YOU REALIZE.

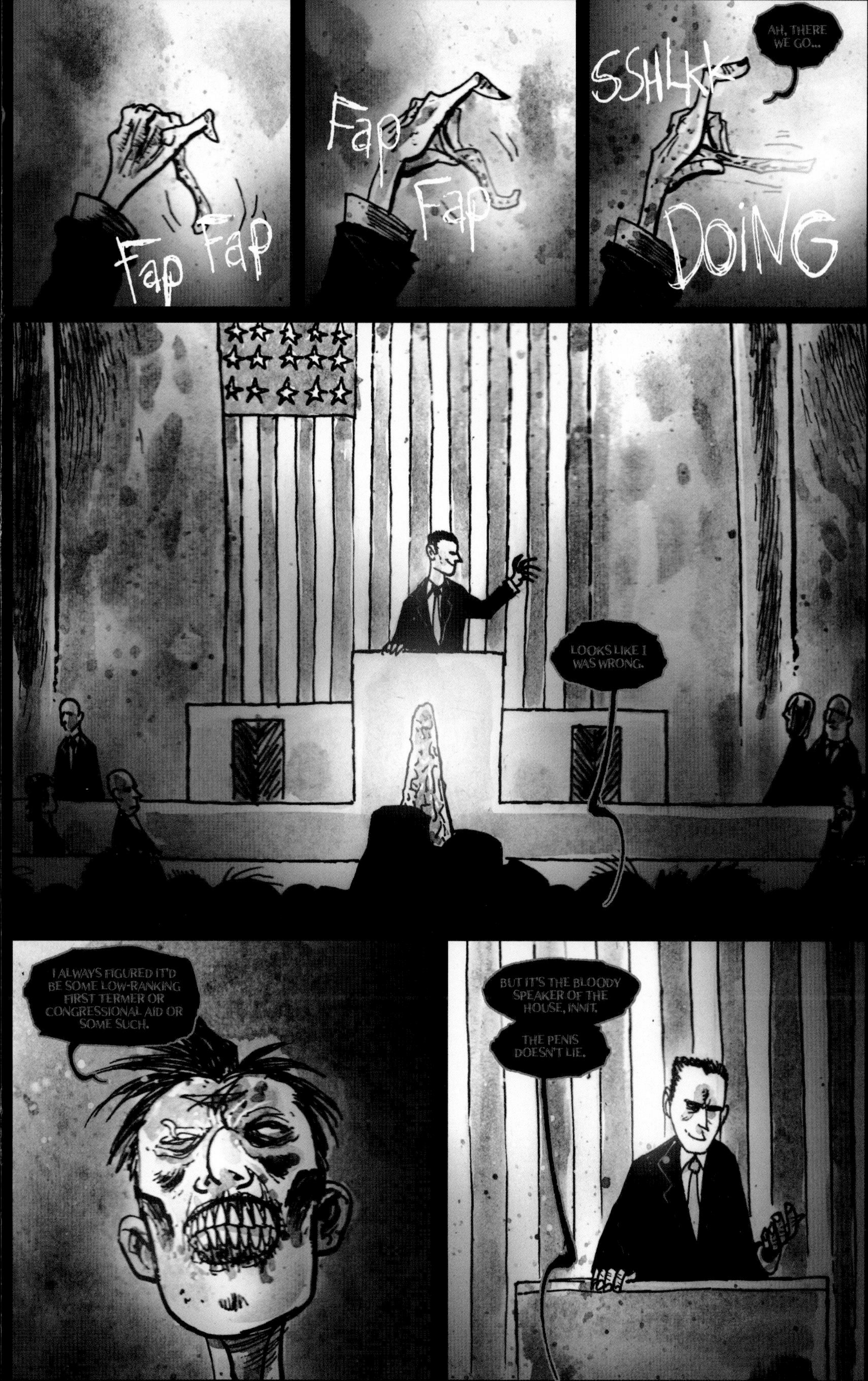
Fap Fap
Fap
Fap
SSHLKK
AH, THERE WE GO...
DOING
LOOKS LIKE I WAS WRONG.
I ALWAYS FIGURED IT'D BE SOME LOW-RANKING FIRST TERMER OR CONGRESSIONAL AID OR SOME SUCH.
BUT IT'S THE BLOODY SPEAKER OF THE HOUSE, INNIT.
THE PENIS DOESN'T LIE.

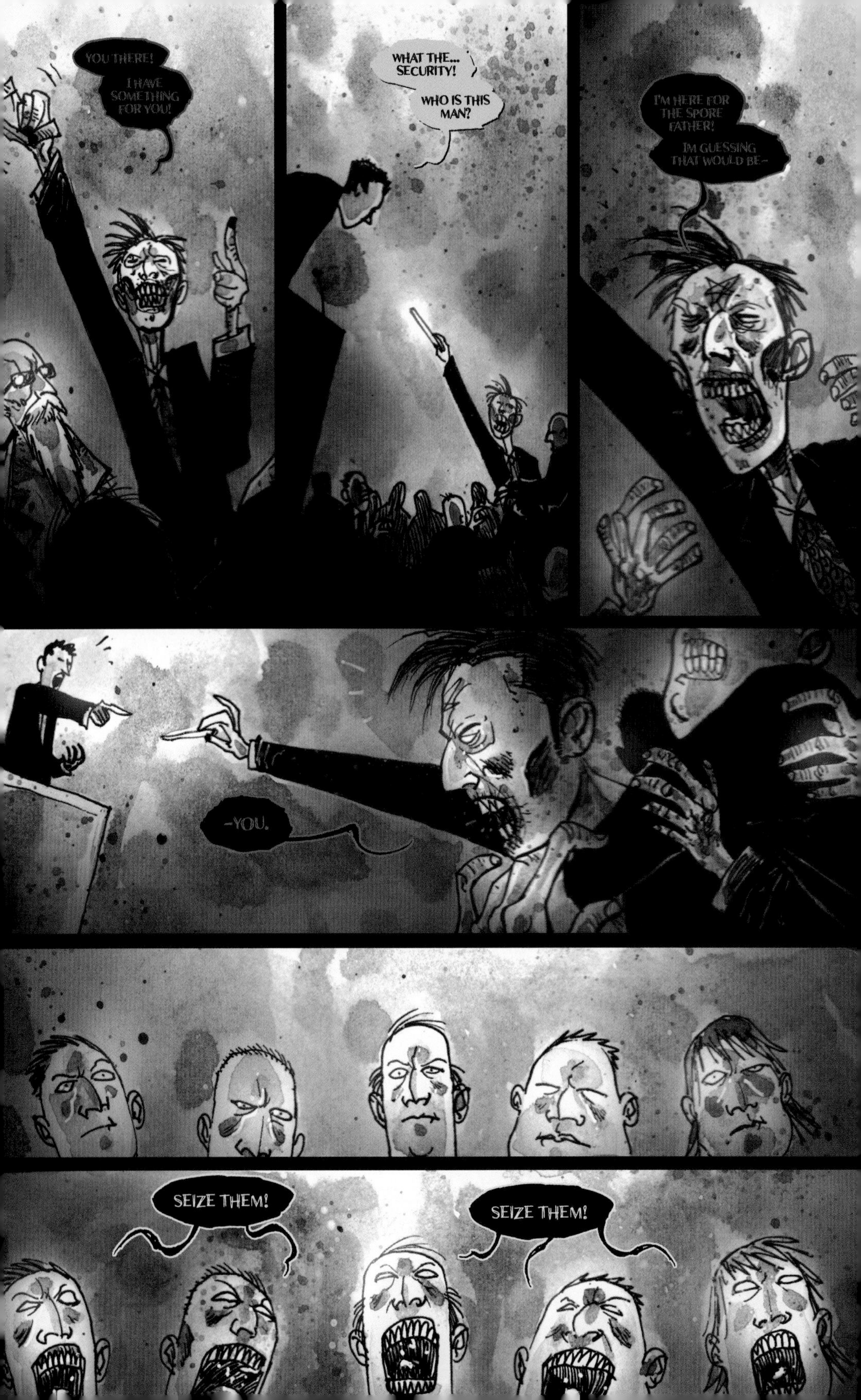
YOU THERE!
I HAVE SOMETHING FOR YOU!
WHAT THE... SECURITY!
WHO IS THIS MAN?
I'M HERE FOR THE SPORE FATHER!
I'M GUESSING THAT WOULD BE--
--YOU.
SEIZE THEM!
SEIZE THEM!

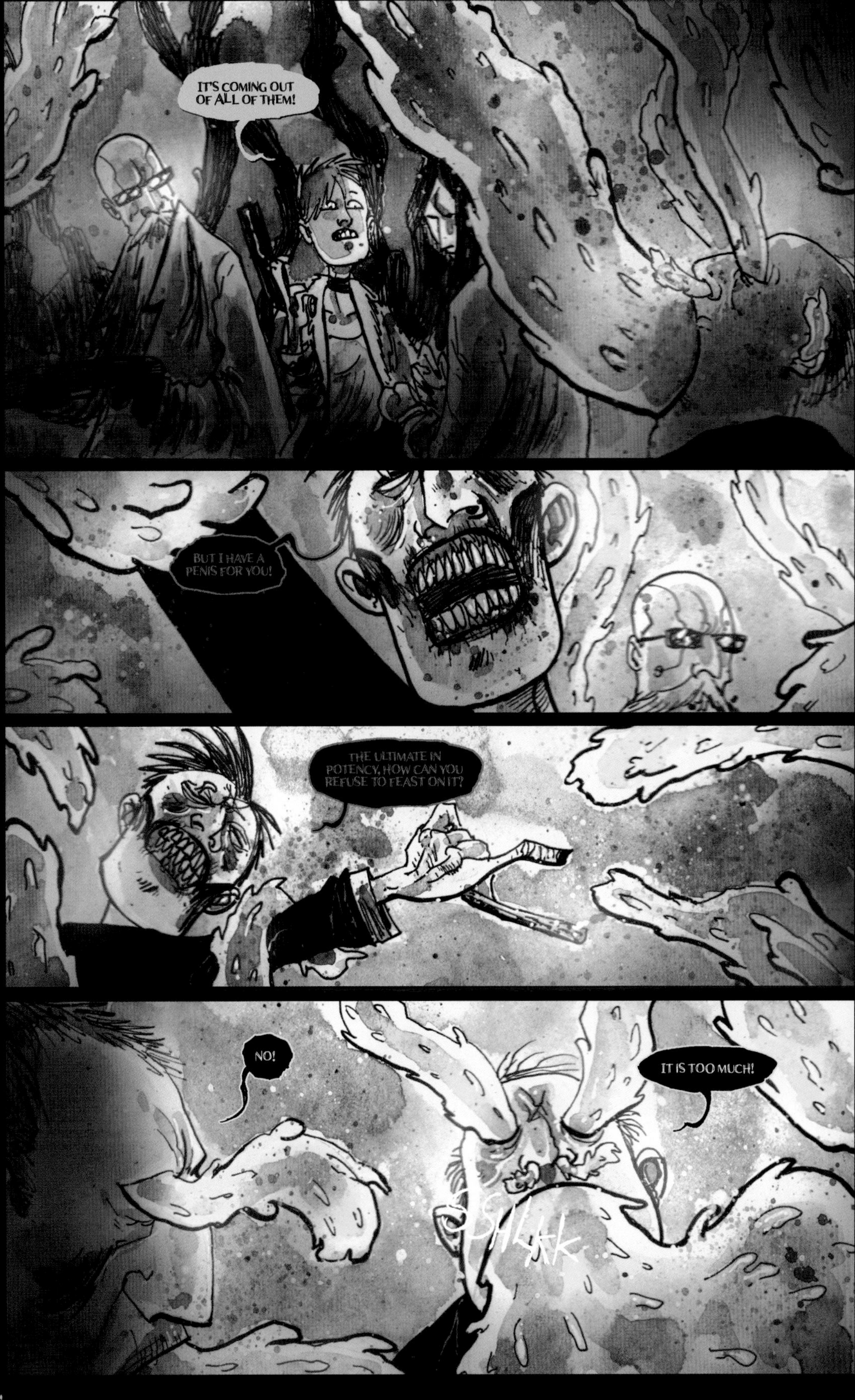
IT'S COMING OUT OF ALL OF THEM!
BUT I HAVE A PENIS FOR YOU!
THE ULTIMATE IN POTENCY. HOW CAN YOU REFUSE TO FEAST ON IT?
NO!
IT IS TOO MUCH!
SSHLUKK

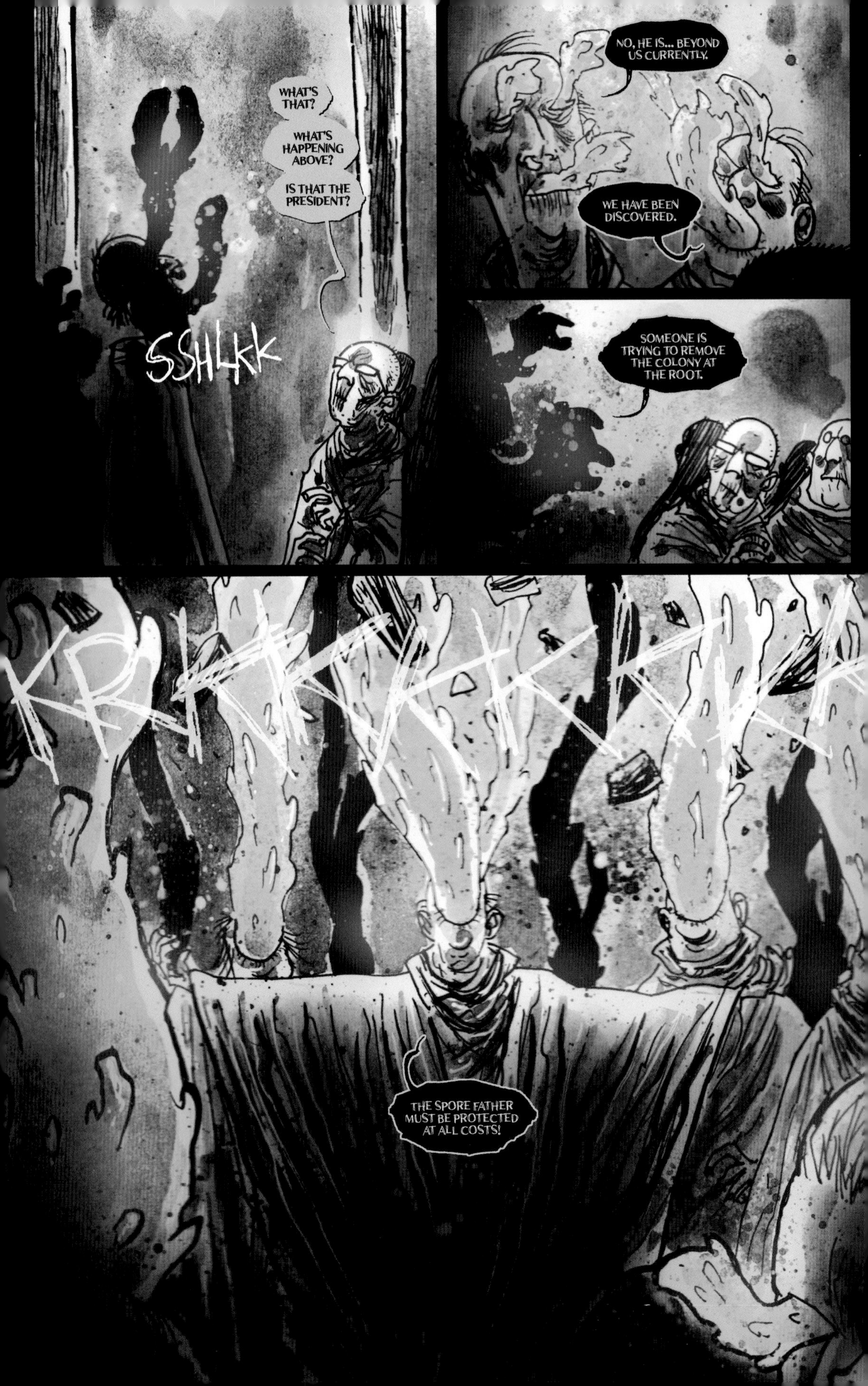
WHAT'S THAT?
WHAT'S HAPPENING ABOVE?
IS THAT THE PRESIDENT?
SSHLKK
NO, HE IS... BEYOND US CURRENTLY.
WE HAVE BEEN DISCOVERED.
SOMEONE IS TRYING TO REMOVE THE COLONY AT THE ROOT.
KRKKKKKKA
THE SPORE FATHER MUST BE PROTECTED AT ALL COSTS!

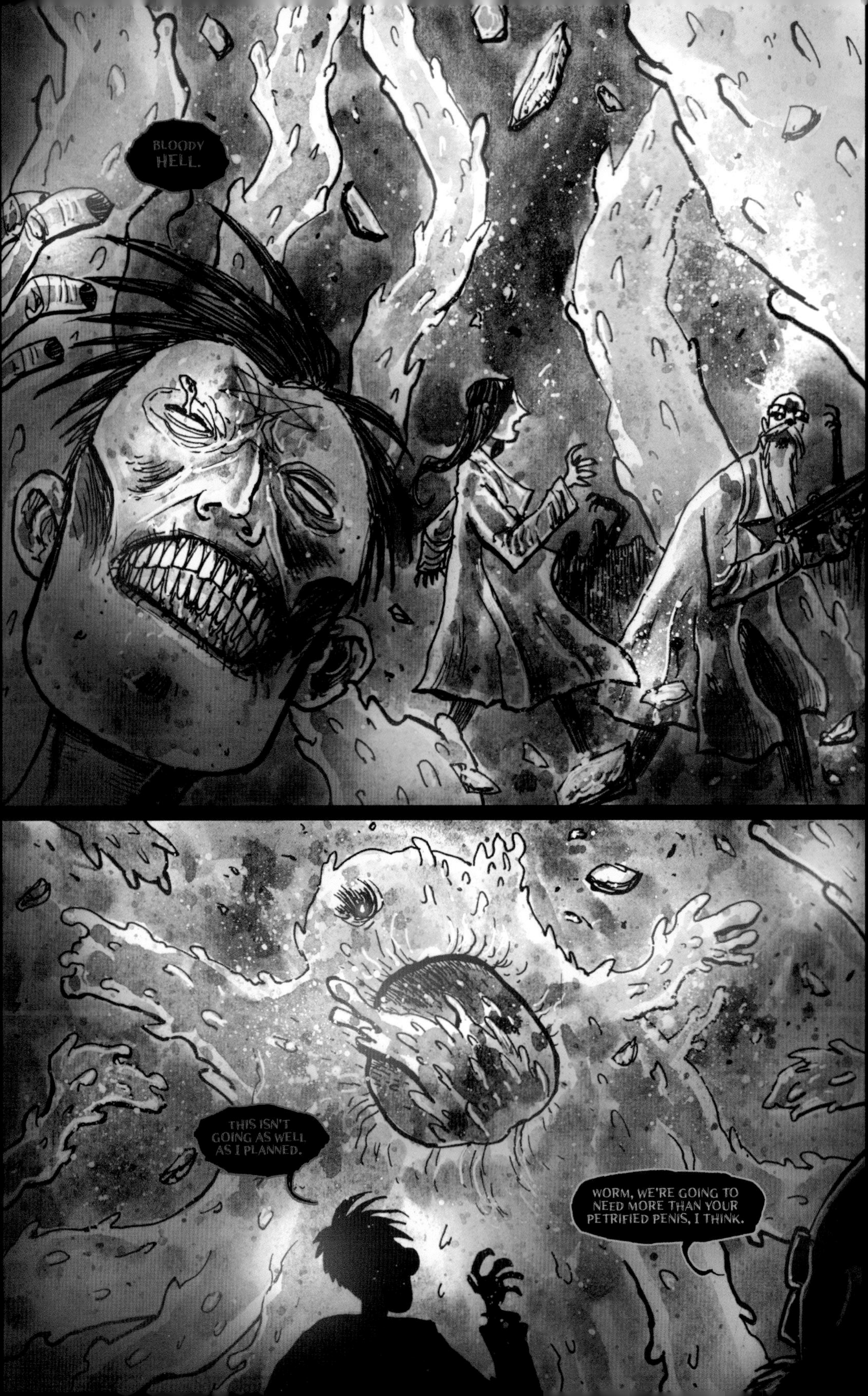
BLOODY HELL.
THIS ISN'T GOING AS WELL AS I PLANNED.
WORM, WE'RE GOING TO NEED MORE THAN YOUR PETRIFIED PENIS, I THINK.

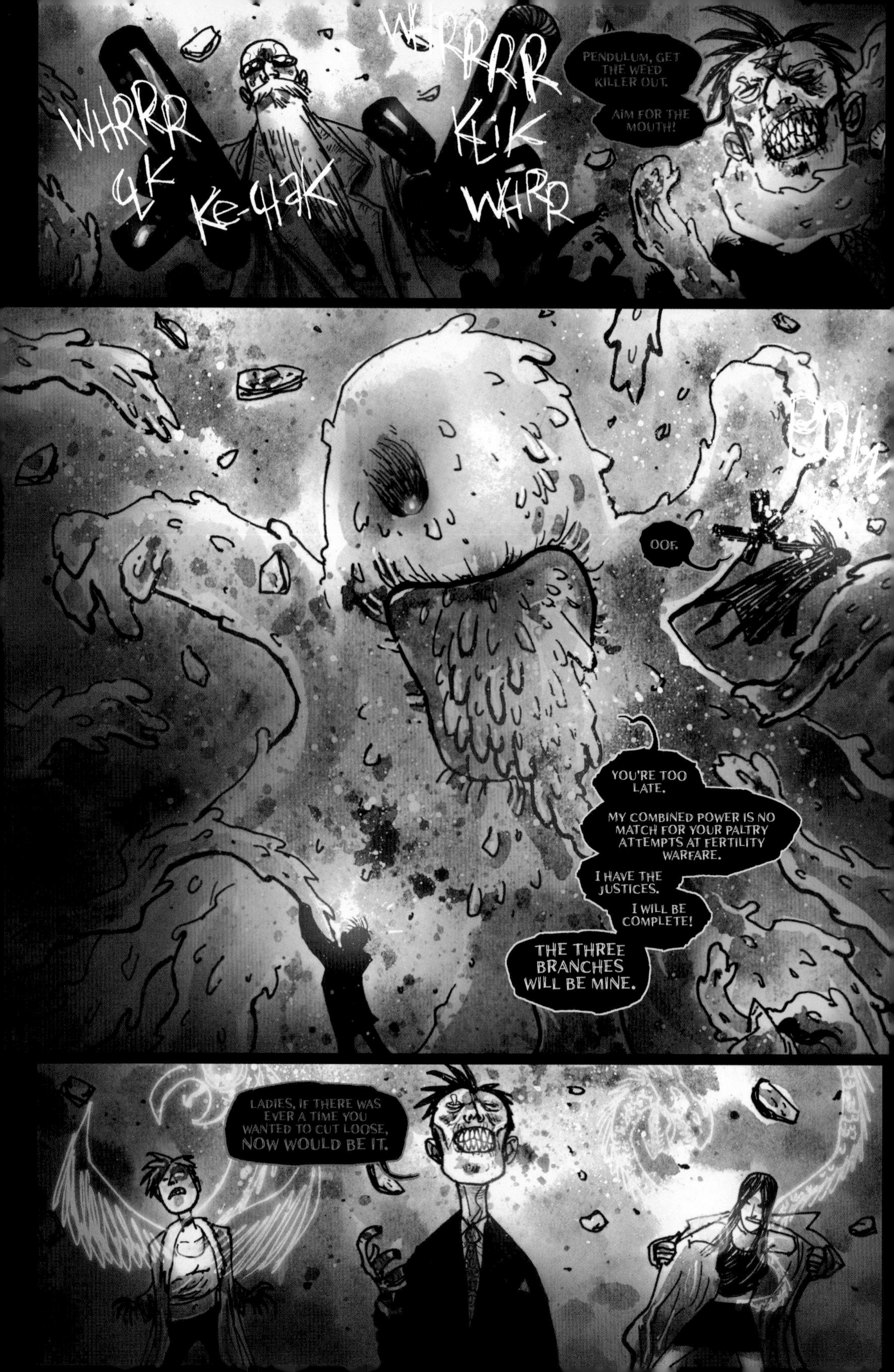
WHRRR
KE-CHAK
KLIK
PENDULUM, GET THE WEED KILLER OUT.
AIM FOR THE MOUTH!
OOF.
YOU'RE TOO LATE.
MY COMBINED POWER IS NO MATCH FOR YOUR PALTRY ATTEMPTS AT FERTILITY WARFARE.
I HAVE THE JUSTICES.
I WILL BE COMPLETE!
THE THREE BRANCHES WILL BE MINE.
LADIES, IF THERE WAS EVER A TIME YOU WANTED TO CUT LOOSE, NOW WOULD BE IT.

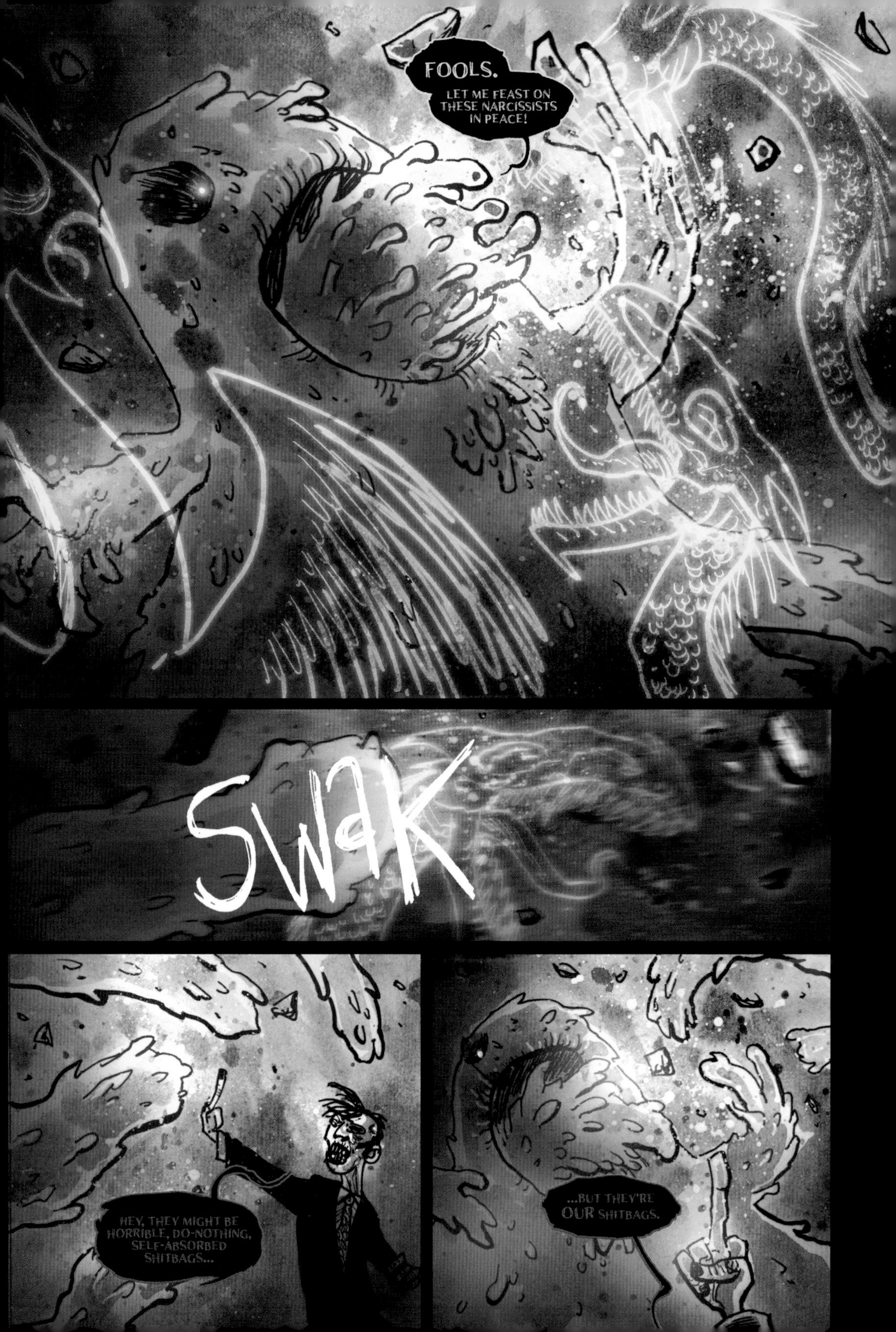
FOOLS.
LET ME FEAST ON THESE NARCISSISTS IN PEACE!
SWAK
HEY, THEY MIGHT BE HORRIBLE, DO-NOTHING, SELF-ABSORBED SHITBAGS...
...BUT THEY'RE OUR SHITBAGS.

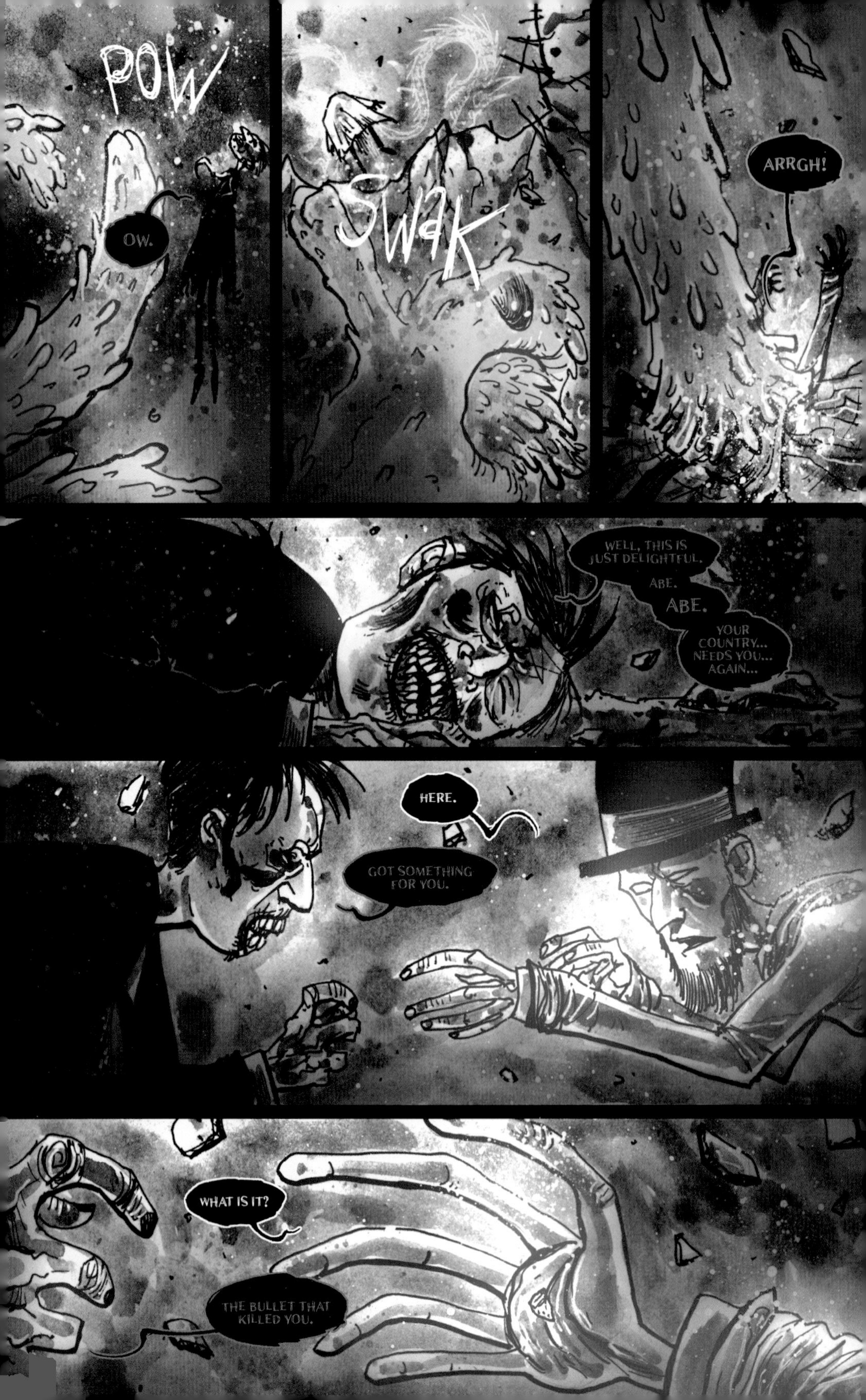
POW
OW.
SWAK
ARRGH!
WELL, THIS IS JUST DELIGHTFUL.
ABE.
ABE.
YOUR COUNTRY... NEEDS YOU... AGAIN...
HERE.
GOT SOMETHING FOR YOU.
WHAT IS IT?
THE BULLET THAT KILLED YOU.

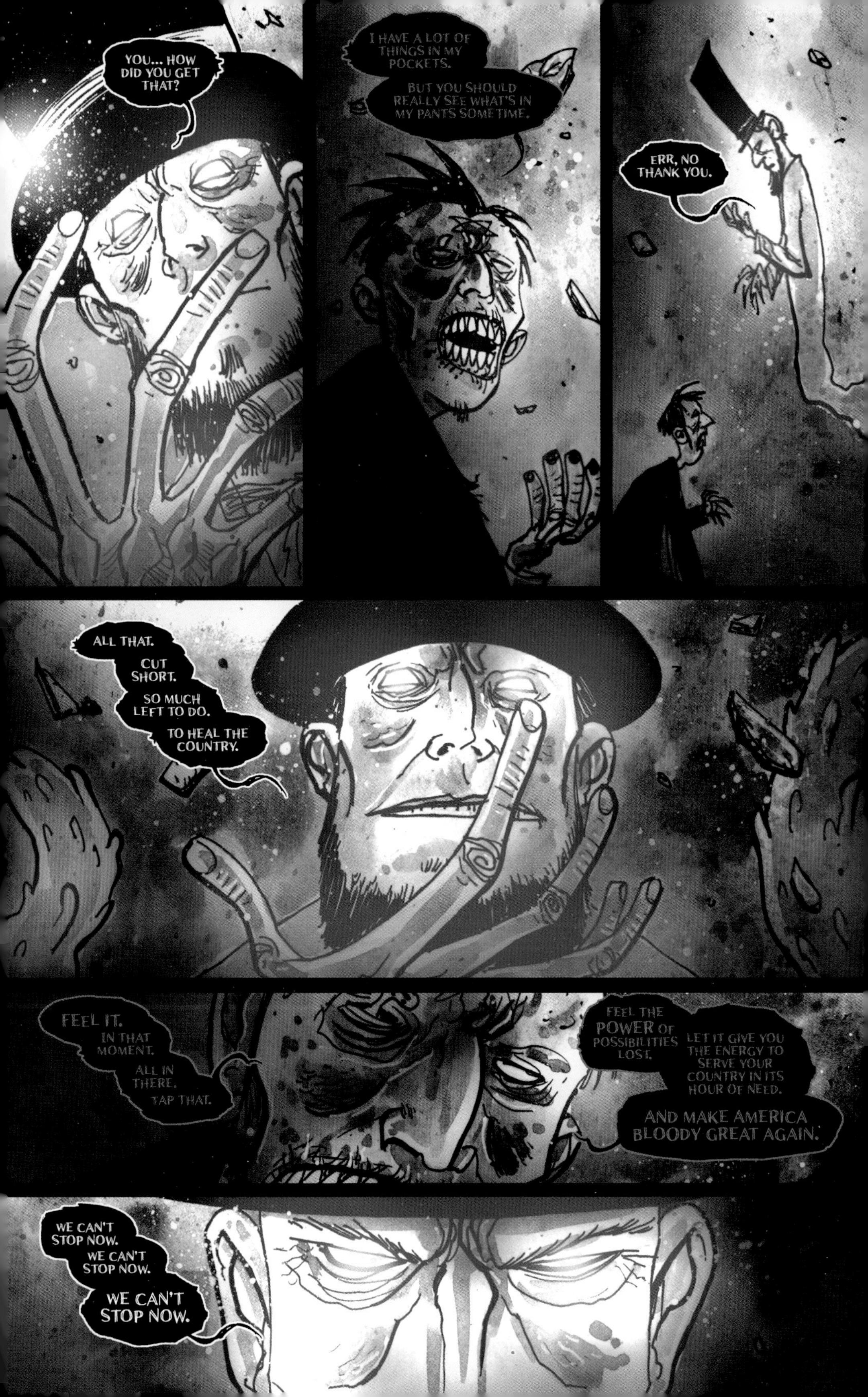
YOU... HOW DID YOU GET THAT?
I HAVE A LOT OF THINGS IN MY POCKETS.
BUT YOU SHOULD REALLY SEE WHAT'S IN MY PANTS SOMETIME.
ERR, NO THANK YOU.
ALL THAT.
CUT SHORT.
SO MUCH LEFT TO DO.
TO HEAL THE COUNTRY.
FEEL IT.
IN THAT MOMENT.
ALL IN THERE.
TAP THAT.
FEEL THE POWER OF POSSIBILITIES LOST.
LET IT GIVE YOU THE ENERGY TO SERVE YOUR COUNTRY IN ITS HOUR OF NEED.
AND MAKE AMERICA BLOODY GREAT AGAIN.
WE CAN'T STOP NOW.
WE CAN'T STOP NOW.
WE CAN'T STOP NOW.

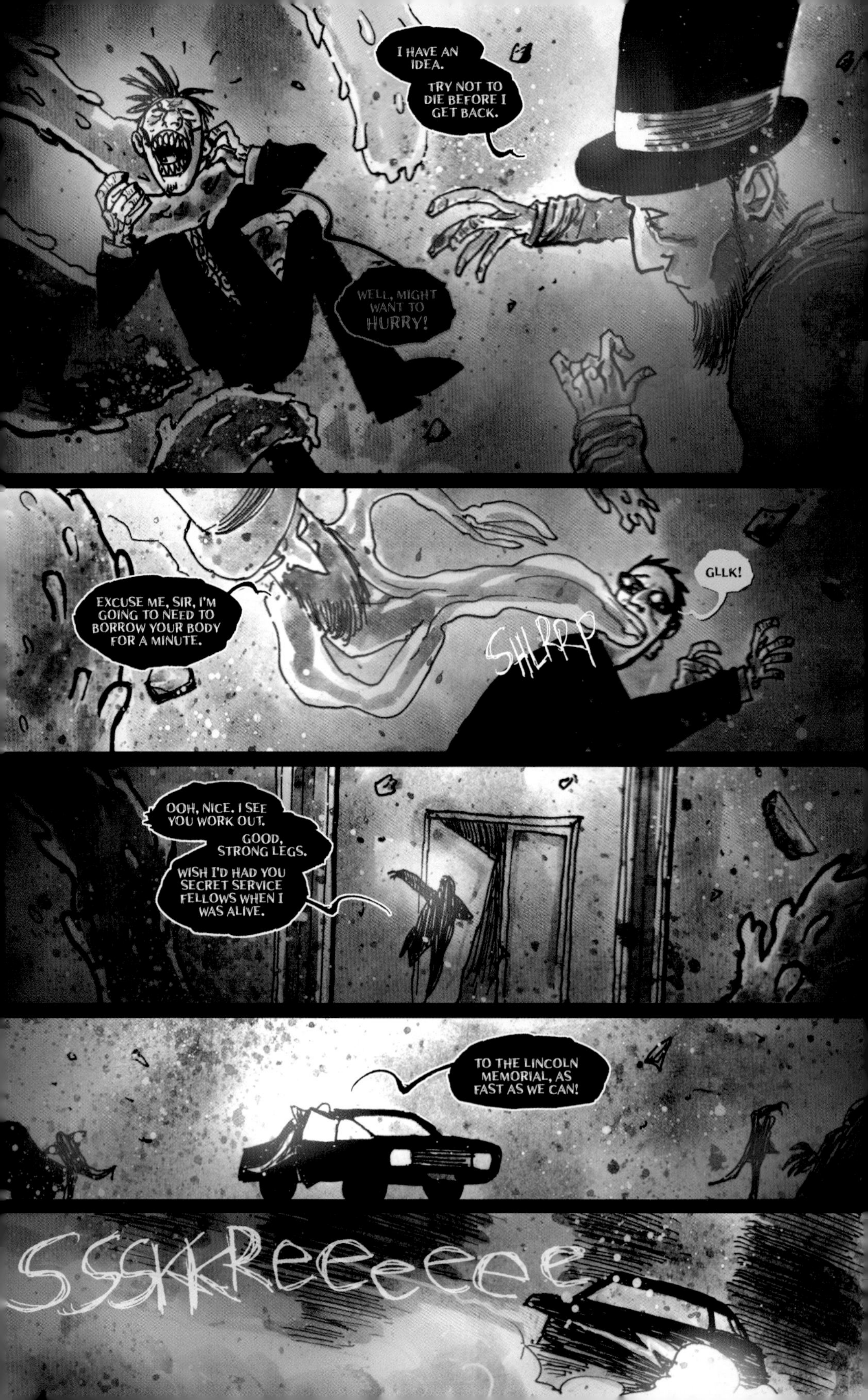
I HAVE AN IDEA.
TRY NOT TO DIE BEFORE I GET BACK.
WELL, MIGHT WANT TO HURRY!
EXCUSE ME, SIR, I'M GOING TO NEED TO BORROW YOUR BODY FOR A MINUTE.
GLLK!
SHLRRP
OOH, NICE. I SEE YOU WORK OUT.
GOOD, STRONG LEGS.
WISH I'D HAD YOU SECRET SERVICE FELLOWS WHEN I WAS ALIVE.
TO THE LINCOLN MEMORIAL, AS FAST AS WE CAN!
SSSKKREEEEEEE

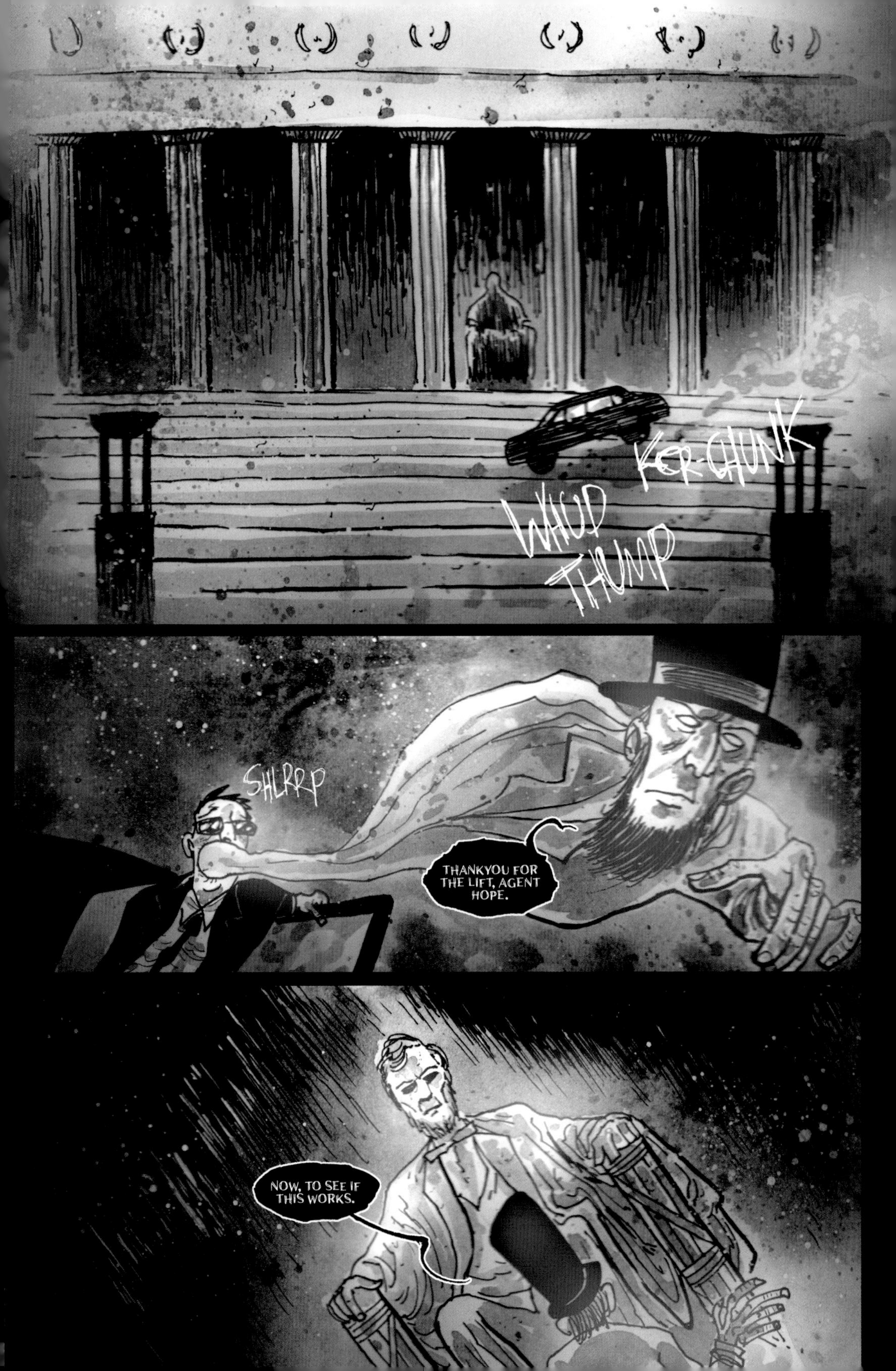
KER-CHUNK
WHUD
THUMP
SHLRRP
THANKYOU FOR THE LIFT, AGENT HOPE.
NOW, TO SEE IF THIS WORKS.

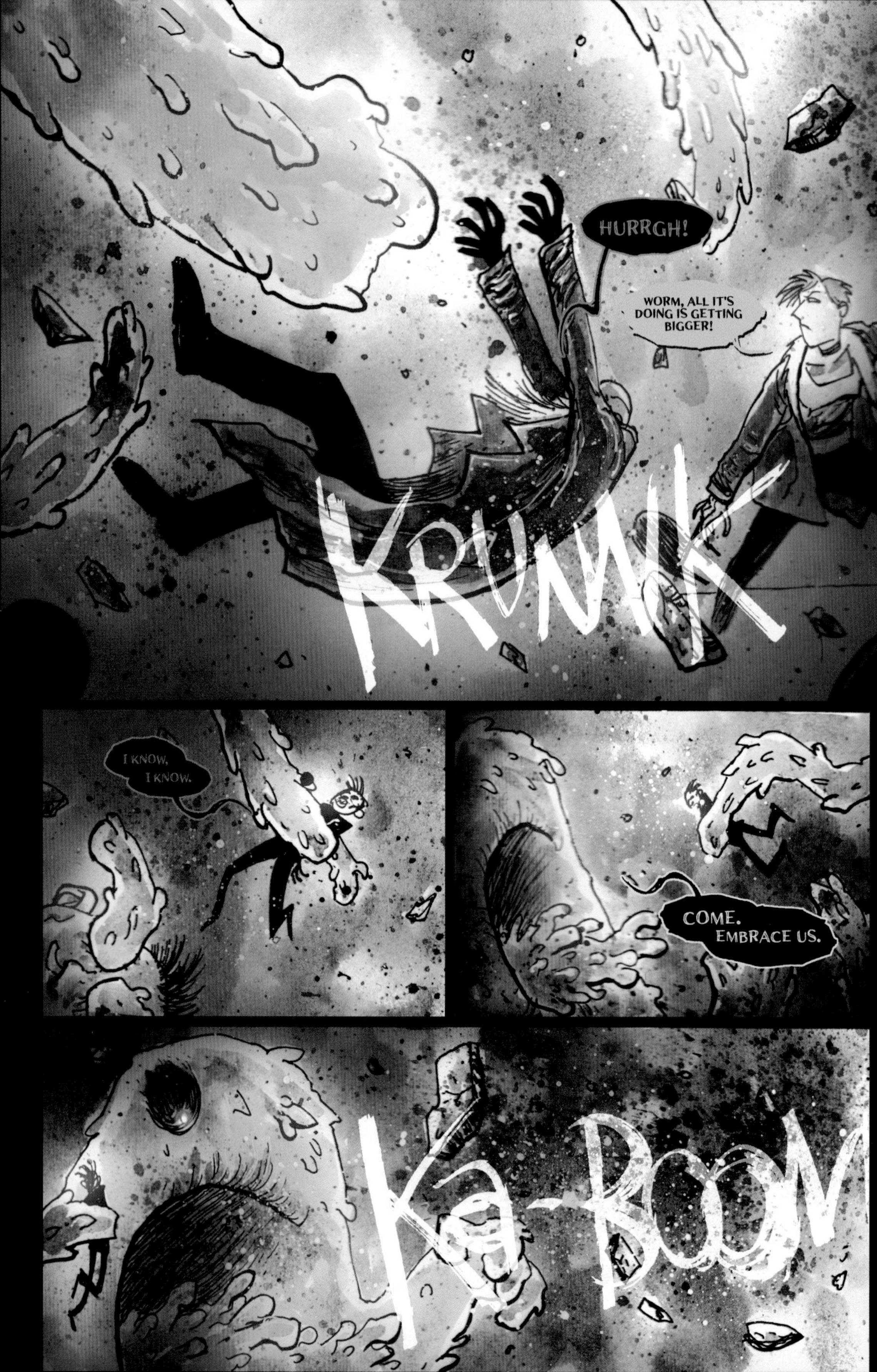
HURRGH!
WORM, ALL IT'S DOING IS GETTING BIGGER!
KRUNK
I KNOW, I KNOW.
COME. EMBRACE US.
KA-BOOM

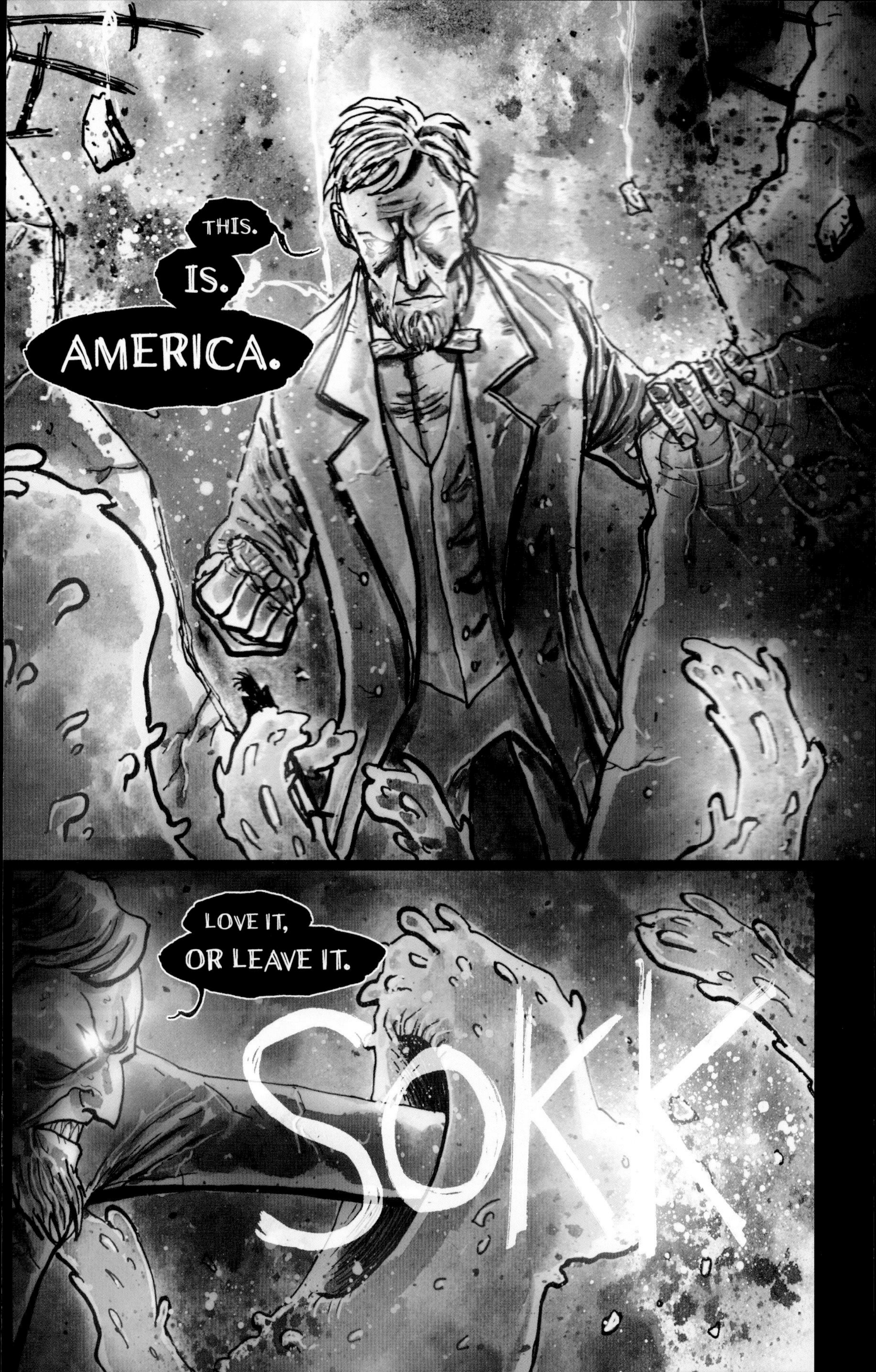
THIS.
IS.
AMERICA.
LOVE IT,
OR LEAVE IT.
SOKK

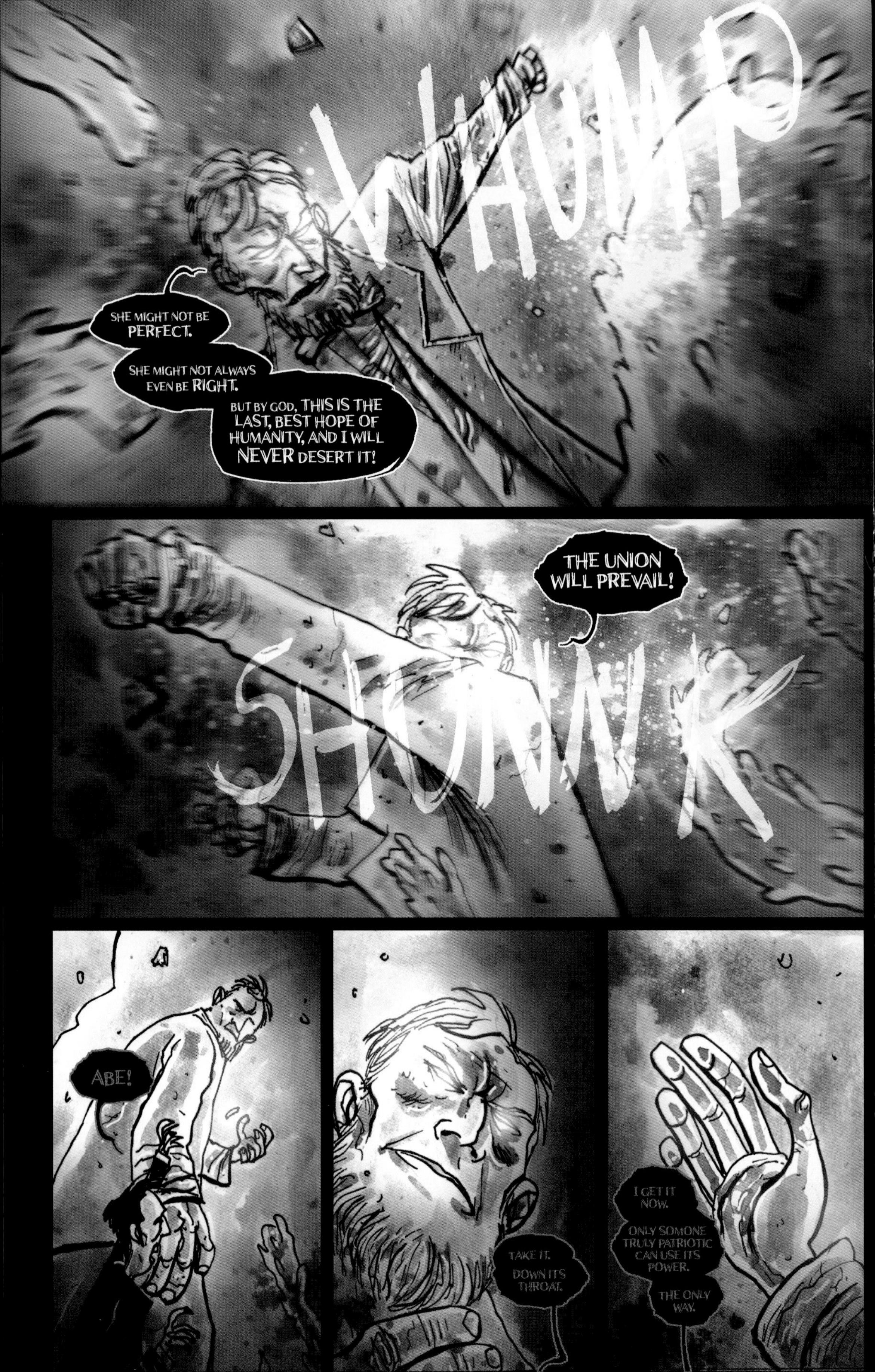
WHUMP
SHE MIGHT NOT BE PERFECT.
SHE MIGHT NOT ALWAYS EVEN BE RIGHT.
BUT BY GOD, THIS IS THE LAST, BEST HOPE OF HUMANITY, AND I WILL NEVER DESERT IT!
THE UNION WILL PREVAIL!
SHUNK
ABE!
TAKE IT.
DOWN ITS THROAT.
I GET IT NOW.
ONLY SOMONE TRULY PATRIOTIC CAN USE ITS POWER.
THE ONLY WAY.

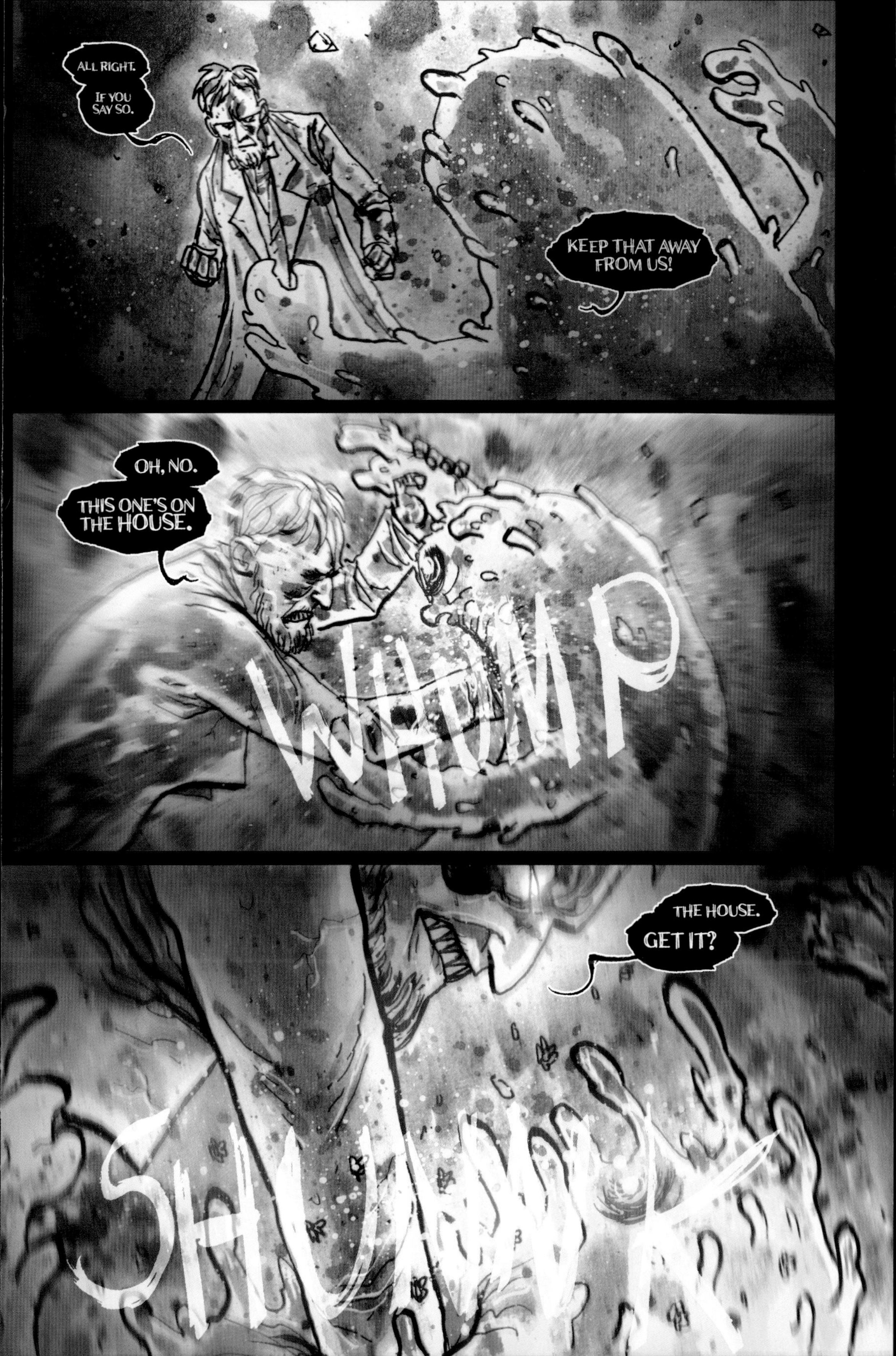
ALL RIGHT.
IF YOU SAY SO.
KEEP THAT AWAY FROM US!
OH, NO.
THIS ONE'S ON THE HOUSE.
WHUMP
THE HOUSE.
GET IT?
SHUNNK

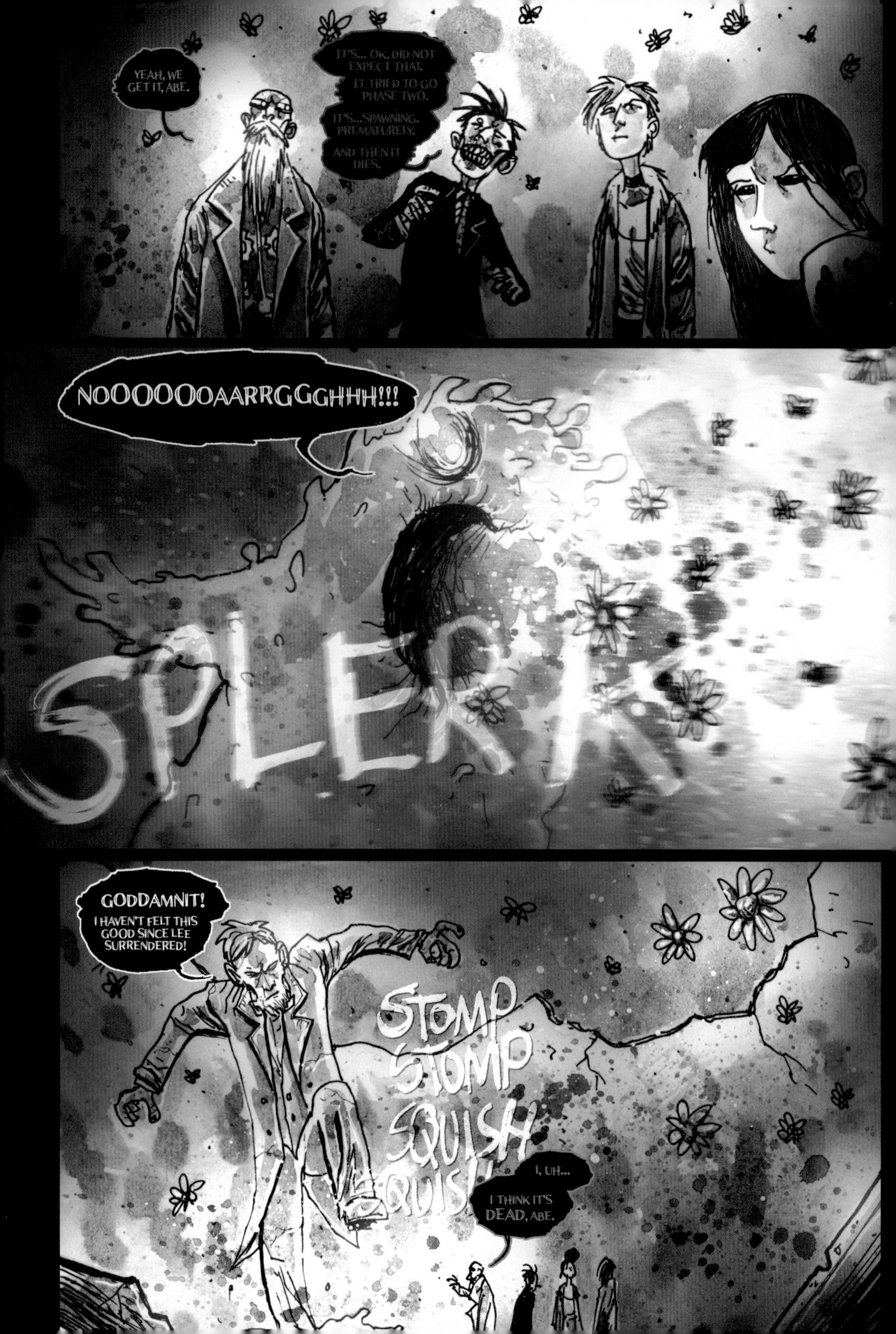

YEAH, WE GET IT, ABE.
IT'S... OK, DID NOT EXPECT THAT.
IT TRIED TO GO PHASE TWO.
IT'S...SPAWNING. PREMATURELY.
AND THEN IT DIES.
NOOOOOOAARRGGGHHHH!!!
SPLERK
GODDAMNIT!
I HAVEN'T FELT THIS GOOD SINCE LEE SURRENDERED!
STOMP
STOMP
SQUISH
SQUISH
I, UH...
I THINK IT'S DEAD, ABE.

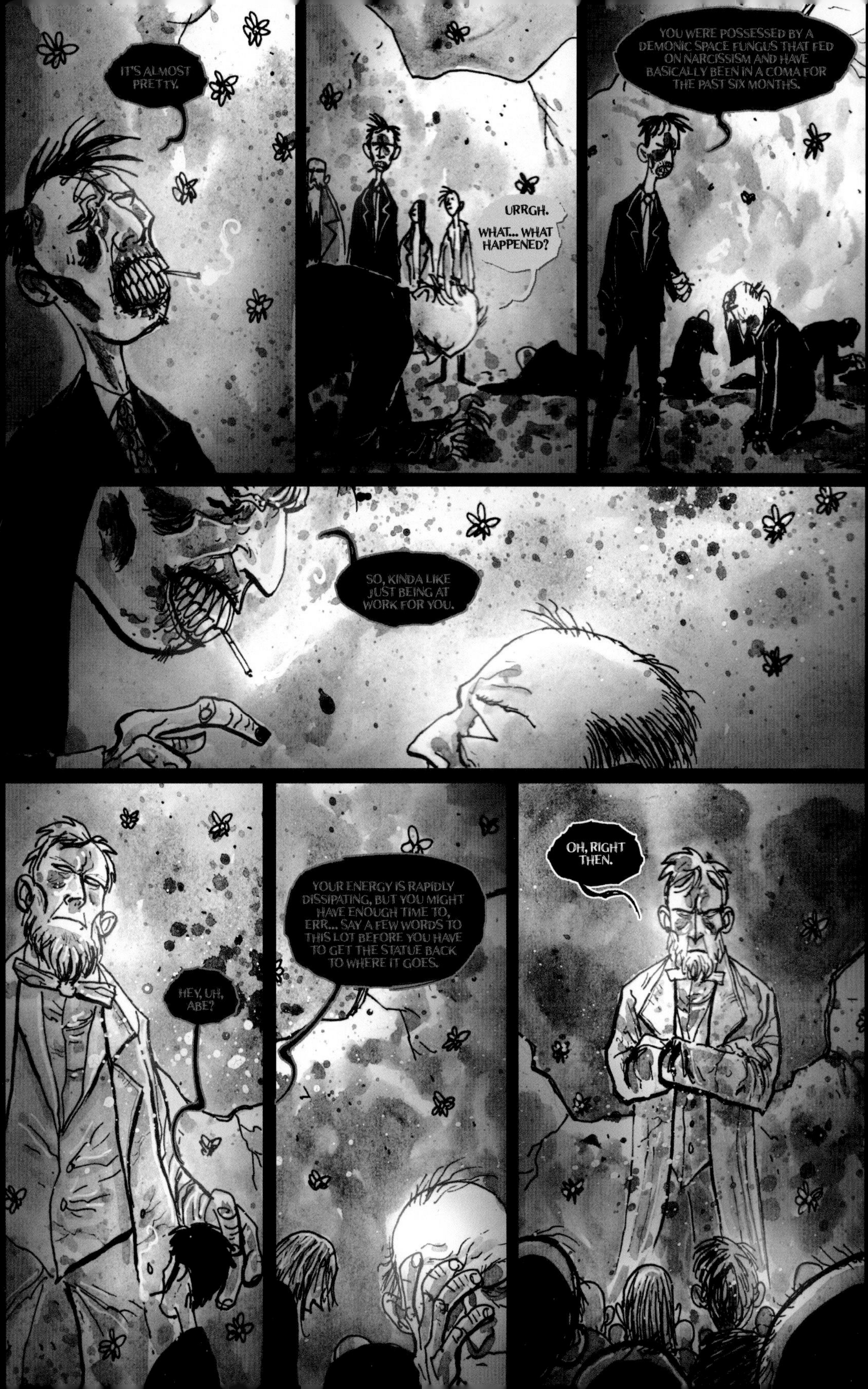
IT'S ALMOST PRETTY.
URRGH.
WHAT... WHAT HAPPENED?
YOU WERE POSSESSED BY A DEMONIC SPACE FUNGUS THAT FED ON NARCISSISM AND HAVE BASICALLY BEEN IN A COMA FOR THE PAST SIX MONTHS.
SO, KINDA LIKE JUST BEING AT WORK FOR YOU.
HEY, UH, ABE?
YOUR ENERGY IS RAPIDLY DISSIPATING, BUT YOU MIGHT HAVE ENOUGH TIME TO, ERR... SAY A FEW WORDS TO THIS LOT BEFORE YOU HAVE TO GET THE STATUE BACK TO WHERE IT GOES.
OH, RIGHT THEN.

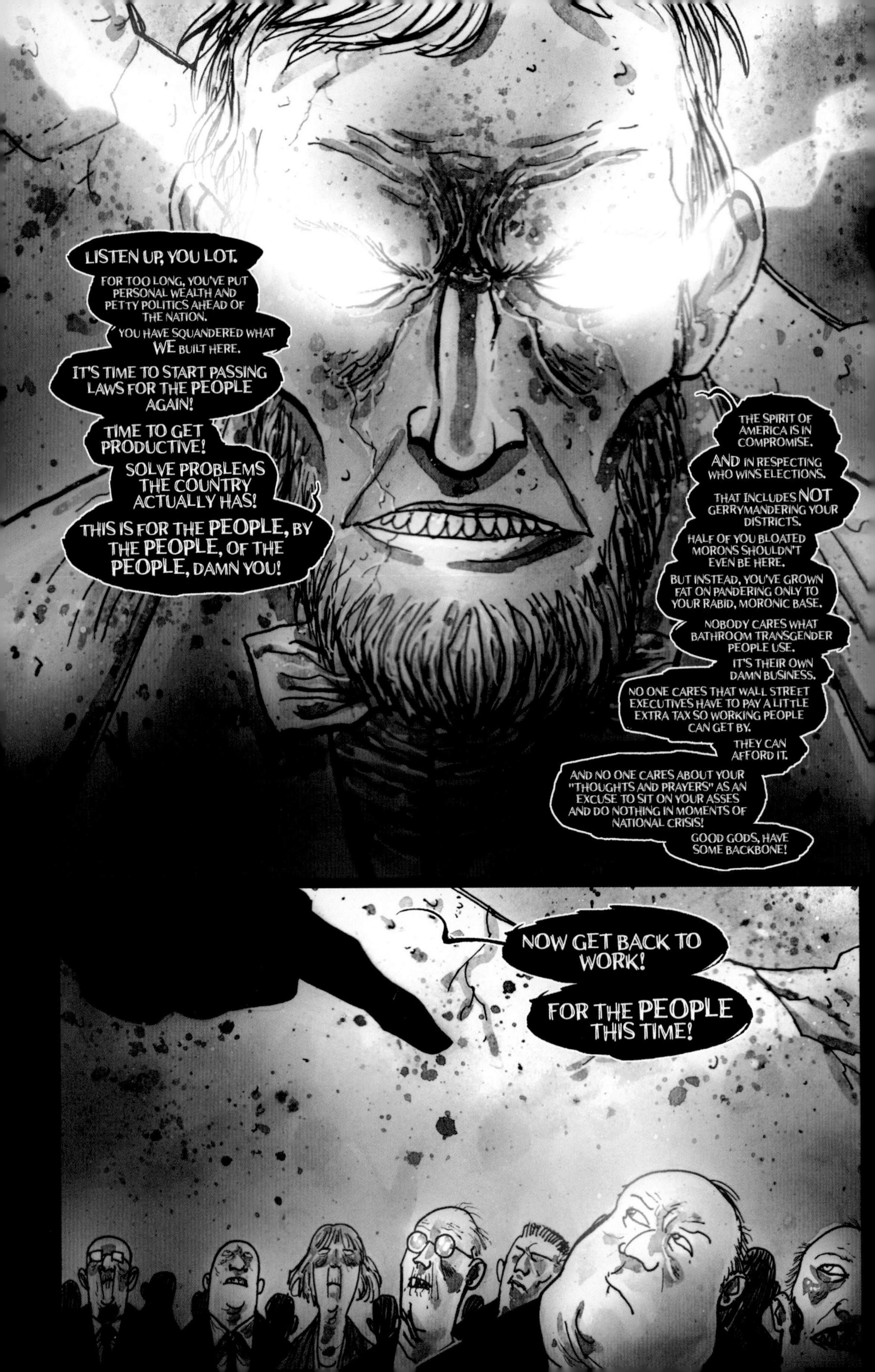
LISTEN UP, YOU LOT.
FOR TOO LONG, YOU'VE PUT PERSONAL WEALTH AND PETTY POLITICS AHEAD OF THE NATION.
YOU HAVE SQUANDERED WHAT WE BUILT HERE.
IT'S TIME TO START PASSING LAWS FOR THE PEOPLE AGAIN!
TIME TO GET PRODUCTIVE!
SOLVE PROBLEMS THE COUNTRY ACTUALLY HAS!
THIS IS FOR THE PEOPLE, BY THE PEOPLE, OF THE PEOPLE, DAMN YOU!
THE SPIRIT OF AMERICA IS IN COMPROMISE.
AND IN RESPECTING WHO WINS ELECTIONS.
THAT INCLUDES NOT GERRYMANDERING YOUR DISTRICTS.
HALF OF YOU BLOATED MORONS SHOULDN'T EVEN BE HERE.
BUT INSTEAD, YOU'VE GROWN FAT ON PANDERING ONLY TO YOUR RABID, MORONIC BASE.
NOBODY CARES WHAT BATHROOM TRANSGENDER PEOPLE USE.
IT'S THEIR OWN DAMN BUSINESS.
NO ONE CARES THAT WALL STREET EXECUTIVES HAVE TO PAY A LITTLE EXTRA TAX SO WORKING PEOPLE CAN GET BY.
THEY CAN AFFORD IT.
AND NO ONE CARES ABOUT YOUR "THOUGHTS AND PRAYERS" AS AN EXCUSE TO SIT ON YOUR ASSES AND DO NOTHING IN MOMENTS OF NATIONAL CRISIS!
GOOD GODS, HAVE SOME BACKBONE!
NOW GET BACK TO WORK!
FOR THE PEOPLE THIS TIME!

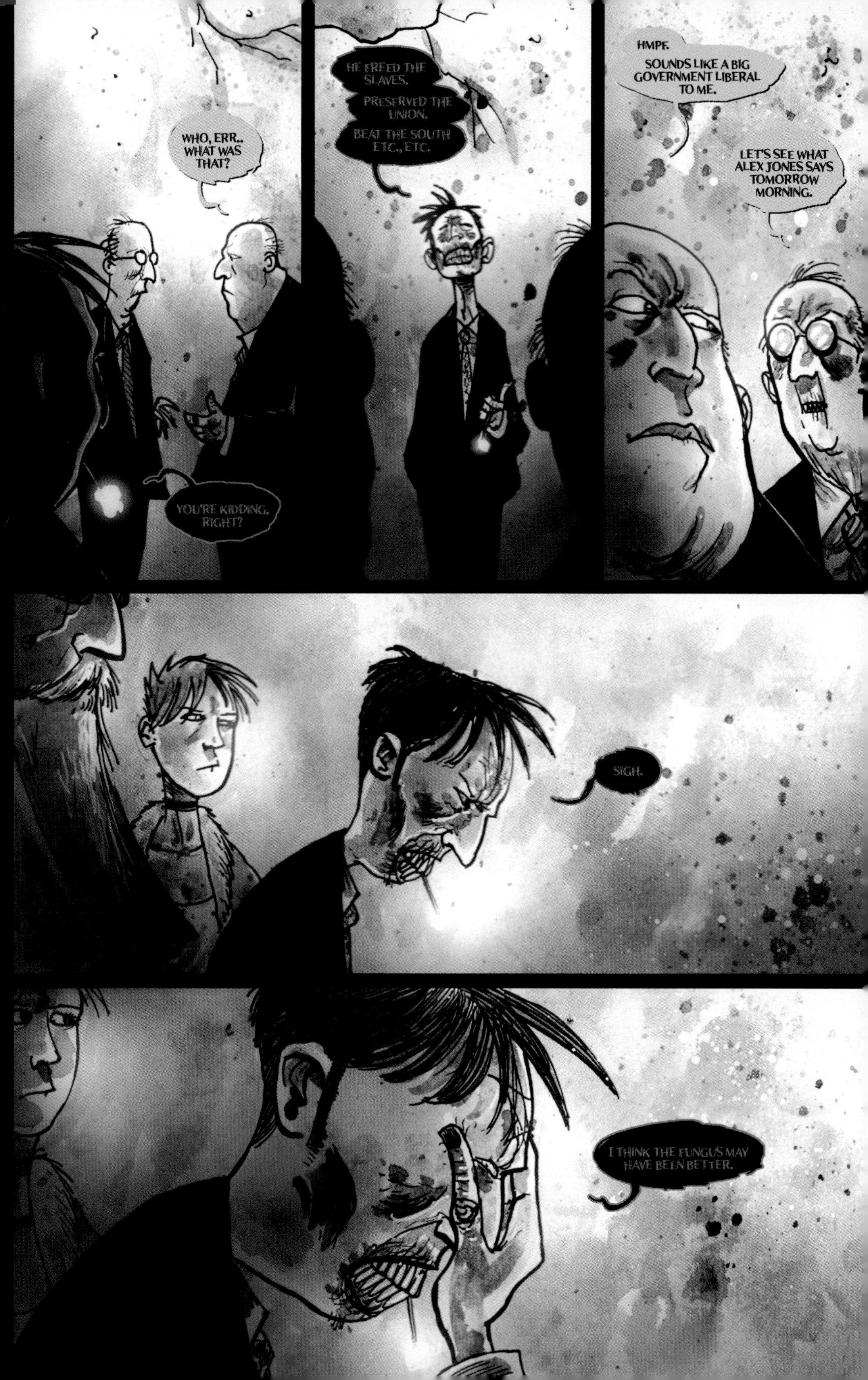
WHO, ERR..
WHAT WAS
THAT?
YOU'RE KIDDING,
RIGHT?
HE FREED THE
SLAVES.
PRESERVED THE
UNION.
BEAT THE SOUTH
ETC., ETC.
HMPF.
SOUNDS LIKE A BIG
GOVERNMENT LIBERAL
TO ME.
LET'S SEE WHAT
ALEX JONES SAYS
TOMORROW
MORNING.
SIGH.
I THINK THE FUNGUS MAY
HAVE BEEN BETTER.

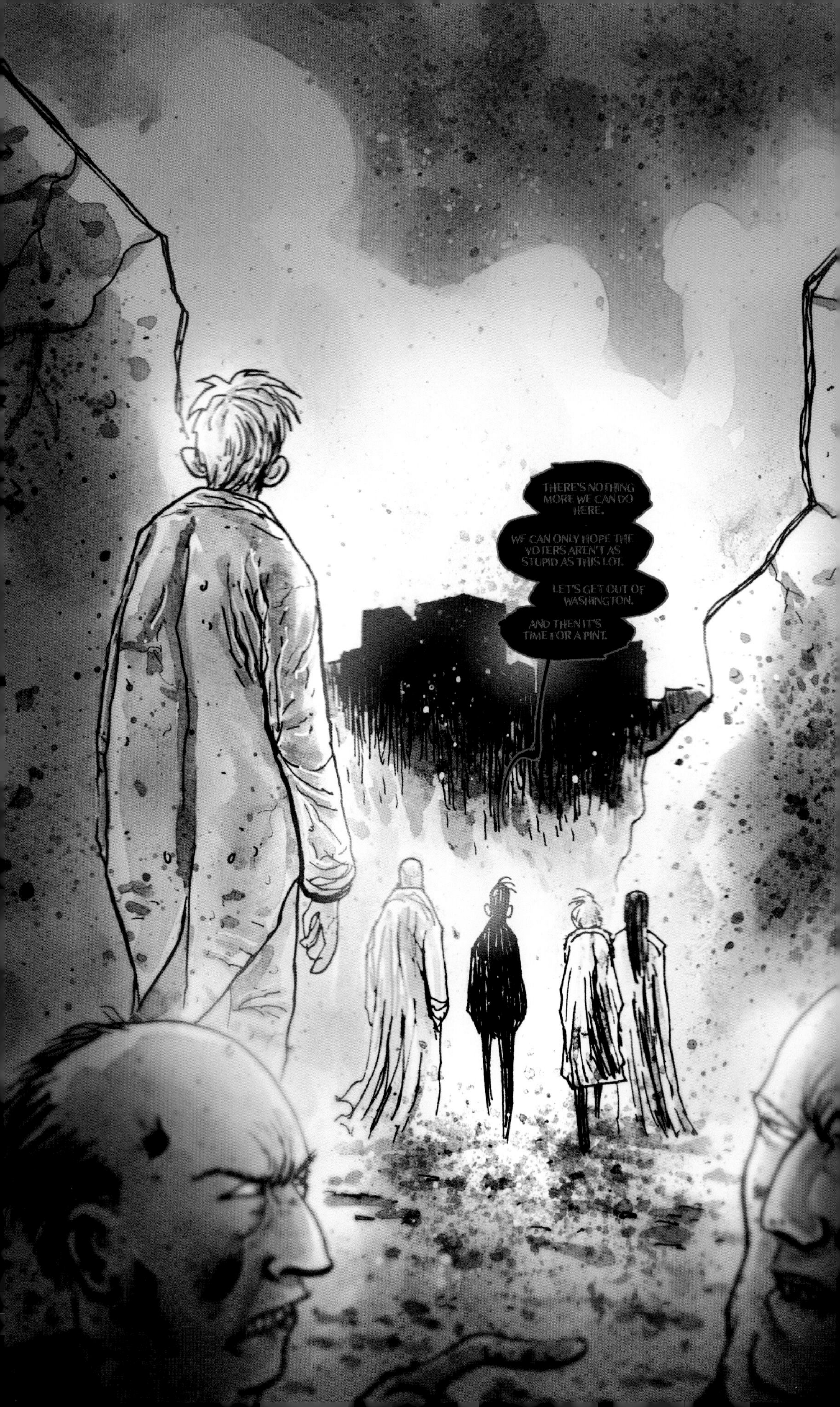
THERE'S NOTHING MORE WE CAN DO HERE.
WE CAN ONLY HOPE THE VOTERS AREN'T AS STUPID AS THIS LOT.
LET'S GET OUT OF WASHINGTON.
AND THEN IT'S TIME FOR A PINT.

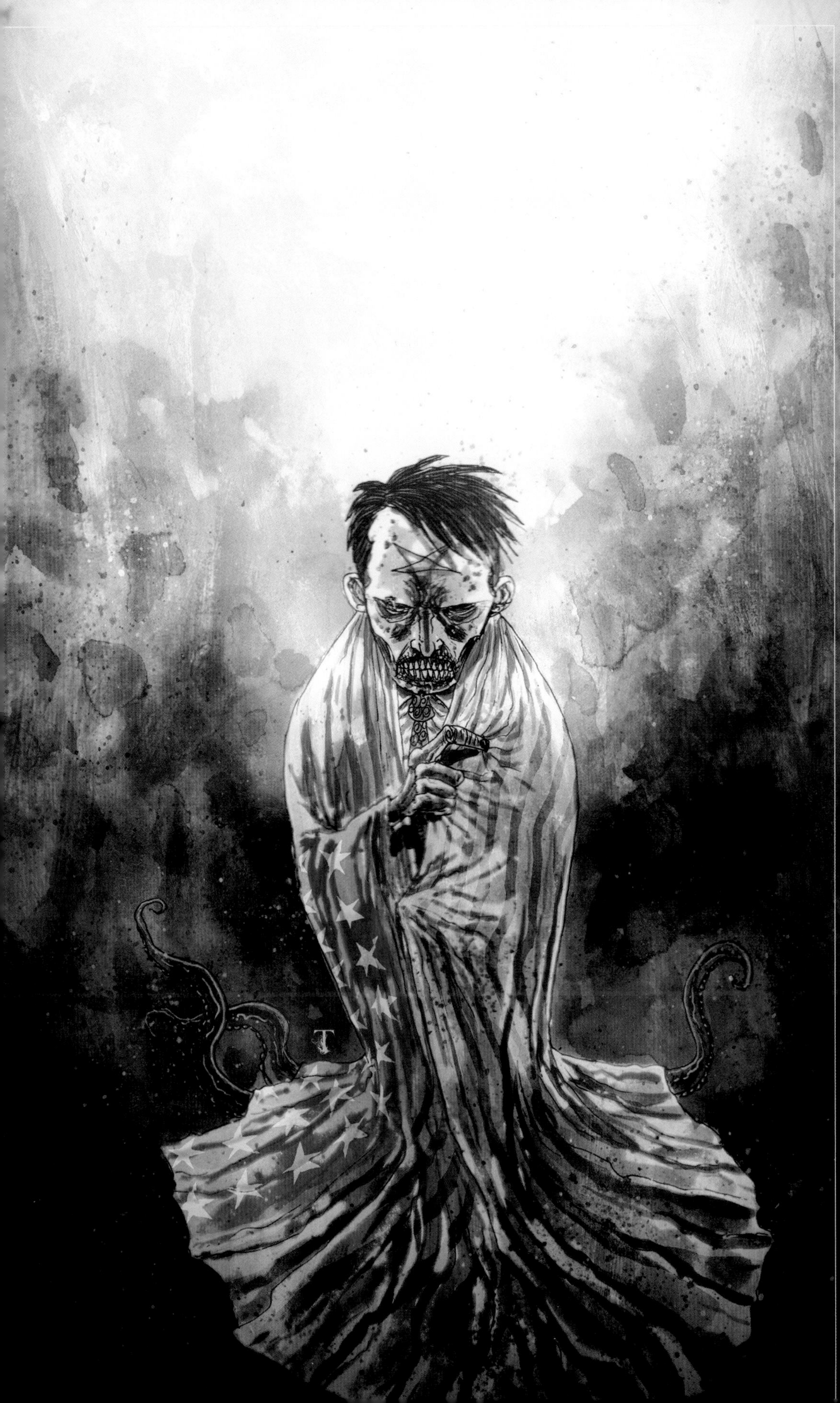

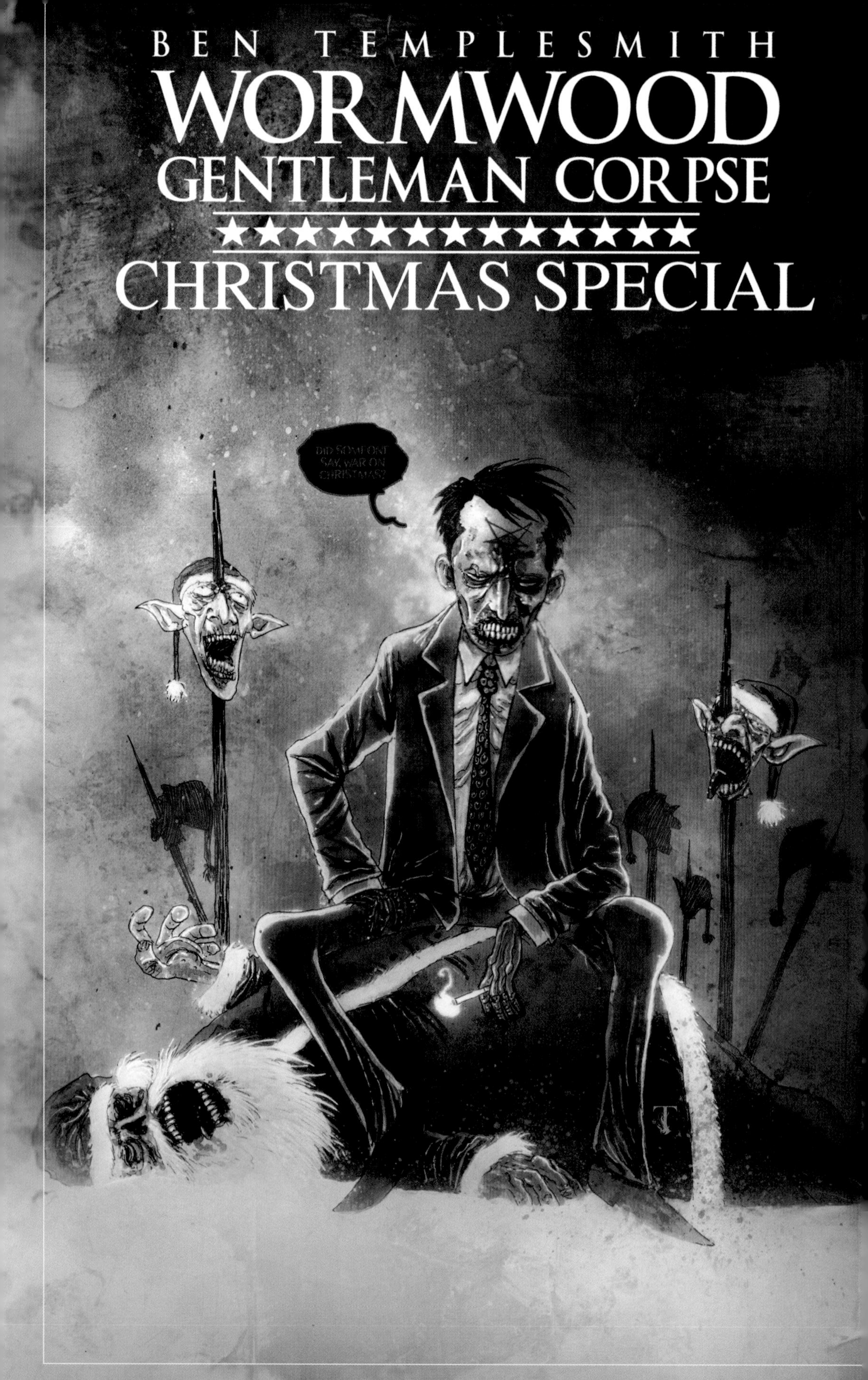
BEN TEMPLESMITH
WORMWOOD
GENTLEMAN CORPSE
CHRISTMAS SPECIAL
DID SOMEONE SAY, WAR ON CHRISTMAS?

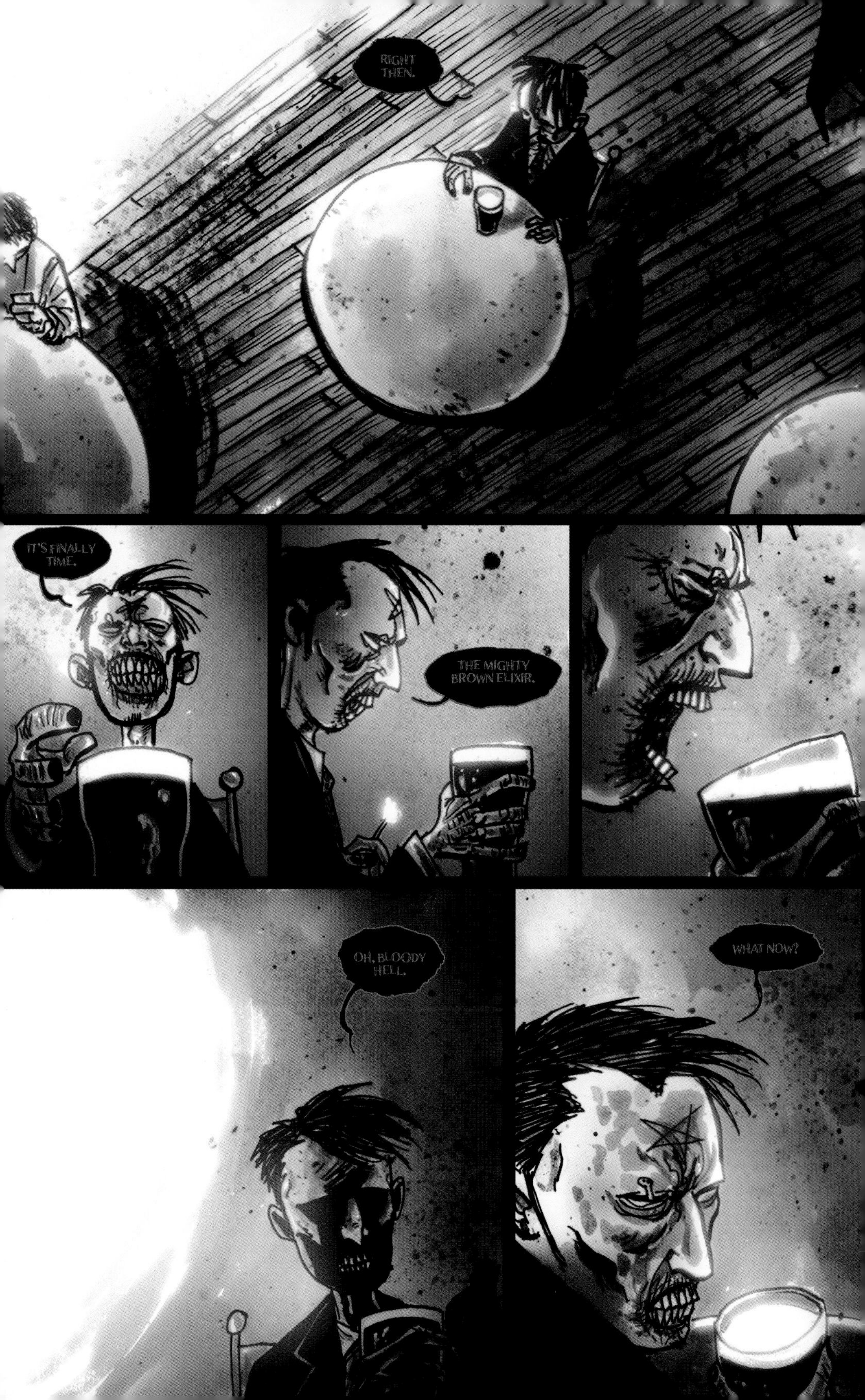
RIGHT THEN.
IT'S FINALLY TIME.
THE MIGHTY BROWN ELIXIR.
OH, BLOODY HELL.
WHAT NOW?

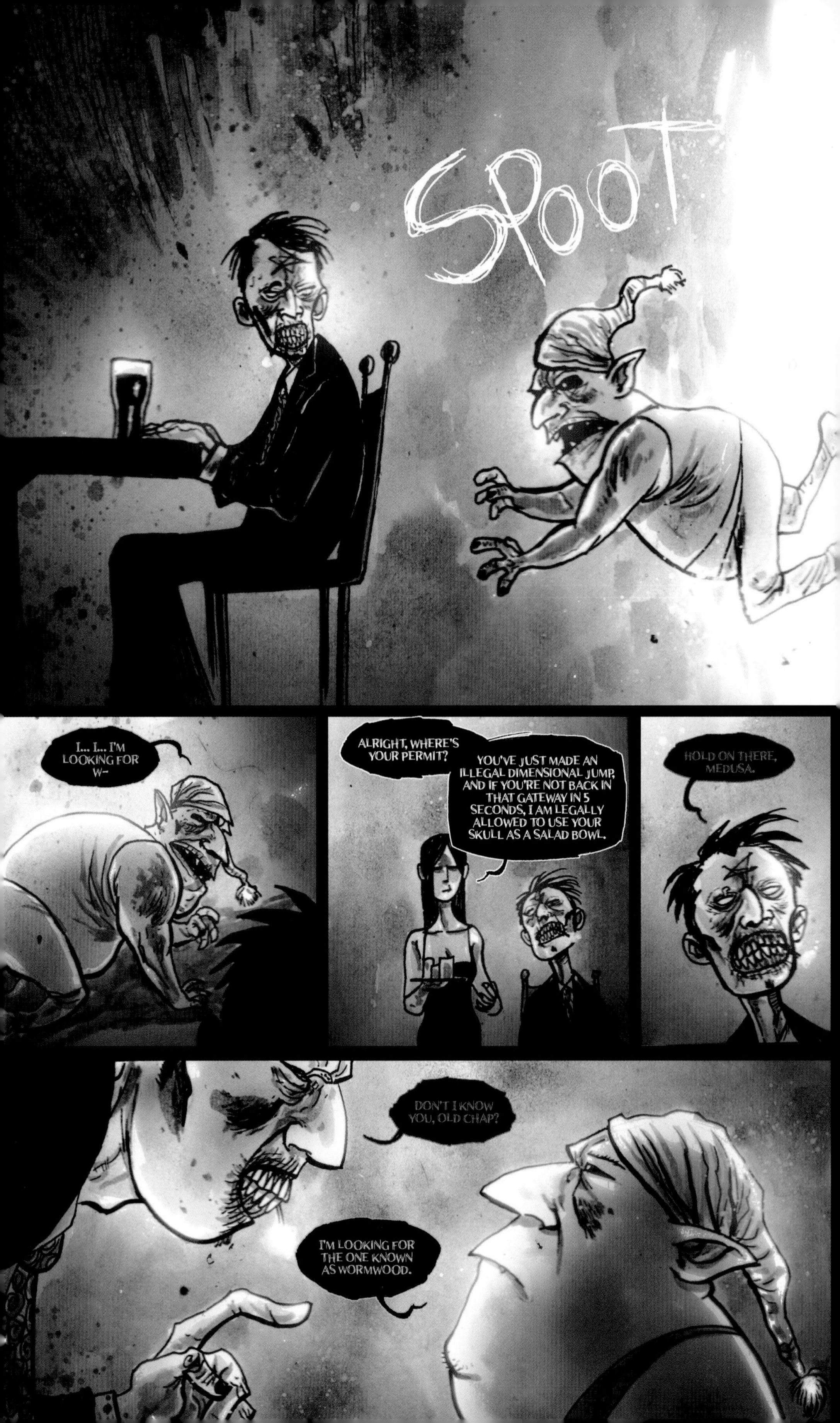
SPOOT
I... I... I'M LOOKING FOR W-
ALRIGHT, WHERE'S YOUR PERMIT?
YOU'VE JUST MADE AN ILLEGAL DIMENSIONAL JUMP, AND IF YOU'RE NOT BACK IN THAT GATEWAY IN 5 SECONDS, I AM LEGALLY ALLOWED TO USE YOUR SKULL AS A SALAD BOWL.
HOLD ON THERE, MEDUSA.
DON'T I KNOW YOU, OLD CHAP?
I'M LOOKING FOR THE ONE KNOWN AS WORMWOOD.

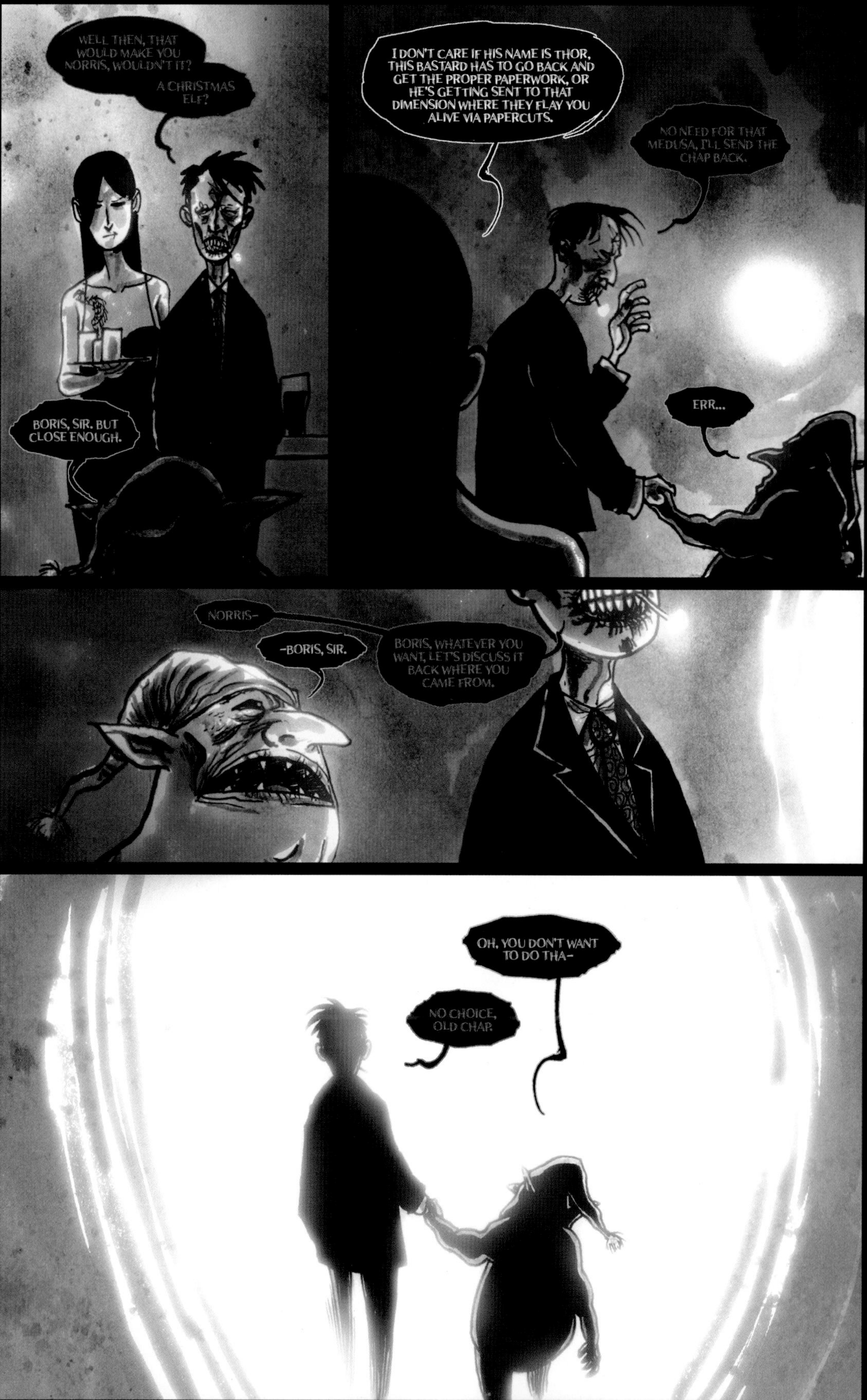
WELL THEN, THAT WOULD MAKE YOU NORRIS, WOULDN'T IT?
A CHRISTMAS ELF?
BORIS, SIR. BUT CLOSE ENOUGH.
I DON'T CARE IF HIS NAME IS THOR, THIS BASTARD HAS TO GO BACK AND GET THE PROPER PAPERWORK, OR HE'S GETTING SENT TO THAT DIMENSION WHERE THEY FLAY YOU ALIVE VIA PAPERCUTS.
NO NEED FOR THAT MEDUSA, I'LL SEND THE CHAP BACK.
ERR...
NORRIS-
-BORIS, SIR.
BORIS, WHATEVER YOU WANT, LET'S DISCUSS IT BACK WHERE YOU CAME FROM.
OH, YOU DON'T WANT TO DO THA-
NO CHOICE, OLD CHAP.

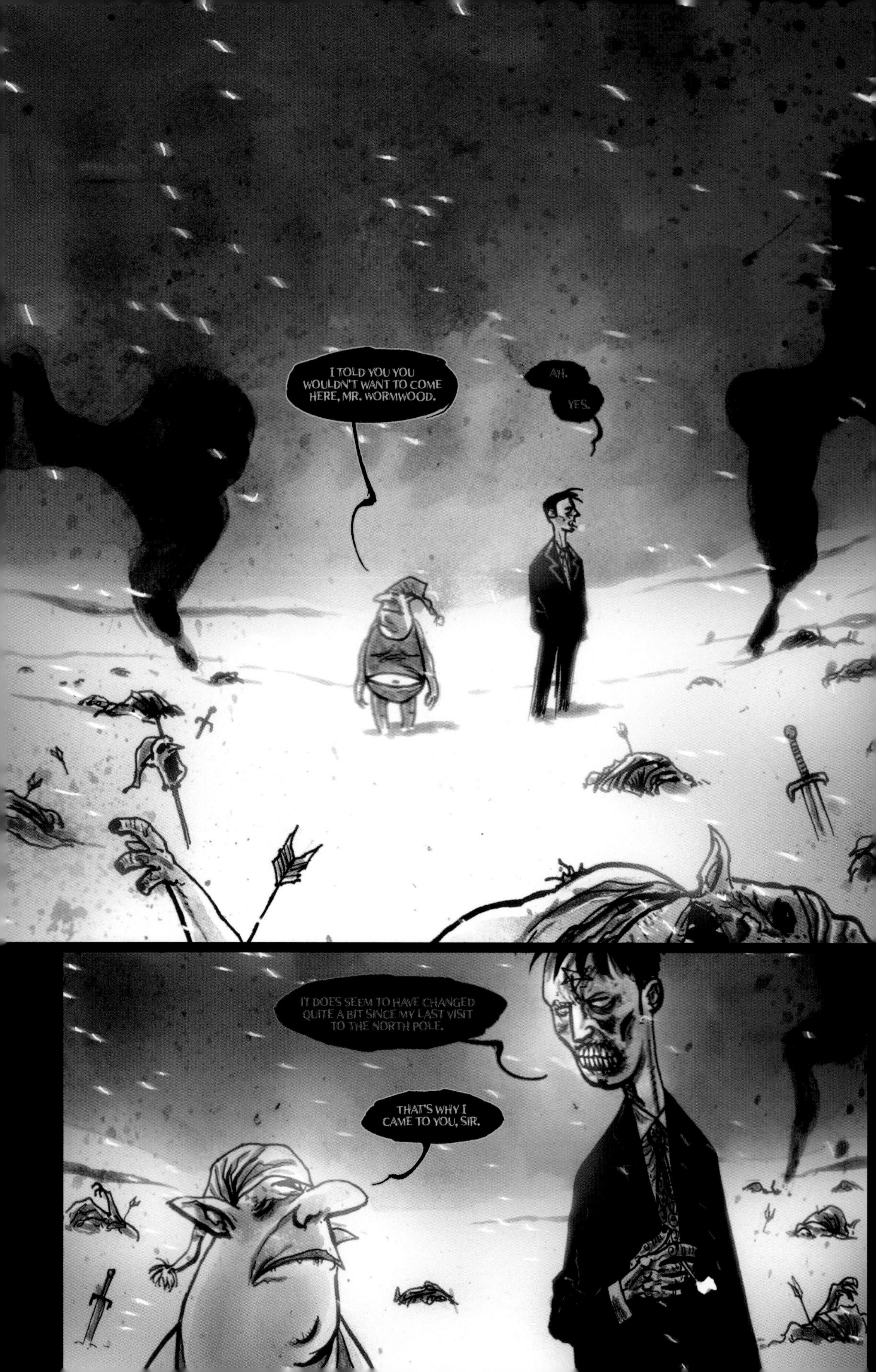
I TOLD YOU YOU WOULDN'T WANT TO COME HERE, MR. WORMWOOD.
AH.
YES.
IT DOES SEEM TO HAVE CHANGED QUITE A BIT SINCE MY LAST VISIT TO THE NORTH POLE.
THAT'S WHY I CAME TO YOU, SIR.

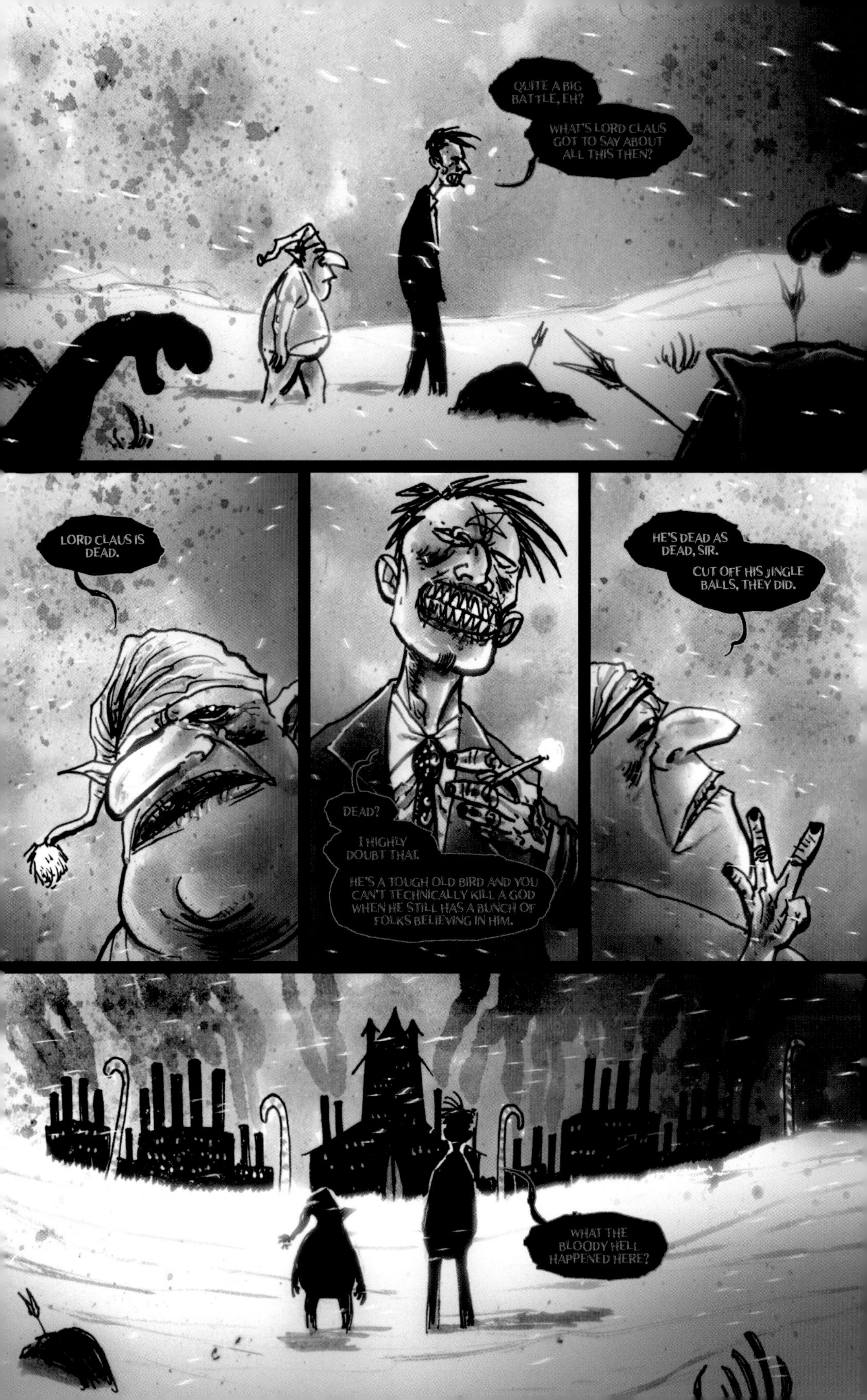
QUITE A BIG BATTLE, EH?
WHAT'S LORD CLAUS GOT TO SAY ABOUT ALL THIS THEN?
LORD CLAUS IS DEAD.
DEAD?
I HIGHLY DOUBT THAT.
HE'S A TOUGH OLD BIRD AND YOU CAN'T TECHNICALLY KILL A GOD WHEN HE STILL HAS A BUNCH OF FOLKS BELIEVING IN HIM.
HE'S DEAD AS DEAD, SIR.
CUT OFF HIS JINGLE BALLS, THEY DID.
WHAT THE BLOODY HELL HAPPENED HERE?

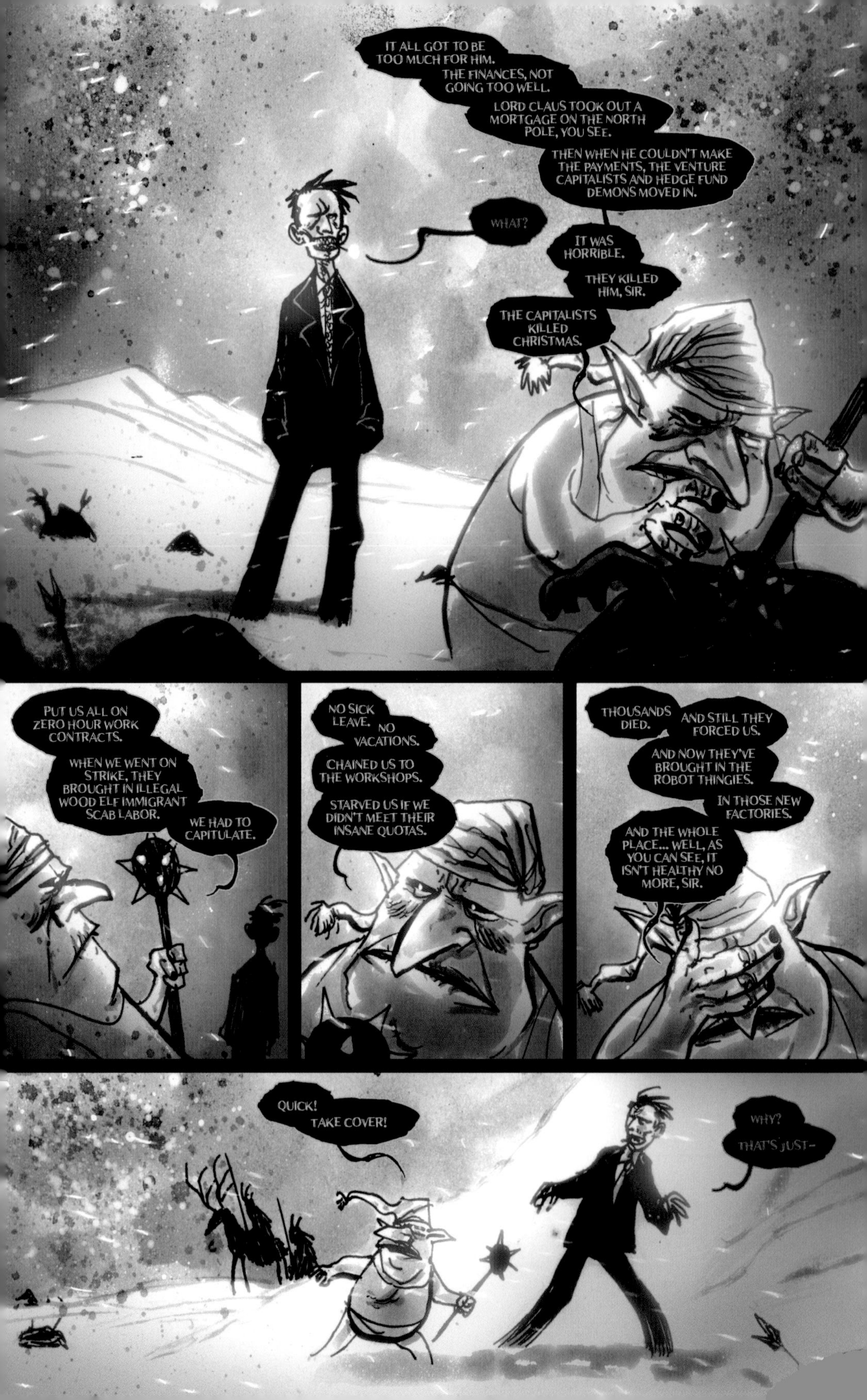
IT ALL GOT TO BE TOO MUCH FOR HIM.
THE FINANCES, NOT GOING TOO WELL.
LORD CLAUS TOOK OUT A MORTGAGE ON THE NORTH POLE, YOU SEE.
THEN WHEN HE COULDN'T MAKE THE PAYMENTS, THE VENTURE CAPITALISTS AND HEDGE FUND DEMONS MOVED IN.
WHAT?
IT WAS HORRIBLE.
THEY KILLED HIM, SIR.
THE CAPITALISTS KILLED CHRISTMAS.
PUT US ALL ON ZERO HOUR WORK CONTRACTS.
WHEN WE WENT ON STRIKE, THEY BROUGHT IN ILLEGAL WOOD ELF IMMIGRANT SCAB LABOR.
WE HAD TO CAPITULATE.
NO SICK LEAVE.
NO VACATIONS.
CHAINED US TO THE WORKSHOPS.
STARVED US IF WE DIDN'T MEET THEIR INSANE QUOTAS.
THOUSANDS DIED.
AND STILL THEY FORCED US.
AND NOW THEY'VE BROUGHT IN THE ROBOT THINGIES.
IN THOSE NEW FACTORIES.
AND THE WHOLE PLACE... WELL, AS YOU CAN SEE, IT ISN'T HEALTHY NO MORE, SIR.
QUICK!
TAKE COVER!
WHY?
THAT'S JUST–

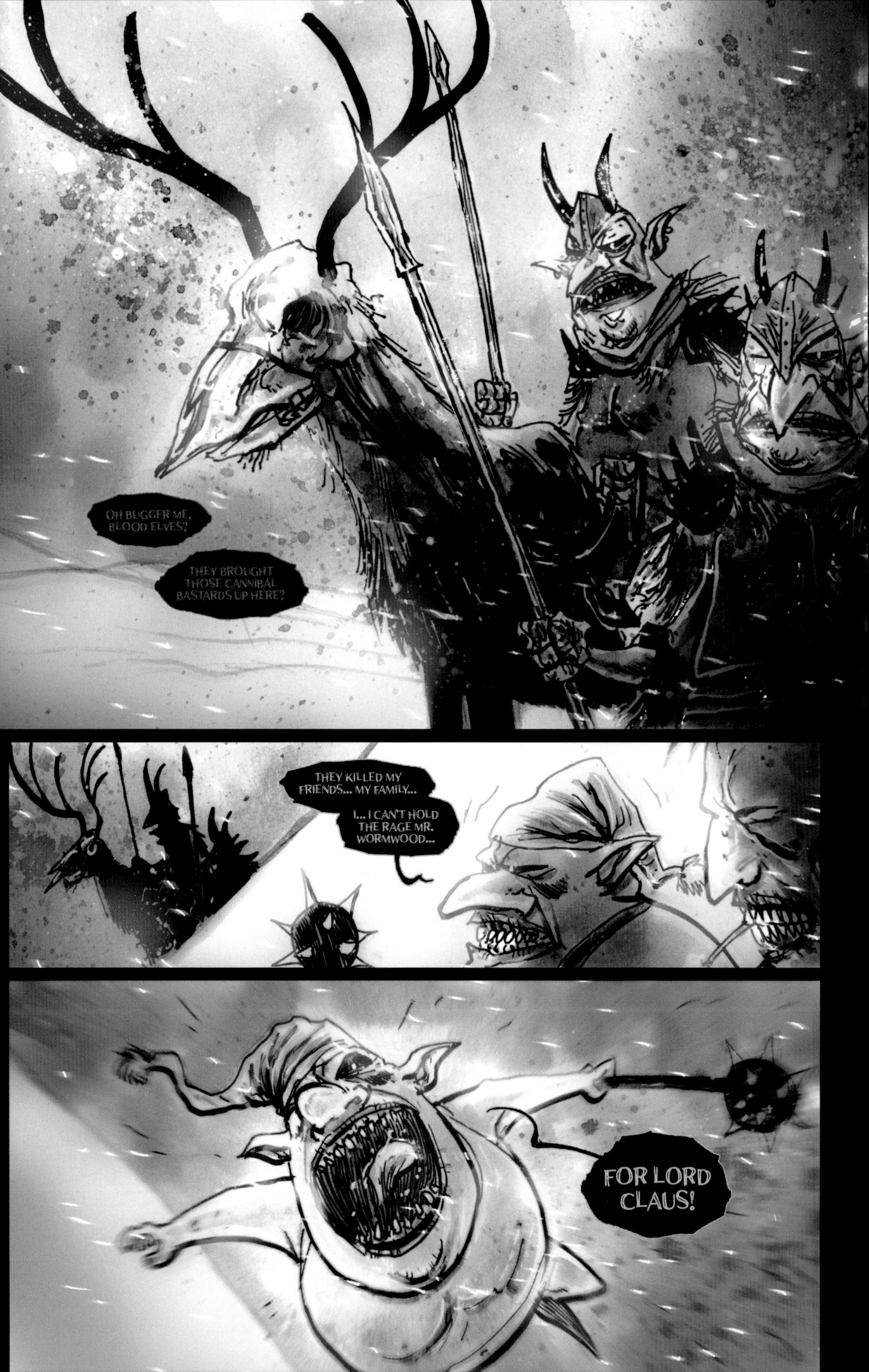
OH BUGGER ME, BLOOD ELVES?
THEY BROUGHT THOSE CANNIBAL BASTARDS UP HERE?
THEY KILLED MY FRIENDS... MY FAMILY...
I... I CAN'T HOLD THE RAGE MR. WORMWOOD...
FOR LORD CLAUS!

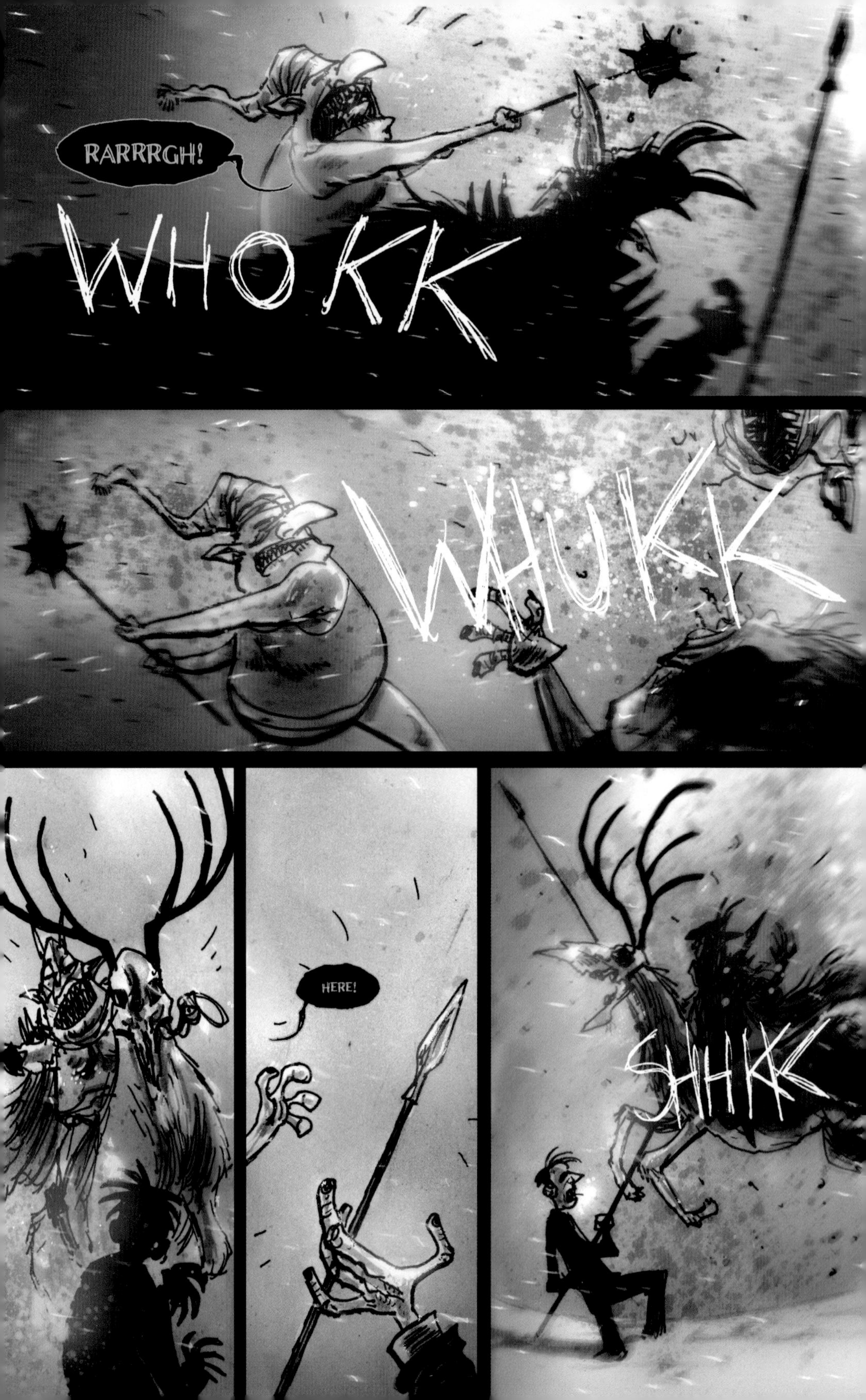
RARRRGH!
WHOKK
WHUKK
HERE!
SHHKK

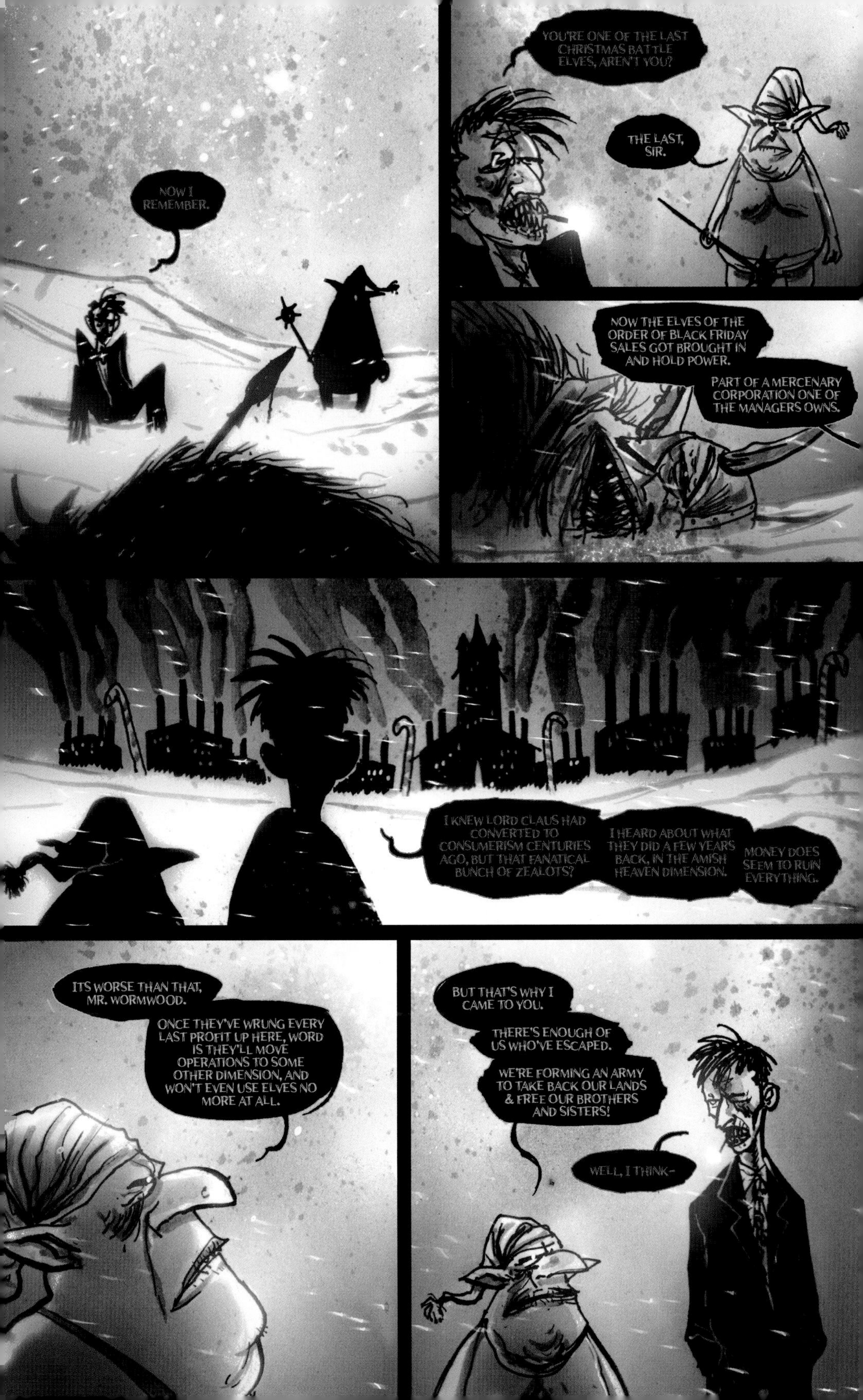
NOW I REMEMBER.
YOU'RE ONE OF THE LAST CHRISTMAS BATTLE ELVES, AREN'T YOU?
THE LAST, SIR.
NOW THE ELVES OF THE ORDER OF BLACK FRIDAY SALES GOT BROUGHT IN AND HOLD POWER.
PART OF A MERCENARY CORPORATION ONE OF THE MANAGERS OWNS.
I KNEW LORD CLAUS HAD CONVERTED TO CONSUMERISM CENTURIES AGO, BUT THAT FANATICAL BUNCH OF ZEALOTS?
I HEARD ABOUT WHAT THEY DID A FEW YEARS BACK, IN THE AMISH HEAVEN DIMENSION.
MONEY DOES SEEM TO RUIN EVERYTHING.
ITS WORSE THAN THAT, MR. WORMWOOD.
ONCE THEY'VE WRUNG EVERY LAST PROFIT UP HERE, WORD IS THEY'LL MOVE OPERATIONS TO SOME OTHER DIMENSION, AND WON'T EVEN USE ELVES NO MORE AT ALL.
BUT THAT'S WHY I CAME TO YOU.
THERE'S ENOUGH OF US WHO'VE ESCAPED.
WE'RE FORMING AN ARMY TO TAKE BACK OUR LANDS & FREE OUR BROTHERS AND SISTERS!
WELL, I THINK-

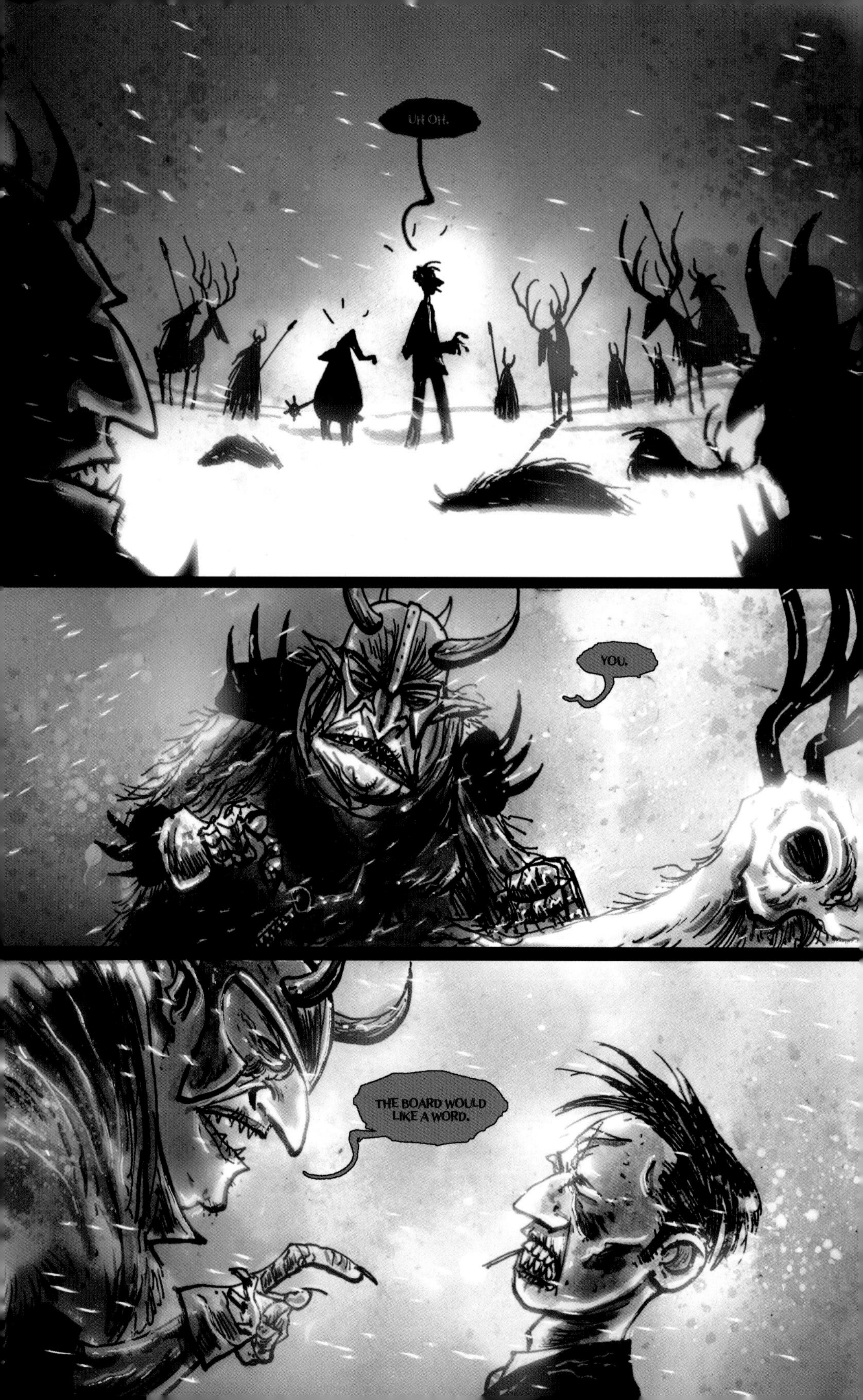
UH OH.
YOU.
THE BOARD WOULD LIKE A WORD.

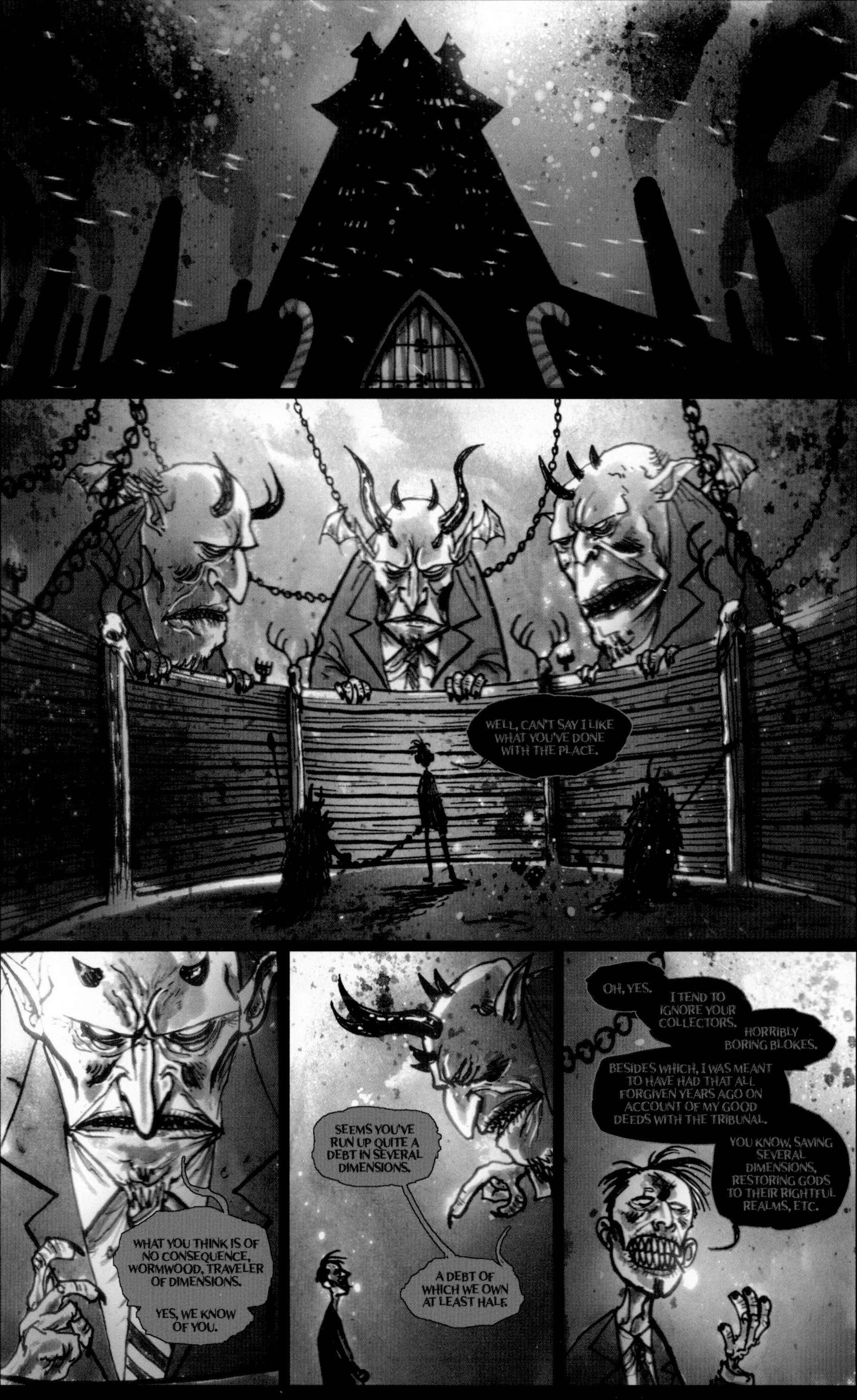

WELL, CAN'T SAY I LIKE WHAT YOU'VE DONE WITH THE PLACE.
WHAT YOU THINK IS OF NO CONSEQUENCE, WORMWOOD, TRAVELER OF DIMENSIONS.
YES, WE KNOW OF YOU.
SEEMS YOU'VE RUN UP QUITE A DEBT IN SEVERAL DIMENSIONS.
A DEBT OF WHICH WE OWN AT LEAST HALF.
OH, YES.
I TEND TO IGNORE YOUR COLLECTORS.
HORRIBLY BORING BLOKES.
BESIDES WHICH, I WAS MEANT TO HAVE HAD THAT ALL FORGIVEN YEARS AGO ON ACCOUNT OF MY GOOD DEEDS WITH THE TRIBUNAL.
YOU KNOW, SAVING SEVERAL DIMENSIONS, RESTORING GODS TO THEIR RIGHTFUL REALMS, ETC.

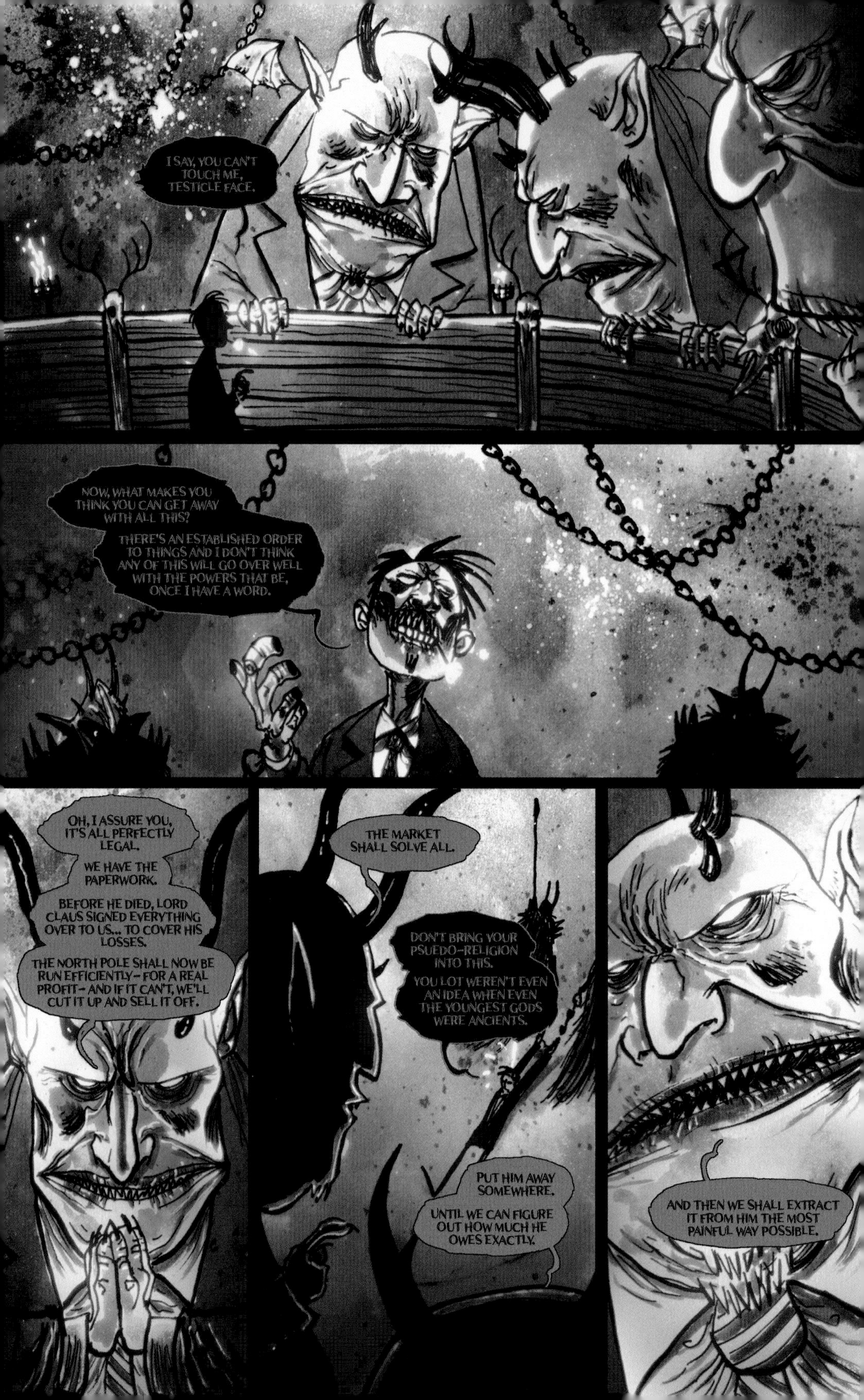
I SAY, YOU CAN'T TOUCH ME, TESTICLE FACE.
NOW, WHAT MAKES YOU THINK YOU CAN GET AWAY WITH ALL THIS?
THERE'S AN ESTABLISHED ORDER TO THINGS AND I DON'T THINK ANY OF THIS WILL GO OVER WELL WITH THE POWERS THAT BE, ONCE I HAVE A WORD.
OH, I ASSURE YOU, IT'S ALL PERFECTLY LEGAL.
WE HAVE THE PAPERWORK.
BEFORE HE DIED, LORD CLAUS SIGNED EVERYTHING OVER TO US... TO COVER HIS LOSSES.
THE NORTH POLE SHALL NOW BE RUN EFFICIENTLY- FOR A REAL PROFIT- AND IF IT CAN'T, WE'LL CUT IT UP AND SELL IT OFF.
THE MARKET SHALL SOLVE ALL.
DON'T BRING YOUR PSUEDO-RELIGION INTO THIS.
YOU LOT WEREN'T EVEN AN IDEA WHEN EVEN THE YOUNGEST GODS WERE ANCIENTS.
PUT HIM AWAY SOMEWHERE.
UNTIL WE CAN FIGURE OUT HOW MUCH HE OWES EXACTLY.
AND THEN WE SHALL EXTRACT IT FROM HIM THE MOST PAINFUL WAY POSSIBLE.

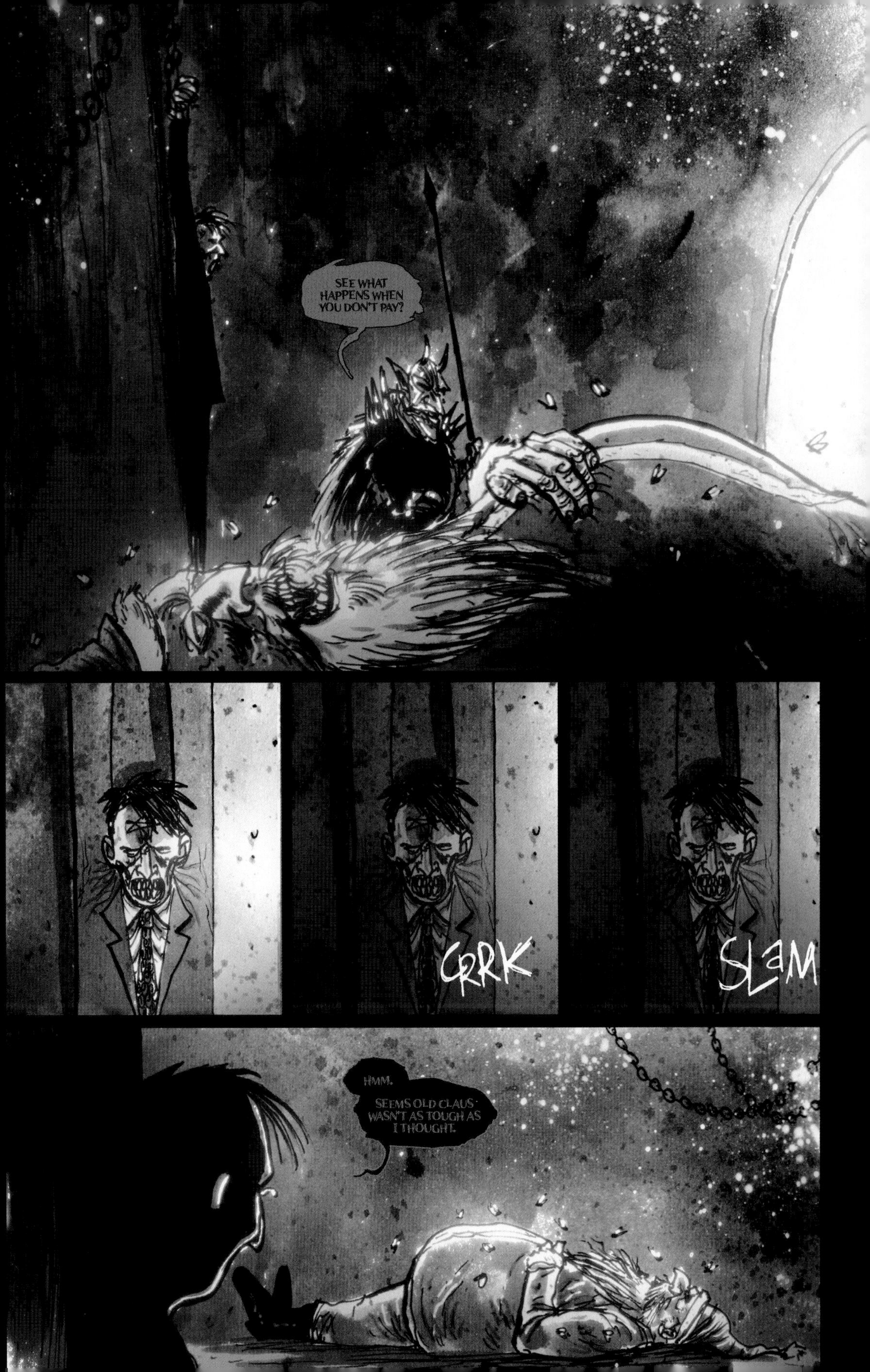
SEE WHAT HAPPENS WHEN YOU DON'T PAY?
CRRK
SLAM
HMM.
SEEMS OLD CLAUS WASN'T AS TOUGH AS I THOUGHT.

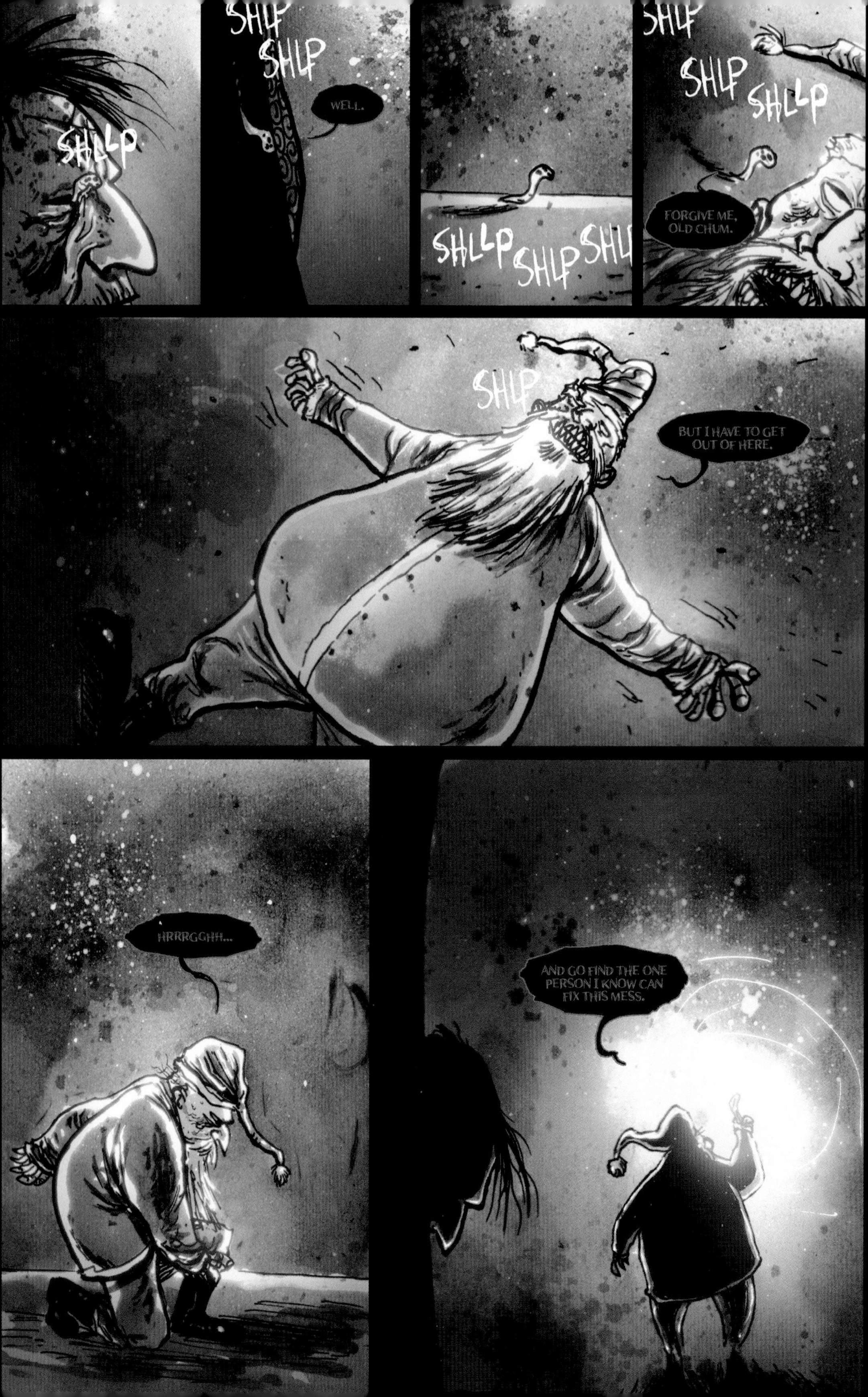
SHLLP
SHLP
SHLP
WELL.
SHLLP
SHLP
SHLP
SHLP
SHLP
SHLLP
FORGIVE ME, OLD CHUM.
SHLP
BUT I HAVE TO GET OUT OF HERE.
HRRRGGHH...
AND GO FIND THE ONE PERSON I KNOW CAN FIX THIS MESS.

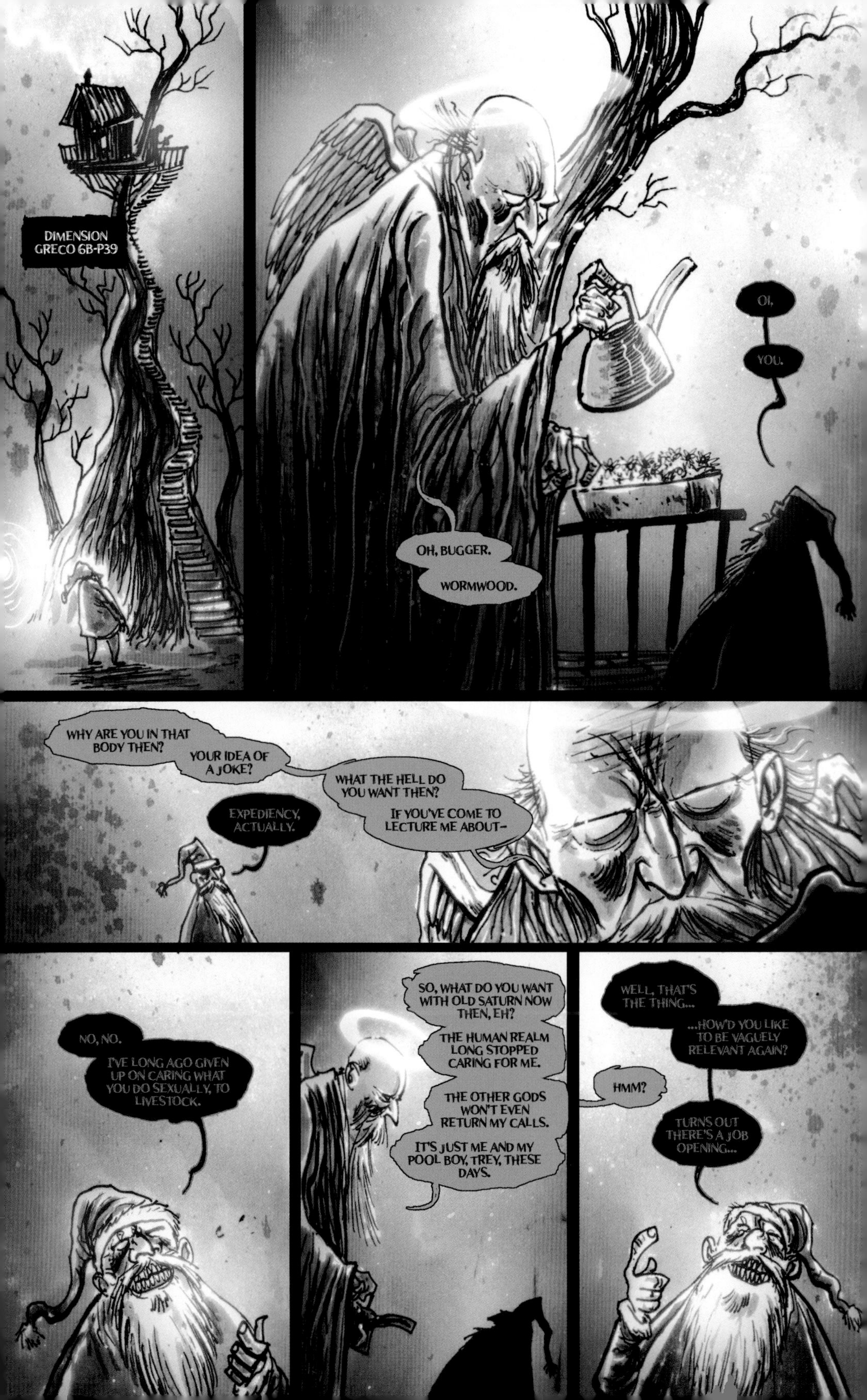
DIMENSION GRECO 6B-P39
OI,
YOU.
OH, BUGGER.
WORMWOOD.
WHY ARE YOU IN THAT BODY THEN?
YOUR IDEA OF A JOKE?
EXPEDIENCY, ACTUALLY.
WHAT THE HELL DO YOU WANT THEN?
IF YOU'VE COME TO LECTURE ME ABOUT-
NO, NO.
I'VE LONG AGO GIVEN UP ON CARING WHAT YOU DO SEXUALLY, TO LIVESTOCK.
SO, WHAT DO YOU WANT WITH OLD SATURN NOW THEN, EH?
THE HUMAN REALM LONG STOPPED CARING FOR ME.
THE OTHER GODS WON'T EVEN RETURN MY CALLS.
IT'S JUST ME AND MY POOL BOY, TREY, THESE DAYS.
WELL, THAT'S THE THING...
...HOW'D YOU LIKE TO BE VAGUELY RELEVANT AGAIN?
HMM?
TURNS OUT THERE'S A JOB OPENING...

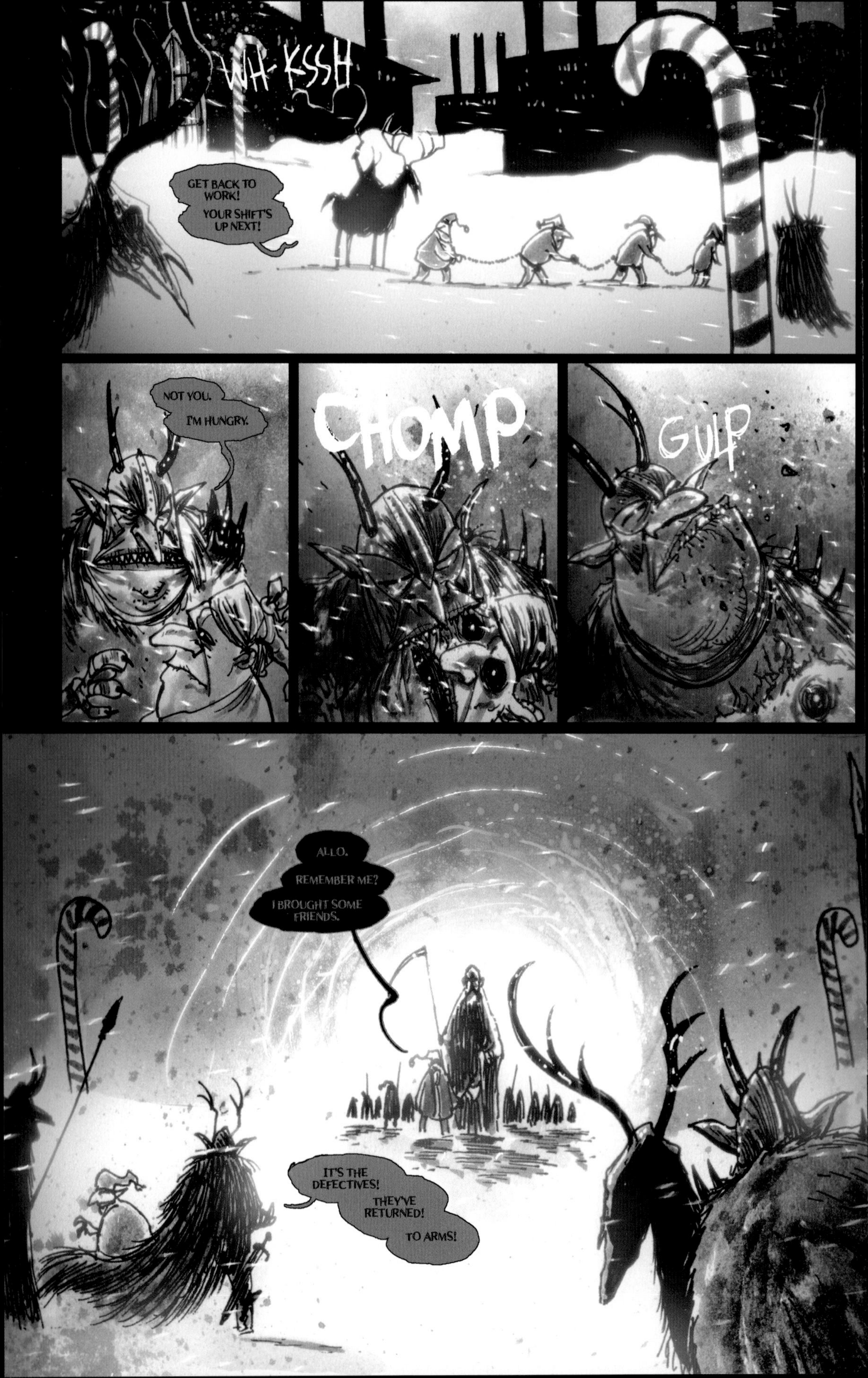
WH-KSSH
GET BACK TO WORK!
YOUR SHIFT'S UP NEXT!
NOT YOU.
I'M HUNGRY.
CHOMP
GULP
ALLO.
REMEMBER ME?
I BROUGHT SOME FRIENDS.
IT'S THE DEFECTIVES!
THEY'VE RETURNED!
TO ARMS!

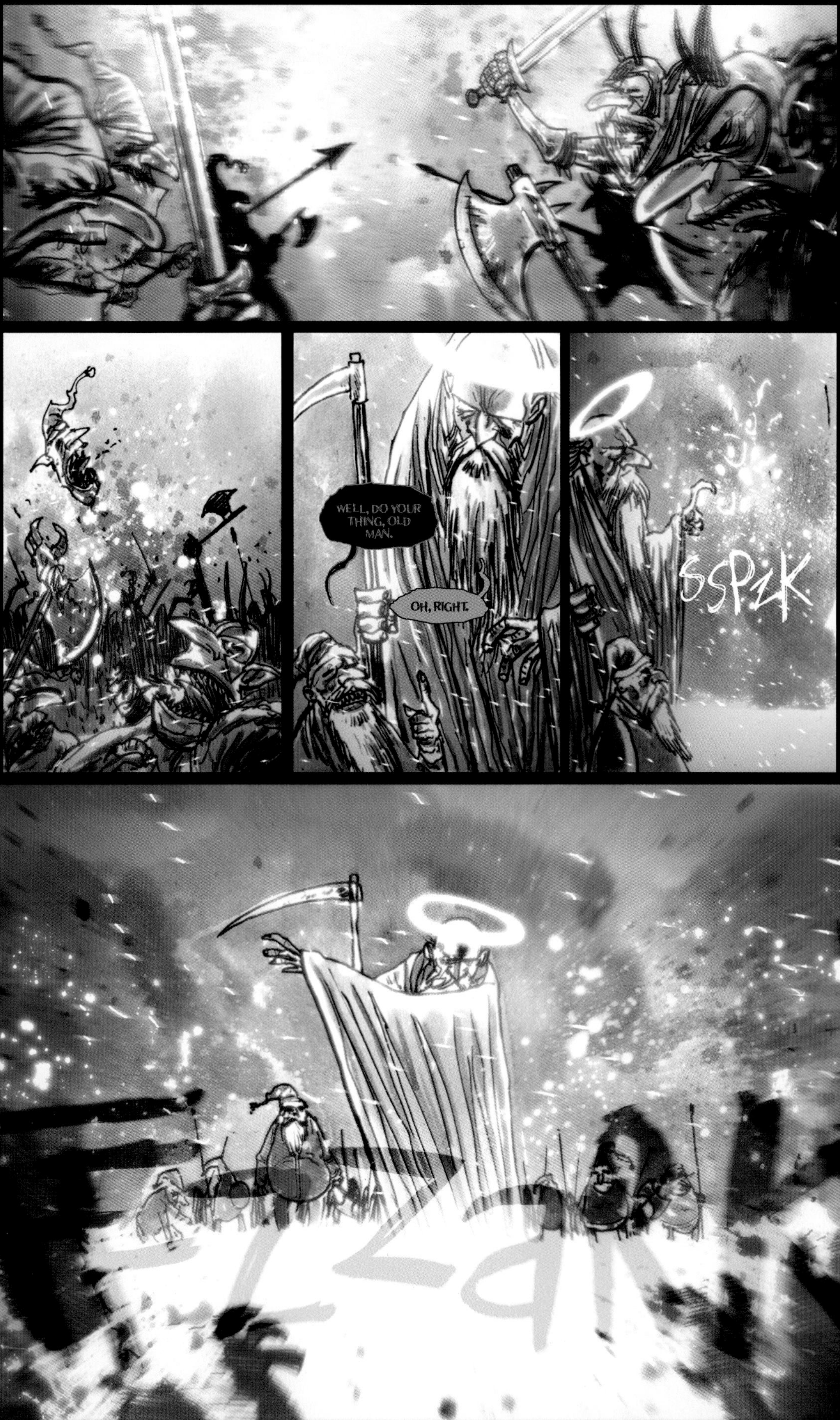
WELL, DO YOUR THING, OLD MAN.
OH, RIGHT.
SSPZK

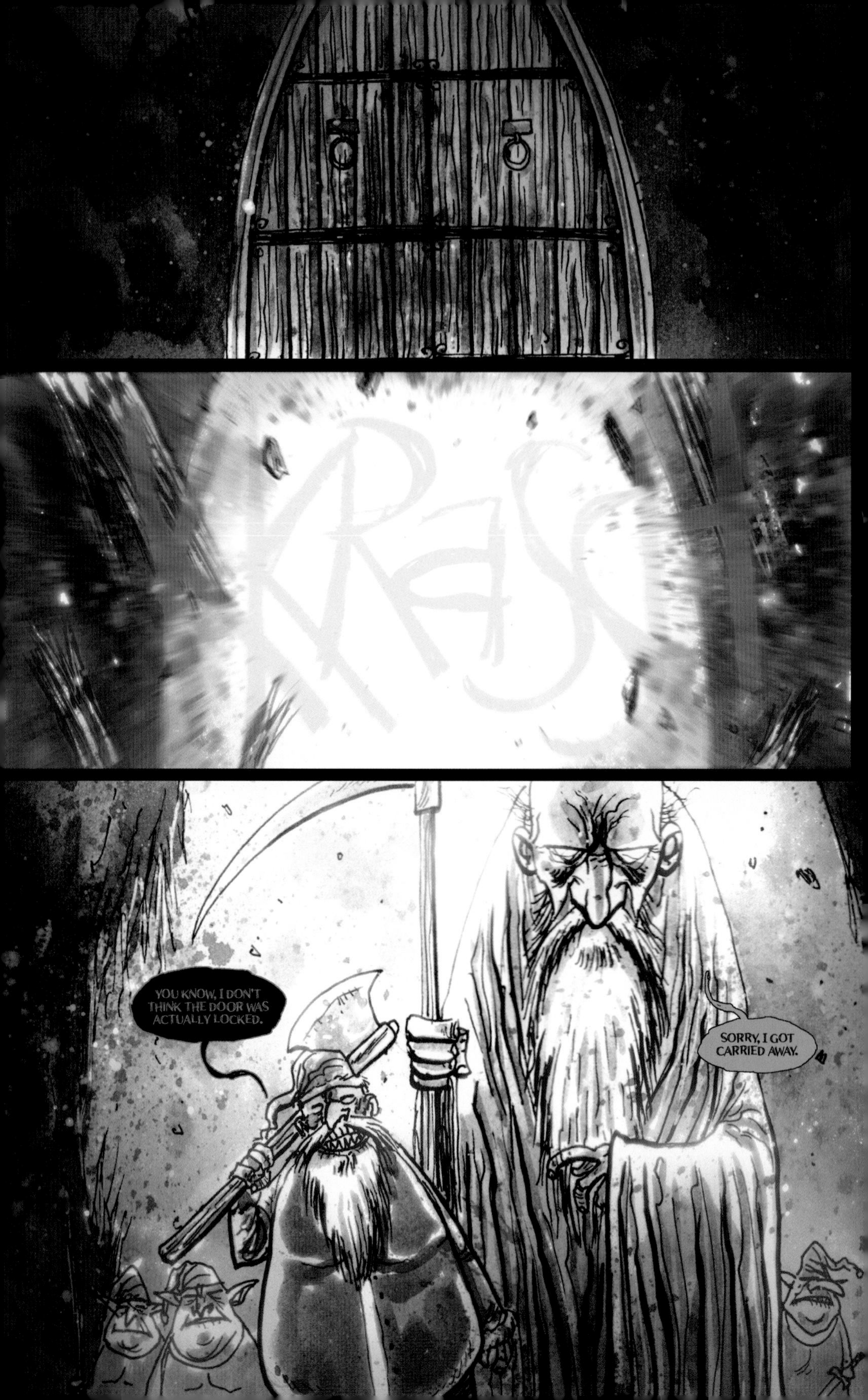
KRASH
YOU KNOW, I DON'T THINK THE DOOR WAS ACTUALLY LOCKED.
SORRY, I GOT CARRIED AWAY.

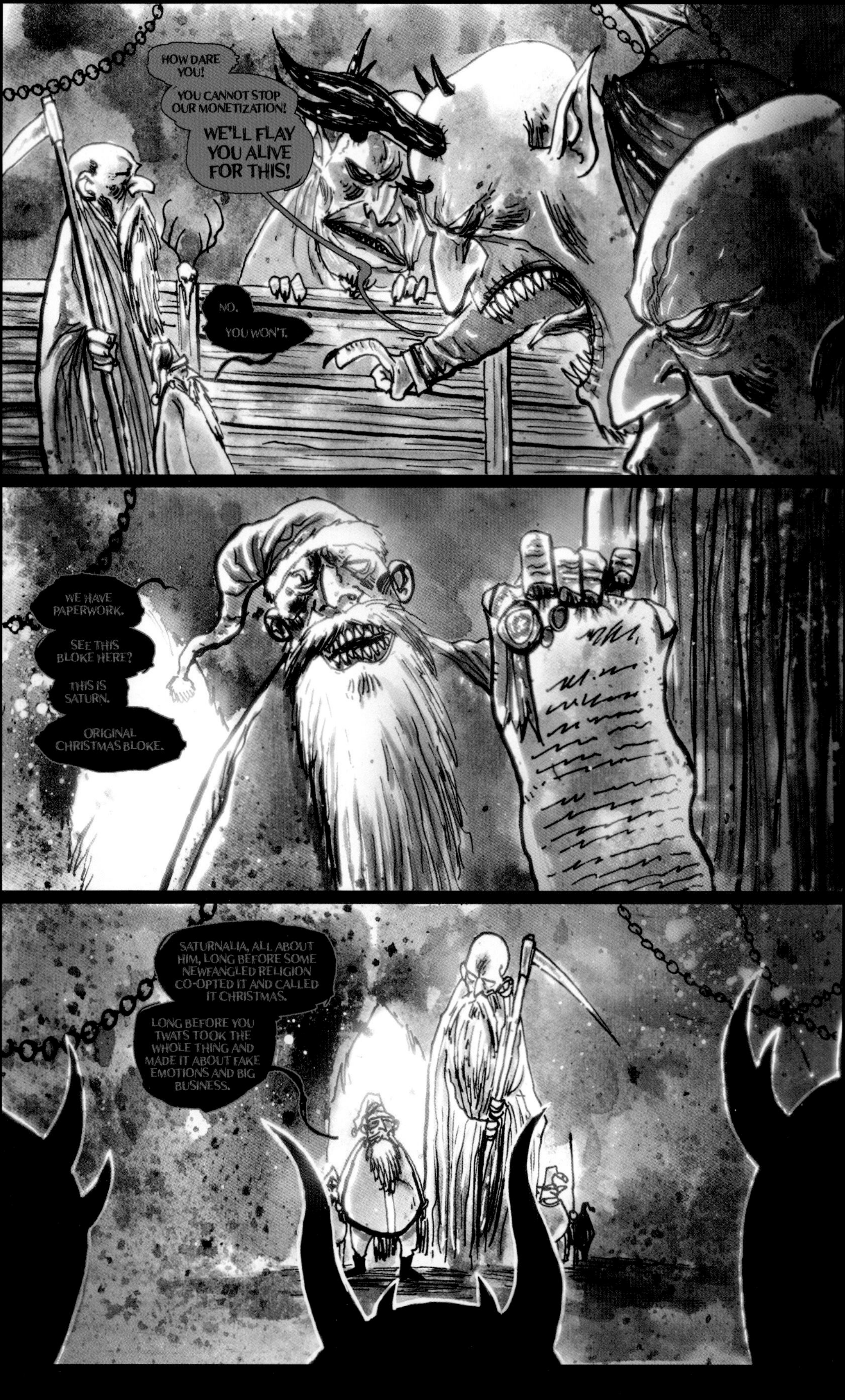
HOW DARE YOU!
YOU CANNOT STOP OUR MONETIZATION!
WE'LL FLAY YOU ALIVE FOR THIS!
NO.
YOU WON'T.
WE HAVE PAPERWORK.
SEE THIS BLOKE HERE?
THIS IS SATURN.
ORIGINAL CHRISTMAS BLOKE.
SATURNALIA, ALL ABOUT HIM, LONG BEFORE SOME NEWFANGLED RELIGION CO-OPTED IT AND CALLED IT CHRISTMAS.
LONG BEFORE YOU TWATS TOOK THE WHOLE THING AND MADE IT ABOUT FAKE EMOTIONS AND BIG BUSINESS.

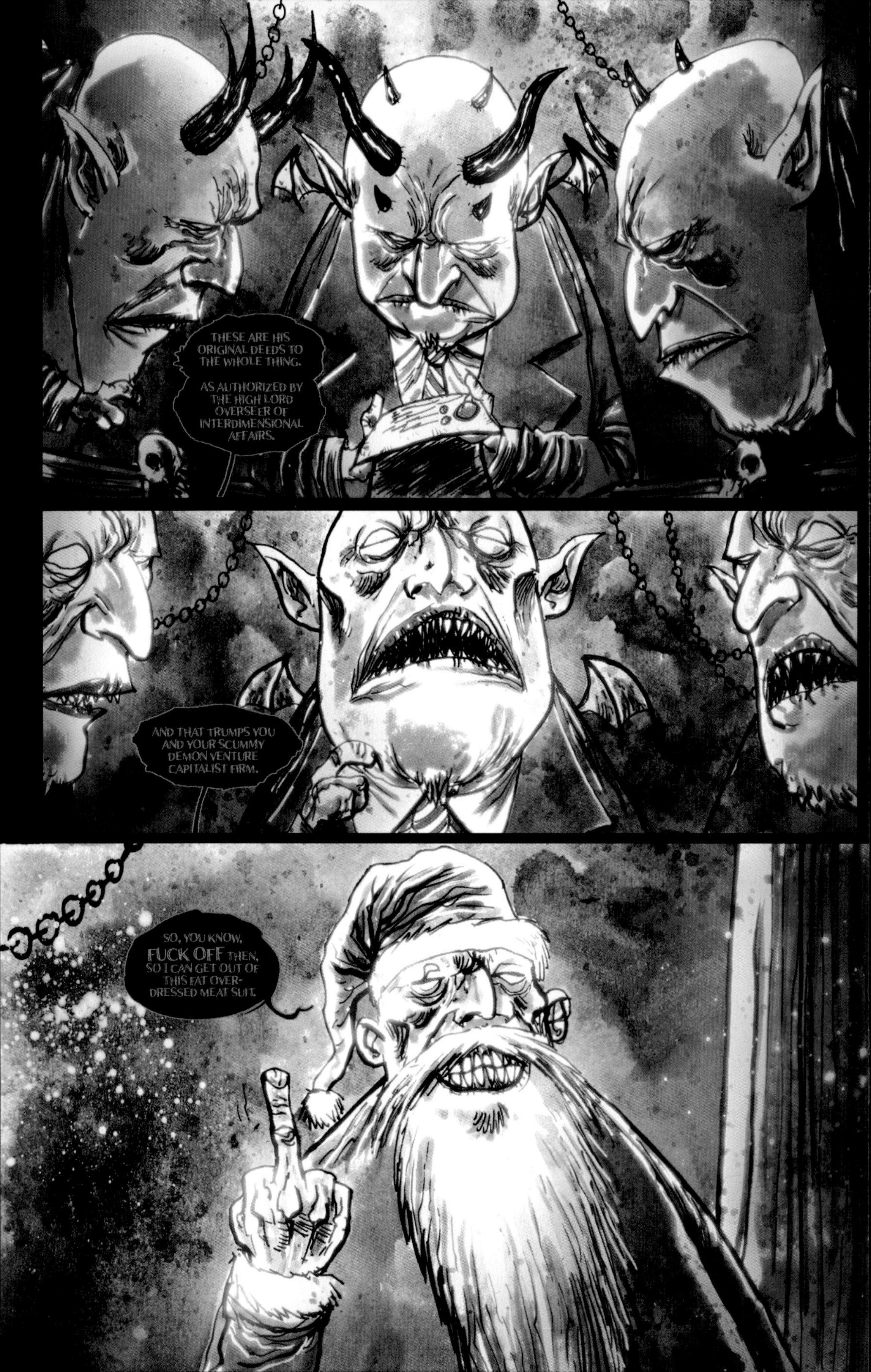
THESE ARE HIS ORIGINAL DEEDS TO THE WHOLE THING.
AS AUTHORIZED BY THE HIGH LORD OVERSEER OF INTERDIMENSIONAL AFFAIRS.
AND THAT TRUMPS YOU AND YOUR SCUMMY DEMON VENTURE CAPITALIST FIRM.
SO, YOU KNOW, FUCK OFF THEN, SO I CAN GET OUT OF THIS FAT OVER-DRESSED MEAT SUIT.

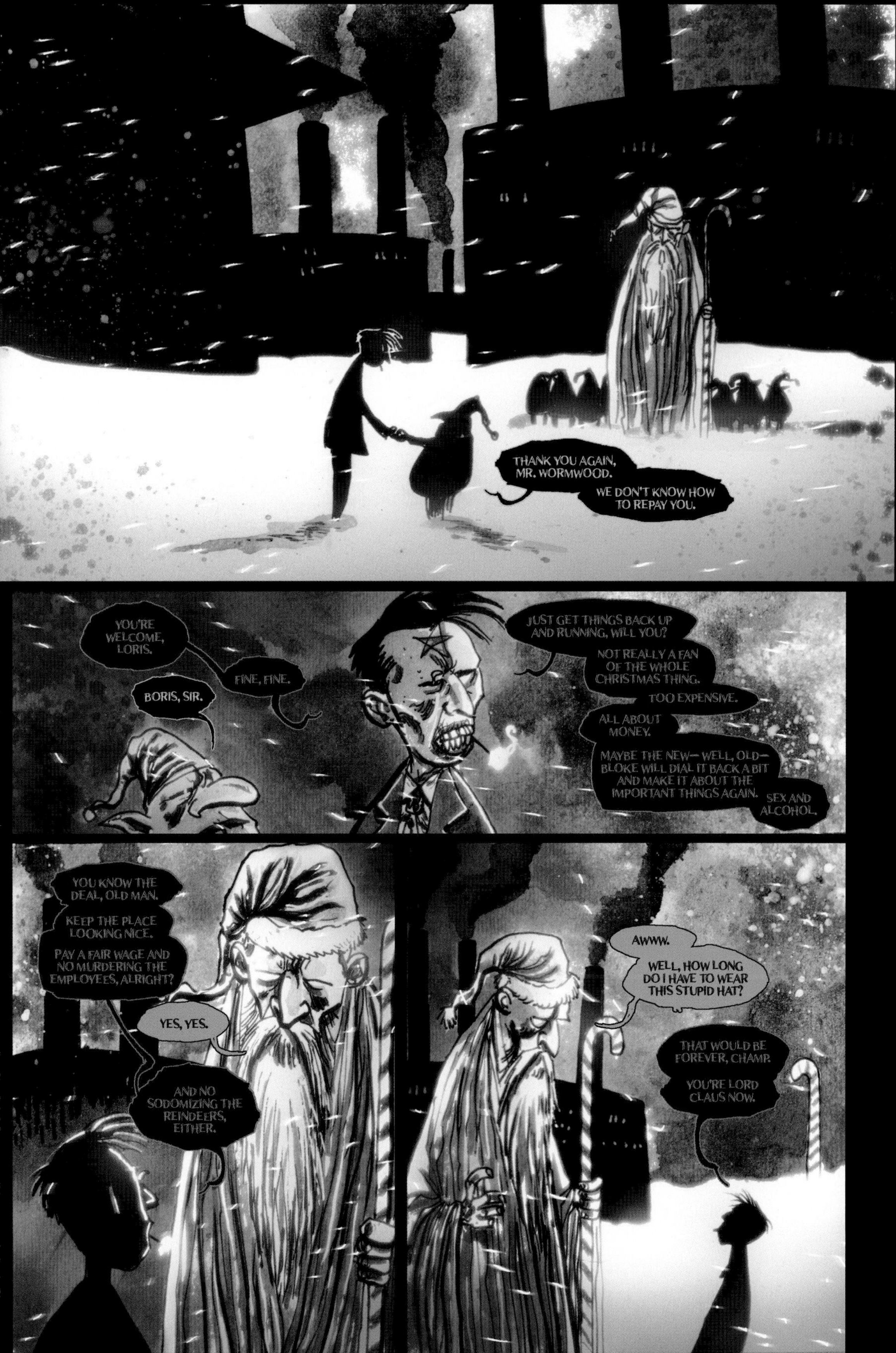
THANK YOU AGAIN, MR. WORMWOOD.
WE DON'T KNOW HOW TO REPAY YOU.
YOU'RE WELCOME, LORIS.
BORIS, SIR.
FINE, FINE.
JUST GET THINGS BACK UP AND RUNNING, WILL YOU?
NOT REALLY A FAN OF THE WHOLE CHRISTMAS THING.
TOO EXPENSIVE.
ALL ABOUT MONEY.
MAYBE THE NEW— WELL, OLD— BLOKE WILL DIAL IT BACK A BIT AND MAKE IT ABOUT THE IMPORTANT THINGS AGAIN.
SEX AND ALCOHOL.
YOU KNOW THE DEAL, OLD MAN.
KEEP THE PLACE LOOKING NICE.
PAY A FAIR WAGE AND NO MURDERING THE EMPLOYEES, ALRIGHT?
YES, YES.
AND NO SODOMIZING THE REINDEERS, EITHER.
AWWW.
WELL, HOW LONG DO I HAVE TO WEAR THIS STUPID HAT?
THAT WOULD BE FOREVER, CHAMP.
YOU'RE LORD CLAUS NOW.

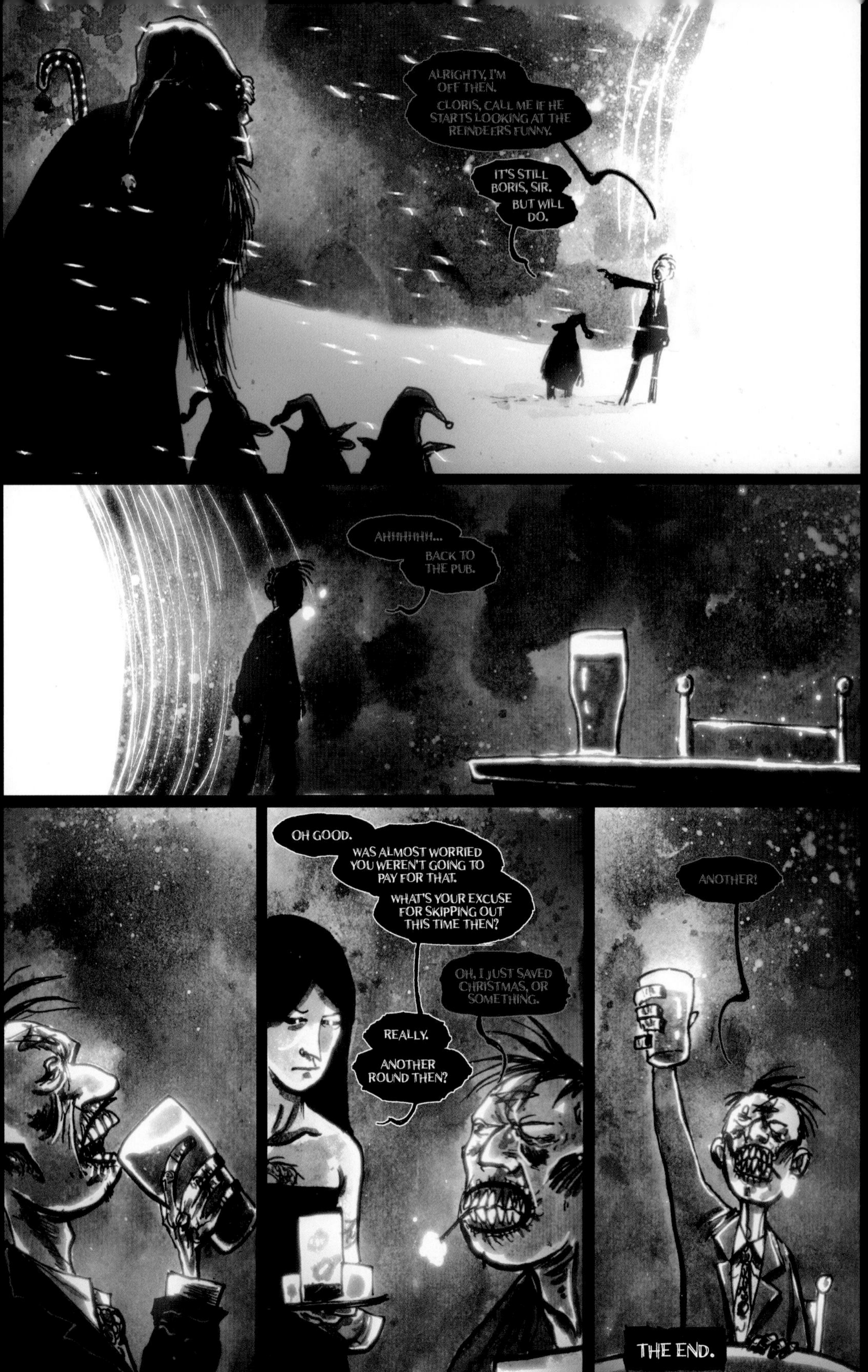
ALRIGHTY, I'M OFF THEN.
CLORIS, CALL ME IF HE STARTS LOOKING AT THE REINDEERS FUNNY.
IT'S STILL BORIS, SIR.
BUT WILL DO.
AHHHHHHH... BACK TO THE PUB.
OH GOOD.
WAS ALMOST WORRIED YOU WEREN'T GOING TO PAY FOR THAT.
WHAT'S YOUR EXCUSE FOR SKIPPING OUT THIS TIME THEN?
OH, I JUST SAVED CHRISTMAS, OR SOMETHING.
REALLY.
ANOTHER ROUND THEN?
ANOTHER!
THE END.

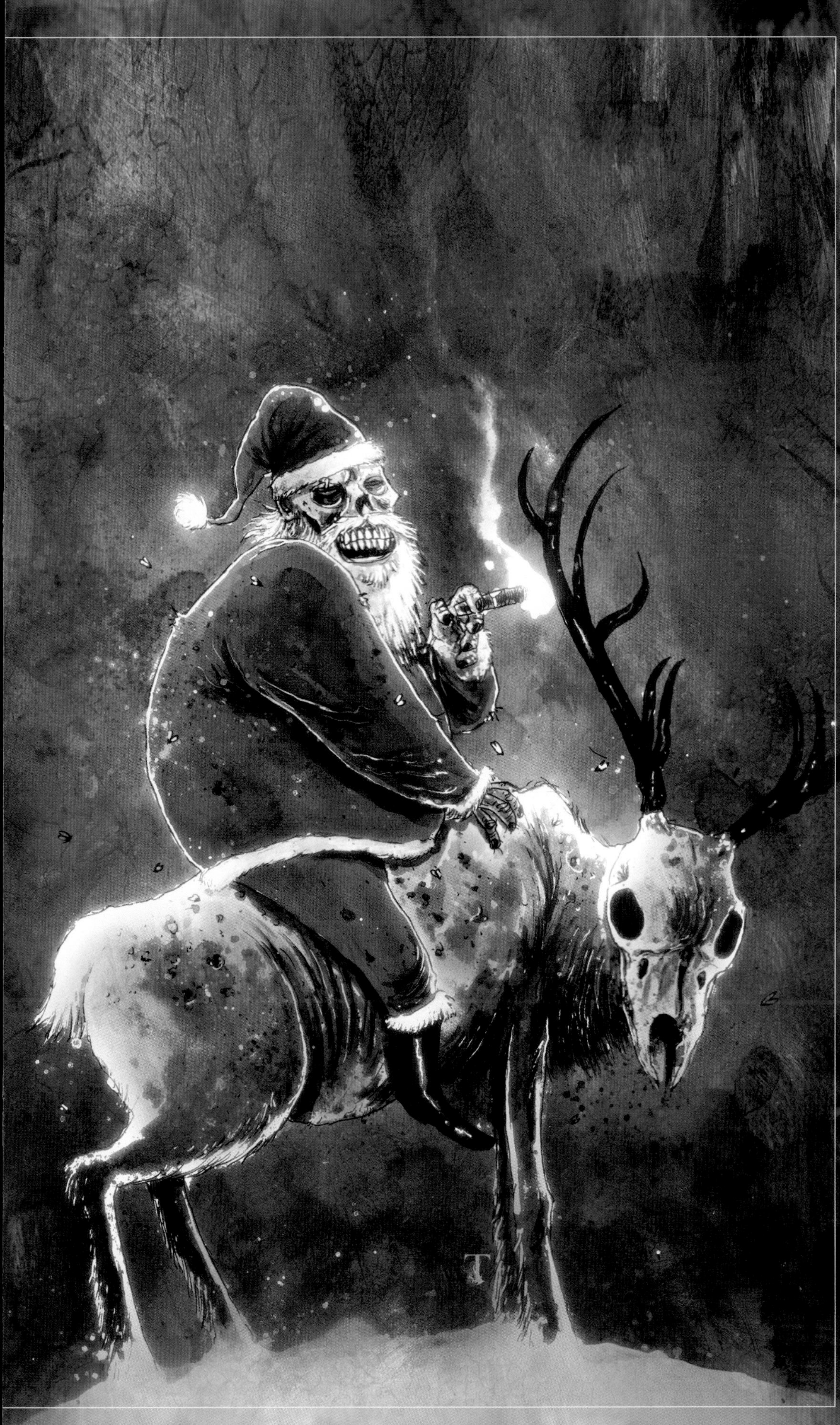

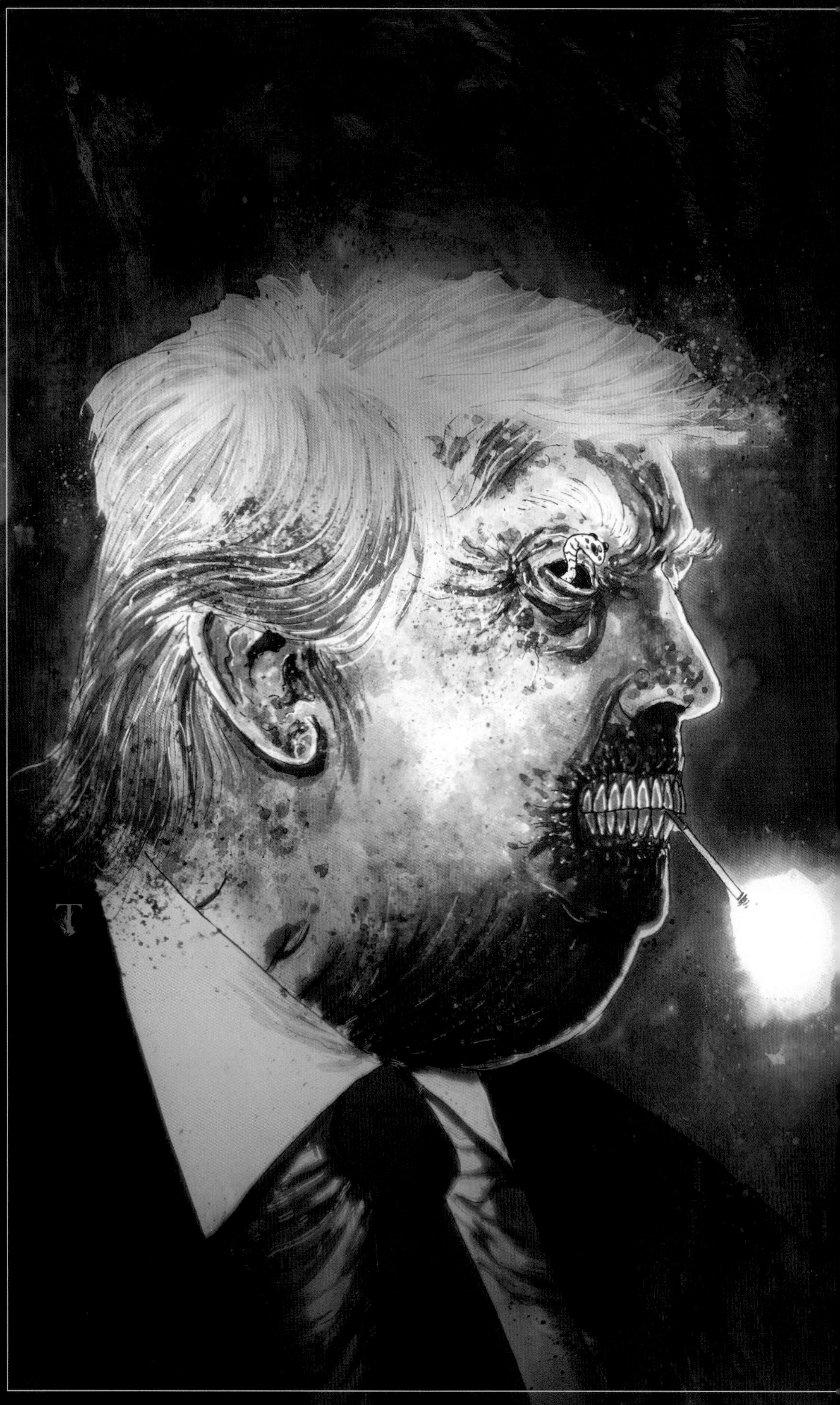

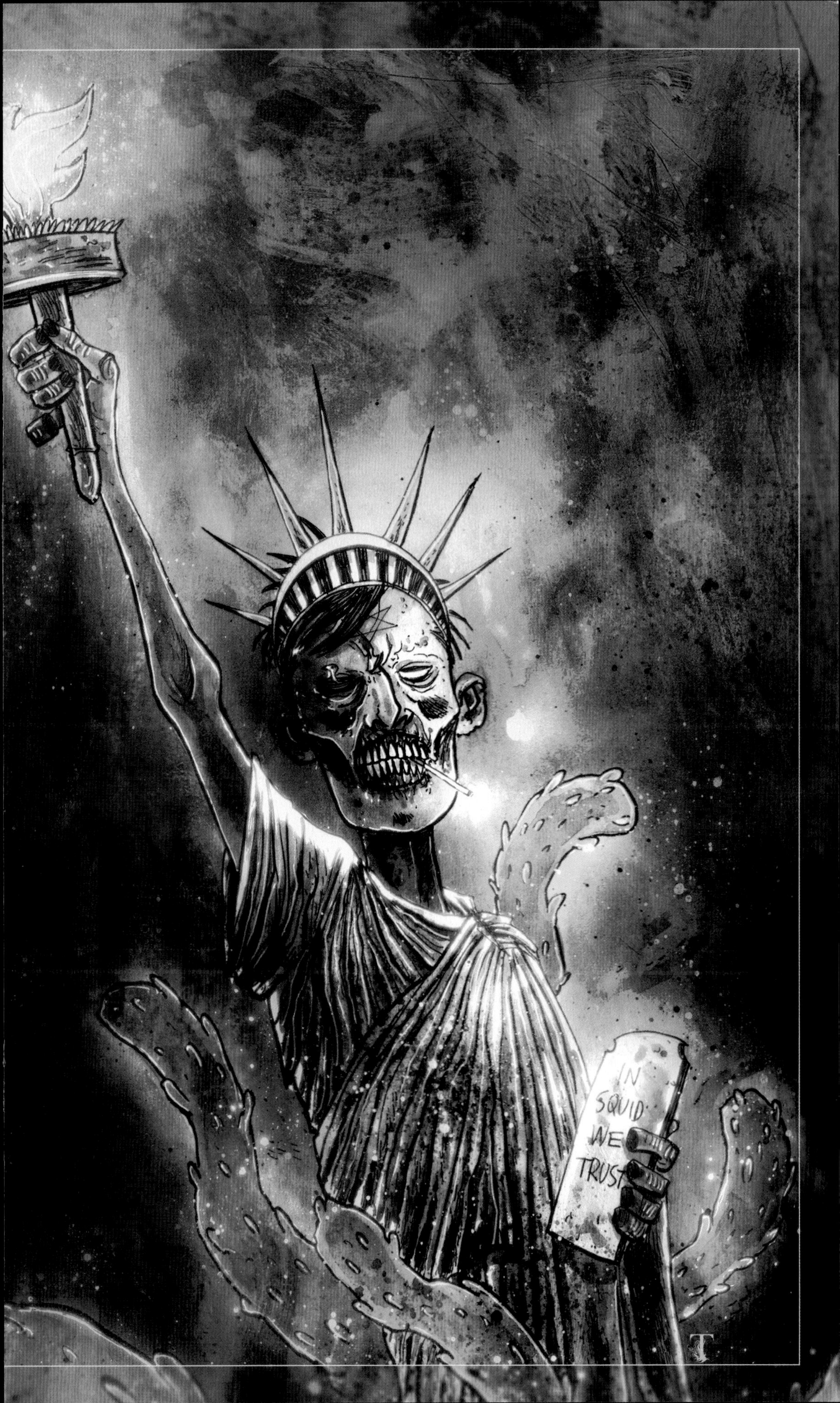
IN
SQUID
WE
TRUST

BEN TEMPLESMITH

WORMWOOD

GENTLEMAN CORPSE

★★★★★★★★★★★★★

MR WORMWOOD
GOES TO
WASHINGTON